THE WISH TO FALL ILL

THE WISH TO FALL ILL

A Study of Psychoanalysis and Medicine

BY

KARIN STEPHEN

CAMBRIDGE

AT THE UNIVERSITY PRESS

1960

CAMBRIDGE
UNIVERSITY PRESS

University Printing House, Cambridge CB2 8BS, United Kingdom

Cambridge University Press is part of the University of Cambridge.

It furthers the University's mission by disseminating knowledge in the pursuit of education, learning and research at the highest international levels of excellence.

www.cambridge.org
Information on this title: www.cambridge.org/9781107475397

First printed 1933
First paperback edition 1960
First published 1960
Re-issued 2014

A catalogue record for this publication is available from the British Library

ISBN 978-1-107-47539-7 Paperback

CONTENTS

PREFACE

Dr Karin Stephen has brought to the study of psychoanalysis an exceptionally critical mind which had previously displayed its capacity in a brilliant career in science and philosophy. In this book she essays the difficult task of conveying the elements of psychoanalytical knowledge to those versed in other fields; I say "difficult" advisedly, because when a student of any other branch of science approaches psychoanalysis he has very few of the direct connecting links to help him which exist in profusion elsewhere in science. In this new field almost everything is strange, unexpected, and often highly unlikely. There are two definite reasons for this. The subject-matter itself, i.e. the workings of the unconscious mind, is concerned with modes of thought extremely alien to those with which we are familiar. Not only so, but we all have within us strong forces which operate without our knowledge and against our will in keeping this unexplored field alien and remote. It is therefore a task of peculiar difficulty to attempt to coordinate knowledge about the unconscious mind with other fields of knowledge.

I have read Dr Stephen's book with interest and consider she has achieved her aim very successfully. Her evident gift of exposition, together with a thorough first-hand knowledge of the subject, has enabled her to convey a great deal of both the principles and practice of psychoanalysis. It would be hard to think of a better introduction to this complex study than that which her book offers.

ERNEST JONES

CHAPTER I

THIS book is based upon a series of eight lectures delivered at Cambridge mainly to medical students. It is essentially *medical* (about illness), and clinical (dealing with cases, giving their history and their main symptoms and the explanations of these).

Theoretical discussion cannot be avoided, because the explanations offered are based upon a theory about the development of the mind and its unconscious motives which is still unfamiliar to many people; but when theory is discussed it will be in connection with actual symptoms, in order to show how, by using the hypothesis here to be put forward, these apparently meaningless mental or physical aberrations become intelligible and are brought out of chaos into order.

But although this book is medical, the lectures having been intended primarily for doctors, no technical language is used, nor are medical knowledge and experience taken for granted, so that it may also interest those who have no intention of studying medicine.

I propose, then, to put forward a hypothesis about the structure and dynamics of the human mind, and to try to explain in terms of this hypothesis certain large classes of human abnormalities, illustrating what I mean by case material, most of which I have myself known at first hand. The hypothesis I propose to work with is the Freudian hypothesis used in psychoanalysis.

In the history of medicine certain kinds of illness, both bodily and mental, have been peculiarly baffling. I mean the sort of symptoms which are often popularly spoken of as "hysterical" or "neurotic" or "mental". When there is something organically wrong with the body, when it has been injured or infected, medicine is at home. But in this other kind of illness, the doctor cannot find anything physical to account for the disturbance.

In modern medicine the term *psychogenic* is used to cover this whole class of abnormalities whose origin appears to be *mental*, as contrasted with the more familiar *organic* illnesses in which the cause is *physical*. For convenience I shall sometimes use the term psychogenic interchangeably with the more familiar one, neurotic.

I do not think my making this distinction between mental and physical causes will be objected to. No doubt a strict definition of what is meant by a "mental" cause would be very difficult, but it is easy to illustrate what is meant. Suppose a girl has red patches on her cheeks; these may be the result of sunburn or of a slap, and in that case they are of *physical* origin, or they may be the result of embarrassment or of anger, and in that case we should all, I imagine, say the cause of the flush was *mental* or *psychogenic*. Reddening of the skin, though actually it is a change from the normal colour, is, however, obviously not an illness, and it would be stretching the meaning of words to call it "neurotic" even when its cause is mental. This illustration is used simply to give a familiar example of a bodily change whose cause is admitted to be "mental".

Of course not all psychogenic events are abnormal and signs of illness. Here, however, we shall for the most part be concerned with illness, and only refer to normal psychogenic events for purposes of illustration and comparison.

It often happens that when a person falls ill it is difficult to decide, merely from the nature of the symptoms, whether the cause is mental or physical. A person may, for instance, be unable to see or hear. Very often a physical examination of the eyes or ears may settle the question by showing that these organs are seriously damaged, and the doctor can then be satisfied that the case is "organic". But sometimes physical examinations fail to reveal anything seriously abnormal, and yet all the same the patient really cannot see or hear. The doctor may then be inclined to call the bodily disturbance "psychogenic" or "neurotic", meaning by this that he puts it down to mental rather than to organic causes. Or, again, the patient may have lost the power of feeling or moving. An examination of the nervous system again may account fully for this, or it may not. Quite often it is inconclusive, and the doctor may be unable to decide whether to call the symptoms psychogenic or organic. It is the same with an enormous variety of pains, swellings, disturbances of the stomach, bowels, bladder, lungs, heart, glands, liver, kidneys, blood supply and so on. It is possible for any of these to get out of order either for organic or for psychogenic reasons, or for the two combined, and although in many cases a differential diagnosis may be easy, in some it is not so.

And besides bodily symptoms, there are also a variety of mental and emotional disturbances which present similar problems. Patients may suffer from confusion, anxiety, depression, or they may develop symptoms of insanity such as delusions or mania, which may be traceable to bodily disease or toxaemia, or may apparently be unassociated with any obvious physical cause. Again, a differential diagnosis is important, and may be difficult.

Probably it is often true that both causal factors, organic and psychogenic, are at work, and it is not so much a question of deciding in favour of the one and rejecting the other as of estimating their relative importance in the particular case, and, from the point of view of treatment, of deciding which approach seems to hold out the best chance of lasting cure.

Until recently, medicine, while making immense advances in the study of the organic side of illness, has paid less attention to the psychogenic side. A patient whose illness could be shown to be organic was sure of receiving serious attention; but, if no organic physical cause could be found to account for the symptoms, doctors, at least until lately, have shown a tendency to wash their hands of the case, as if an illness which was not organic was no concern of theirs and needed no further attention. While nothing was known of the psychogenic causes of disease, this was perhaps the only thing to be done. But in recent times Freud's work has gone far to alter the position. We now know a great deal more than we did about the mental and emotional maladjustments from which psychogenic illness springs.

Freud built up his theories mainly on the study of one kind of psychogenic illness, the *neuroses*, whose symptoms include bodily disturbances and also a variety of mental abnormalities such as morbid anxiety, depression, phobias, obsessions. Psychoanalytic study of the other group of psychogenic illnesses which belong to insanity and are technically termed "psychoses" is less advanced, but enough work has been done on them already to suggest that the theories which explain the neuroses will throw much light also on the psychoses, though there are obviously important differences between these two kinds of psychogenic illness which further work should bring to light and define.

As a result of Freud's investigations of psychogenic illnesses, they now no longer appear simply as senseless or wilfully tiresome, but can be explained as being the outcome of a struggle with psychological difficulties and dangers comparable to the physiological struggles of the body with such physical difficulties and dangers as infections, poisons, or injuries, in terms of which the symptoms of organic illness can be explained.

Just as a swelling or a rise of temperature is a physiological reaction to a physical attack from bacterial toxins which threatens bodily health, so an outbreak of anxiety or a functional paralysis may be understood as a reaction to a psychological danger.

In this book I shall not attempt to discuss organic illness but shall be concerned only with Freud's theory of the nature of these psychological dangers which he holds responsible for psychogenic illness, and with the meaning of the psychogenic symptoms which, if Freud is right, are to be understood as reactions to them.

In dealing with organic illnesses medicine has already a great mass of well-established knowledge to rely upon, but while next to nothing was known of the causes of psychogenic illnesses they presented a stumbling-block, so much so, indeed, that actually the word "neurotic" degenerated into a term of abuse. It would almost seem as if doctors, unable to deal with such patients, had tried to comfort themselves by supposing that it was the patient's own fault that he did not get well.

But moral indignation is surely out of place in the science of medicine. In medicine our subject-matter is the functioning of living beings and we are concerned to discover why these functions sometimes go wrong and, if possible, to devise ways for making them go right again. Praise for health and blame for illness do not belong here.

All the same, the doctor who says his neurotic patient is being ill on purpose is very near the truth. It is quite true that neurotic patients *do* fight, with all their might, to retain their symptoms.

And if this view of their symptoms as reactions to danger is correct, then, according to their lights, they are right to do so. Of all the possibilities which they recognise as being open to them, their illness appears to them to be the least evil—it has been created with extraordinary skill to protect them from an even more terrible situation which seems to them to be the only alternative. It enables them to carry on somehow, though at a heavy cost to their physical health or mental and emotional capacity. The symptoms provide them with some sort of *modus vivendi* which does work, however expensively; and this being so, I doubt whether, even when it is possible, it is really in the patient's interests to deprive him of his symptoms until the need for them has also diminished. To take away his symptoms might be to plunge him into the very danger which he most dreads and which the illness was unconsciously created to avert.

But although it is dread that drives neurotics to take refuge in symptoms, it must not be supposed that they are conscious of the things of which they are so terrified, or even that they are always conscious that they are terrified at all.

The symptoms are defences against a danger situation which they cannot tolerate, but this danger is not consciously recognised. How deeply their organism feels the reality of the danger is proved by the sacrifices they will make to escape it, but the feeling itself is truly unconscious and they are completely unaware that their illness has any purpose behind it.

Ultimately this danger situation by which the neurotic is unconsciously actuated has to do with powerful impulses in himself of which he dare not become aware. These impulses are forcibly kept out of consciousness by something equally powerful in himself which automatically blinds him to what is really going on inside him. It *dissociates* a part of the personality from the rest, simply because the alternative, conscious recognition, feels intolerable. There are various ways in which this dissociation may be brought about and maintained, but the most typical is *repression.*

When repression works efficiently we hear nothing about what is being kept out of consciousness. Life goes on smoothly as if it did not exist. Indeed, much of what passes for normal life is, I think, carried on in this way.

But what has been repressed does not therefore cease to exist: it is always pushing against the opposing barrier, trying to get back to conscious awareness and overt expression, and this pressure is obscurely recognised as a danger which may be reacted to, if there is any weakening of the repressing force, by an outbreak of anxiety, whose real origin, however, still remains unknown to the patient.

Some further defence will now be required if anxiety is to be avoided, and I suggest that this defence may be supplied by symptoms. The view which will be put forward in this book is that *neurotic symptoms are defences designed to prevent anxiety from developing when repression threatens to give way*. They are a second best—a compromise resorted to when repression alone threatens to be inadequate, and some outlet has to be permitted.

And if we can argue by analogy from the neuroses to the other group of psychogenic illnesses, the psychoses (insanity), we may lay down the general proposition that the ultimate reason for every kind of psychogenic illness is the need at all costs to ward off the danger situation which would develop if repression were to fail, thus allowing the impulses which have been banished into the unconscious to return again to consciousness.

This, in brief outline, is the theory of psychogenic illness which I shall try to illustrate all through this book. It rests upon the assumption that consciousness is not the whole of mental life, but that, on the contrary, there may exist, outside it, powerful impulses which may interfere with consciousness while yet remaining entirely unknown to it. I shall not attempt here to prove the possibility of such interference from the unconscious, which has now become a commonplace for most people, but shall content myself with a few illustrations.

The spontaneous occurrence of dissociations of personality and the experimental facts of post-hypnotic suggestion show that sometimes, at any rate, a part of the personality or isolated impulses can be split off from the consciousness, and that this dissociated part can affect feeling and behaviour while yet remaining entirely unknown. There is actually also a good deal of evidence suggesting that, not merely in abnormal cases, but in all of us, the conscious part of the mind is not the whole of it.

Many of the conscious conclusions and decisions with which we carry on our everyday life appear to be simply the end-points of unconscious mental processes not unlike those which can be set up artificially in post-hypnotic suggestion. Often indeed people make use of their unconscious faculties quite deliberately to supply the solutions of problems which baffle their conscious thinking.

Everyone, probably, at some time or other has put a difficulty in his mind to simmer, and by and by found that the solution has presented itself to him. This happens with some people strikingly in the case of mathematical speculations. They puzzle and puzzle, and then, suddenly, perhaps, when they are occupied with other matters, the answer flashes into their minds. It is the same with music. Sometimes when one has been trying in vain to recall a tune and finally given it up, it seems to happen that, apparently just because one has stopped making conscious efforts, one finds oneself humming it. Something has supplied one with what one was looking for, something unconscious in oneself. Forgotten lines of poetry, names or faces, the words of a foreign language, and a thousand other things all behave similarly; indeed all our thinking which we call conscious and voluntary must ultimately be based on the fortunate circumstance that, out of the vast reservoir of our memory and experience, the unconscious can, in general, be relied upon to supply us with the appropriate items which are relevant to our conscious purposes, when we need them. This universal drawing upon unconscious material underlies the whole of our conscious lives, but it is usually only when a hitch occurs that our attention is drawn to it. We then find that our conscious purposes fail to evoke what they need, and it may be that, instead of what we wanted, we are supplied with something quite different. Some other purpose outside consciousness has tampered with our source of supplies and some unconscious preoccupation has overridden our conscious intentions.

This overriding of conscious intention by the forces of the unconscious is just what happens in psychogenic illness. According to the psychoanalytic hypothesis, psychogenic symptoms are produced by impulses which have been dissociated from the rest of the self: they are the result of a partial breakdown of the repressing force which attempts to keep these impulses dissociated.

The next question to be considered is why this dissociation should have occurred at all and why it should be necessary to maintain it so forcibly, and the answer seems to be that dissociation is produced to avoid the intolerable pain of privation and frustration.

The frustration of powerful instincts produces a damming up of the impulses which are denied an outlet, and the tension thus created may throw the organism into an unendurable psychophysical condition which must be dealt with somehow. The only way out may be to deny the whole thing and keep on denying it. But although this painful situation is caused by the thwarting of instinct, mere external privation does not seem to give rise to neurosis. The first normal reaction to this is not repression of desire but an attempt to get what is denied, and it is only when this attempt is blocked, not by *external* difficulties, but by conflict with other *internal* forces, that the intolerable tension is produced which may have to be dealt with by the denial and repression of the impulses concerned.

Neurosis, then, arises when some powerful impulse is thwarted, not simply by the absence of what it craves in the external world, but rather on account of internal conflict with some other powerful impulse. The privation here comes from within and not from without.

The most obvious of such situations occurs perhaps when desire for a satisfaction conflicts with fear, real or imaginary, of the results of getting it. Suppose a baby has almost suffocated at the breast as sometimes happens: fear will now conflict with the primary impulse of hunger, which normally would urge it to suck the breast again.

A similar conflict will arise if destructive aggressive impulses are aroused simultaneously with other impulses either of desire or fear directed to the same object. The baby who has not been able to satisfy itself at the breast may be torn between desire for the nipple and anger at the experience of disappointment, being thus simultaneously attracted and repelled by the same stimulus.

Or one child who has been robbed by another, wishing to attack, and at the same time fearing to do so, may be impelled to set upon the enemy and simultaneously to flee from him. The resulting deadlock of conflicting impulses may produce this state of intolerable strain of which I have just spoken. The upshot may be the abandoning of the original wish. The baby may turn away from the breast—it has repressed hunger and given up the milk: or the child may give up competing with a powerful antagonist and become his submissive imitator—it has repressed rivalry and given up the thing of which it was robbed.

As will be explained later, repression is not the most satisfactory way of dealing with such situations, but everyone, I think, has at times made use of it. The strain seems to be greatest in the early years of life when the urges of instinct may be strong and out of all proportion to the small child's capacity for getting what it wants, so that rage and fear come powerfully into conflict with desire, and instinct repression may seem to be the only possible solution. Analysis of psychogenic symptoms seems to show that the underlying repressed instincts from which ultimately they derive their energy are, to a large extent, immature, their dissociation dating back to conflicts which occurred early in life.

But we do not need to remember our childhood in order to get an idea of the way that repression works. Everyone knows what it feels like to try voluntarily to banish the thought of whatever is connected with painful incidents of failure, humiliation and disappointment. These adult situations are not different in essentials from the childish ones just described, and the conflict which leads to repression is, here too, an internal one. If it were not for internal checks we should not take such situations quietly; on the contrary we should struggle or revenge ourselves. But education and discipline have endowed us with a powerful organisation of counter-forces which do not allow us to burst out and discharge tension in this spontaneous way. Our reasons for checking ourselves may be rational or not; at any rate we do not, and very likely cannot, let ourselves go in such situations, and thus we should be in danger of suffering the torments of undischarged tension if we did not make up our minds to ignore the whole affair. This solution of the problem of disappointment by refusing to be aware of it may be reached voluntarily, but very often it is achieved involuntarily. We all succeed in ignoring a great deal that would otherwise disturb us profoundly. Interest and attention are simply withdrawn automatically. Furthermore, recognition of whatever tends to rearouse the conflict is shut out from conscious awareness, and so a respite from intolerable tension is won by a sort of mental blindness.

When Freud first recognised in his patients this involuntary repudiation of whatever it would be too painful or disturbing to recognise, he put it down to what he then called censorship, describing what happens as if there were a *censor* seated on the threshold of consciousness who examined the ideas which try to enter and refused permission to the dangerous ones. He might equally well have invented a Customs Officer hunting for contraband on the frontier. The idea of an active barrier forcibly excluding parts of the self from conscious awareness is a discovery of the very greatest significance, and fundamental to the psychoanalytic hypothesis, but the simile of the censor is now felt to be unnecessarily anthropomorphic and the tendency is to replace it by the less figurative notion of repression.

Another variety of what is essentially this same defence-mechanism of repression consists in withdrawing attention not from the painful situations themselves, but rather from the conflicting emotions which they arouse. A great deal of the training of our civilisation is directed towards acquiring this technique of repressing emotion so that in the end we are able to go through even very difficult situations without conscious disturbance. A civilised person, for instance, is able to endure the presence of rivals and even to congratulate them and put up with defeat cheerfully, recognising the defeat but not reacting to it with a turmoil of foiled ambition, humiliation or despair. Such cultural achievements rest, to a considerable extent, upon the dissociation and repression of painful emotional conflicts. Most of us have learnt this technique and use it with more or less success. It must be regularly employed by surgeons who have learnt to dissociate the emotions connected with cutting and bloodshed. This extraordinary capacity for repression, together with the closely allied capacity for deceiving not only each other but even themselves, seems to be one of the great distinguishing marks of human beings. One may even go so far as to say that civilisation as we know it is largely based on this strange power which we have developed. We could, in fact, hardly get on without it. At the same time this type of repression by dissociating emotion carries with it the danger that it may succeed too well, and then we find ourselves, undisturbed, it is true, but with no emotion available for life, so that nothing matters to us. This is, I think, the explanation of the feeling of apathy and emotional inadequacy from which many people suffer. The price we pay for the emotional stability and the escape from suffering which successful repression brings is emotional impoverishment and the sacrifice of the energy used up in maintaining the repression. This impoverishment may go to great lengths, for, since repression cannot solve conflicts but can only shelve them, it happens inevitably that, in spite of all efforts to ignore them, fresh objects or situations will continually be presenting themselves which threaten to awaken the repressed conflicts, and fresh efforts of repression will be needed to exclude them from consciousness. On the other hand, when repression is working well, but not too well, it has the advantage of giving us a considerable measure of emotional stability and spares us much suffering, though only at a price. The price may be worth paying, undoubtedly it *is* worth paying, provided we do not pay too much. One might say that the healthy person is one who has bought stability and freedom from anxiety cheaply enough to outweigh his losses by his gains; the neurotic has made a bad bargain, gaining less relief and paying too heavy a price. The situation which repression brings about is this: henceforth there are two opposing forces at work—on the one hand, there is the vigorous refusal to become aware of anything which might awaken painful conflicts, leading always to more and more repression and impoverishment of consciousness: on the other hand, there is the pressure from the banished impulses which are always trying to break through the barrier and avail themselves of any weakening of the repressing forces to express themselves in thought and action. So long as the original conflict remains unsolved, the threat of its reawakening is a constant potential source of anxiety.

While the repression works efficiently, there is nothing to show but some impoverishment of consciousness. This impoverishment is so widespread that, unless it goes to great lengths, we regard it as a part of normal character development.

But if repression is inadequate, so that the banished impulses threaten to win their way through in spite of it, then the danger situation may be met by the development of symptoms, as a second line of defence, and the person is then no longer to be regarded as quite normal, though, as a matter of fact, a certain number of such symptoms are so common as to pass without remark.

The first intimation of the weakening of repression may be the development of anxiety. This anxiety might itself be regarded as a symptom, since it is a reaction to the danger of the return of the repressed, but as it does nothing to relieve the situation it seems more convenient to look upon it simply as a danger signal. This may be thought of as the *anxiety situation*, and all the other manifestations of psychologic illness may then be classed as symptoms whose object is to act as defences against the development of anxiety situations.

This can be done in two ways, either by reinforcing the repression, or else by affording the repressed impulses a partial outlet. Symptoms may, therefore, be of two kinds, according to whether they consist in repudiating the efforts of the repressed impulses to break through into consciousness, opposing more and more vigorous repression the stronger the attempt to force the barrier, like building up a higher and stronger dam in a reservoir that threatens to overflow; or whether they abandon the attempt to hold the repressed impulses under entirely, and take the alternative way of controlling and disguising their expression, since they cannot be kept altogether unsatisfied; like regulating the overflow from the reservoir in which the water can no longer be completely contained, by the creation of a new channel. If the defence takes the line of further repression, the symptoms may, as we have seen, appear in the form of obvious physical or mental or emotional impoverishment. The patient who is struggling not to be aware of impulses connected with seeing and touching may make himself safe from temptation by becoming psychogenically blind or paralysed, and so settle his problem. Or he may show surprising *amnesias* (loss of memory), he cannot remember things which ordinary people remember, places, events, words; or he shows emotional inadequacies, he feels nothing when the people he cares for die, or when he achieves the things he most wishes for.

We are accustomed to take for granted a considerable amount of amnesia and emotional impoverishment as normal to our civilisation: when it goes beyond what is customary we call it a symptom of psychogenic illness. It indicates that the patient is hard put to it to maintain the repressions of ordinary civilisation and that these are in danger of breaking down before the onslaughts of the forces which have been banished to the unconscious. In the effort to meet this danger more energy is now withdrawn from consciousness than normally happens, and the loss of perception or memory or feeling is exaggerated beyond what we have learnt to expect.

In this danger situation, repression may be further reinforced, not merely by withdrawal of attention or emotion from such objects or situations as threaten to arouse conflict, but by a particular emphasis on some *other* thing which rivets the attention and keeps it safely occupied, like applying a counter-irritant in pain, or like a conjurer who keeps up a flow of conversation and gesticulates with his right hand to distract the attention of the audience from the important point concerning what his left hand is doing; or perhaps there may be exaggeration of the very opposite of what must not be admitted, as happens in the case of militant prudishness or excessive cleanliness, or foolhardy recklessness. This defence-mechanism is called "over-compensation" and, within limits, is normal and universal; it is only to be reckoned as morbid when it takes on an exaggerated compulsive quality so that any failure to maintain it causes serious distress, marked indignation, or anxiety.

These defences, then—distraction of attention, dissociation of emotion and over-compensation—are some of the ways in which simple repression may be reinforced. They succeed in so far as anxiety is no longer aroused by the forbidden object or action, either because it itself, or the disturbing emotion connected with it, is successfully ignored.

But when repression threatens to break down, the danger may be met, not by more repression and reinforcements of repression, but in quite an opposite way, that is, by allowing partial satisfaction to the repressed impulses which are threatening to break through. In this case the symptoms will show a different picture, not consisting of impoverishments or over-compensations but of peculiar kinds of gratification, corresponding to the impulses which have been repressed.

Usually the impulses are still denied open gratification and get their satisfaction only in disguised and displaced ways. In the symptoms thus produced it is often possible to recognise either the repressed impulse, or the repressing force, or, more frequently, a compromise between the two.

Everyone makes use, to some extent, of these various mechanisms for dealing with impulses which, for some reason or other, must not be openly satisfied, but which refuse to be completely denied. Whether we are to call any given defence pathological or normal seems to depend really on three factors. One is the amount of energy used up and the extent of impoverishment of conscious life which it involves, another the extent to which the repression succeeds, and the third how we feel about the displaced outlet which the repressed impulse may succeed in creating for itself, I mean whether we approve of it or regard it as harmful or silly.

Probably there is no one, however apparently normal, who has the full use of his capacities; some sacrifice of power is always being made to avert the anxiety which privation has at some time aroused, and whose reappearance is dreaded. But in normal people what is being repressed represents only a small part of their total capacity, most of it is finding more or less satisfactory discharge, and this residuum is either simply lost by complete repression or is producing symptoms of negligible importance.

As regards the other defence-mechanisms of disguised or displaced gratifications, it is even more difficult to draw hard and fast lines between normal and pathological. All the highest achievements of culture technically called "sublimations" as well as the morbid symptoms of psychogenic illness fall into this category of displaced gratifications. It is remarkably hard to say what it is that makes one displacement a sublimation and another a symptom, and yet we can all feel the difference—singing, oratory, playing musical instruments, painting, writing, scientific research are obviously in a different class from, for example, stammering, delusions of being poisoned, inability to do handwork, compulsion to be constantly washing, and so on. In both cases unconscious significance is transferred from earlier on to later objects or activities, but, whereas in symptoms this unconscious significance, by introducing conflict, serves only as an interference, in the case of sublimation it acts as a reinforcement so that an object or activity, already interesting in its own right, may now, for unconscious reasons, be pursued with added zest.

I recognise that in thus attempting to trace back to a common unconscious origin activities at such opposite poles in our scale of values as sublimations and symptoms I risk arousing alarm or hostility, and I think this is because most people feel instinctively that repressed impulses are necessarily impulses of which we have reason to be ashamed. This is, as a matter of fact, by no means true.

Actually, people often repress not only what would be called bad impulses but also many that would be called good. But this ethical way of looking at the matter is in any case out of place here: the discussion of values does not belong to medical psychology, which is not concerned with the goodness or badness of the material it studies any more than botany is concerned with the relative aesthetic merits of vegetables or flowers.

The problem for medical psychology is simply this: given that anyone is suffering from an internal conflict of repressed impulses, what outlet are those impulses finding?

In so far as anyone is healthy, that is, free from repressed conflict, medical psychology has nothing to say about his case. At present, however, few of us are free. We do not become subjects for medical treatment until our symptoms seriously disturb the course of our lives, but most of us are obliged to repress some impulses the open expression of which is forbidden because it would arouse intolerable anxiety, and which must therefore go unsatisfied or else find indirect expression.

The case of people who are seriously neurotic is thus perhaps actually not so very different in kind from that of many people who would be counted normal, but it is quite different in the extent of the capacities involved, and in the actual results as regards living. Life for neurotics is more or less completely dominated by the necessity to avoid anxiety at all costs, and the greater part of their capacities are either sacrificed to repression, so that their conscious life, though not obviously eccentric, is profoundly circumscribed and impoverished, or wasted in positive symptoms which make them noticeably abnormal.

If, therefore, I now quote some of the minor symptoms which we all develop from time to time, it must not be taken to mean that we are all neurotic. All that is necessarily implied by the presence of symptoms is that some attempt at repression is being made which is not working quite smoothly. In the course of our everyday life we all produce trivial aberrations of conduct, hardly worthy, perhaps, to be called symptoms, but which illustrate the sort of way in which symptom-formation works. They seem to be brought about either by a reinforcing of existing efforts at repression which have threatened to give way, or else by a partial breaking through of something which was meant to be repressed. One may try again and again to write or post a letter or pay a bill, it is always forgotten—the envelope is posted without the address, or without the stamp. All this difficulty in accomplishing a simple everyday act suggests reluctance which may not be conscious, however, and which certainly has not been allowed consciously to interfere with carrying it out.

The reason why such apparently trivial matters are interfered with is usually not obvious from the face value of the actions themselves. When there is difficulty in performing actions of this sort it is usually because they are somehow associated with other interests of more real importance which have been repressed for quite adequate reasons. It is not that particular bill or letter which matters much, but something else connected with it, which is in danger of being recalled by it. It is really this earlier thing which must stay repressed and *must not* be permitted to return to consciousness, and the trivial present-day events fall under repression, too, not in their own right, but just in so far as they threaten to revive those other more serious preoccupations.

Anything which is associated with an important repressed preoccupation is always liable to suffer sympathetic repression. It is not safe to be aware of it. This mental blindness, due to unrecognised association with something repressed for an anxiety reason, may be extended to other people, events, periods of one's own past history, or character traits of one's own, even very important ones. Actual physical blindness may even occur occasionally, in cases where to see would arouse intolerable conflict. A case occurred in which a wife, though she had the normal use of her eyesight for every other purpose, was unable to see her husband at all. It was as if he alone of all the things in the room were invisible. Here I should judge that the function of sight itself had probably a deep anxiety significance and also that the husband aroused in her a conflict of emotions which could not be adequately discharged and so would throw her into a state of anxiety if permitted to develop.

Psychogenic blindness like this can be paralleled artificially in hypnotism, but here it need not be associated with any deep sources of anxiety. The subject while hypnotised is given several pieces of paper, some marked with a cross, some plain, and is told that he can see only the plain ones. After waking, and now remembering nothing of all this, he will pick out of a heap of such papers only the plain ones, actually avoiding the marked ones, and when all the plain ones have been taken he will assure you that there are none left.

Inability to understand, actual deafness, and even complete clouding of consciousness may be called in where it is necessary, for anxiety reasons, in order not to attend to something—to shut it out of conscious awareness. Many analysts have come across this. In the case of one of my own patients, whenever I said anything to her which was likely to arouse painful feelings she told me she had not heard anything I had said, or else fell sound asleep. Boredom is quite often (though certainly not always) a minor manifestation of the same protective mechanism.

In these illustrations of psychogenic loss of perception of greater or less severity it is the forces of repression that have triumphed. But everyday slips as well as more important symptoms may originate also in the other way, by the breaking through of some unwelcome impulse which has succeeded, momentarily, in evading the barrier of repression.

A friend, whose permission I have to use his slip, was discussing this question of the meaning of "accidental" occurrences in a very sceptical spirit. He did not think there was nearly enough evidence and remarked rather contemptuously: "one or two instances like that would never convict me". Quite involuntarily a secret sense of guilt, which he was probably successfully ignoring, slipped out and expressed itself through his lips; unconsciously he was perhaps thinking "How might I betray myself if I were caught off my guard?" Most of us feel dimly that we have things to hide which slips may reveal. We all speak of being "caught out" or "detected" when such slips are brought to our notice. After his own slip my friend was a little more convinced.

Another friend heard this at an architects' dinner. Among the after-dinner speakers was an architect who was reputed to have a sharp eye to business. This man was speaking about the dangers of spoiling the countryside by reckless building, but he was anxious to make the point that one must not imagine that all building necessarily spoils the landscape. On the contrary, judiciously used, it might actually improve it. "A skilful architect", he pointed out enthusiastically, "can often obtain such very pleasing contracts—er—contrasts." Such slips are accidents in the sense that they were not consciously intended, but they are not due to "pure chance".

I have used these everyday illustrations because they are familiar and because most people would agree that in these cases the failure to do or say what was intended has a meaning, and can be explained by saying that the person did not *want* to perceive, or really *meant* the thing which in fact he said by mistake; it broke through in spite of his conscious intentions, it was meant, though it was not meant to be said.

In these illustrations the somewhat private thoughts behind the slips were not hard to guess. We understand them easily because they belong to the sort of things that any of us would admit might happen to ourselves, and although what slipped out involuntarily may not have been clearly in consciousness, very likely it was not seriously repressed either. But I must say that these explanations which one can see so easily do not altogether satisfy me. I think that although they are on the right lines they probably do not go deep enough to account for the disturbance. I doubt if consciousness or voluntary behaviour are ever disturbed for trivial reasons, and I think we should probably find that when this seems to happen it is because the trivial action is associated with some other matter of real importance emotionally, and that the interference is really to protect this other important matter which *has* to be repressed at all costs.

But even in these trivial slips and errors I am perhaps assuming too easily that everyone will agree with the view that they result from the intrusion of unconscious impulses. Some people, I know, take the line that it is making too much fuss over such trifling "accidents" to read into them hidden meanings, and prefer to explain them as the result of fatigue or ill health or some momentary distraction of attention. When we are tired or ill or inattentive these slips certainly do seem to happen more easily.

No doubt in the case, for instance, of loss of consciousness under chloroform, or following a blow on the head, the most important factors are usually organic, and it may be that physiological research will some day reveal more subtle alterations of innervation or blood supply which may adequately explain some types of aphasias (mistakes in words) or amnesias (forgetfulness). At present, however, speculation along these lines is still only at the stage of guess-work, and even if the time comes when these gaps in our knowledge of physiology are filled, I think such explanations will still fall a long way short of covering the whole field. In the case, for instance, of a slip which in a moment of carelessness substitutes one rather similar word for another, I doubt whether physiology will ever be able to tell us why those particular words out of the sentence were chosen for distortion and why that particular word-resemblance was made use of. To explain these things we have to take into account the particular psychology of the person in whom this speech accident occurred. In the present state of our knowledge it seems to me that the correct attitude about such things as lowered vitality or absent-mindedness is that they are very often only contributing circumstances, they open the door to the unconscious, they lower the threshold, weaken the resistance. So they prepare the ground; but what actually avails itself of this opportunity depends upon the preoccupations, whether conscious or unconscious, of the particular individual.

It may always be necessary that there should be some modification of the chemistry of the body before what is normally outside the consciousness is able to take control. But even assuming that this is so, it does not get us much further, for we do not yet understand what the chemical changes may be which raise or depress the threshold of consciousness. On the other hand, we *are* beginning to know something about the repressed material which often *avails itself of these physiological conditions* to gain expression, and it frequently seems as if what took this opportunity was indeed something which we have good reason for ignoring. Also it must be admitted that we quite often make slips and forget things we know when we are apparently perfectly well and paying full attention.

Forgetting some perfectly familiar word is another instance of the sort of curious "accident" that happens to everybody occasionally. The word is certainly not in the consciousness, and yet it cannot really be said to be unknown, since, when possible words are suggested, we know whether they are to be accepted or rejected; therefore, in a sense, we do know all along. Our ideas seem to circle round the forgotten word, almost like iron filings on a surface, arranging themselves in relation to a magnet hidden beneath it.

Freud gives an illustration of an attempt of his own to recall the name of a certain small country on the Riviera. After exhausting the resources of conscious effort he gave up in despair, and let his mind drift, waiting to see what names would present themselves. He thought of Monte Carlo, Piedmont, Albania, Monte Video, Colico. The name Albania attracted his attention, and was immediately followed by Montenegro, probably helped by the contrast, white-black. Then he noticed that, substituting Montenegro for Albania, he had four names all containing the syllable Mon: Monte Carlo, Piedmont, Montenegro, Monte Video, and one more ending in "ico", and immediately he thought of the right word—Monaco. "Incidentally", he said, "I could quite easily find out what made me forget the name for the time being. Monaco is the Italian for Munich, and it was some thoughts connected with this town which acted as an inhibition."

Here, then, we have Freud, knowing the word Monaco perfectly well, but unable to recall it because of unpleasant associations, that is to say, knowing it unconsciously. And we have this unconscious knowledge controlling the choice of random names which presented themselves to his mind when he let it wander and no longer attempted to direct it, and finally, although conscious voluntary effort to find the lost word had failed, this other method succeeded in recalling it.

Freud was not the first, no doubt, to make use of this passive technique for recovering lost memories, but he was the first to realise its immense possibilities. Under the name of "free-association" it is now used by all psychoanalysts and is their most valuable instrument for overcoming the barrier which shuts off what has been dissociated from the consciousness of the personality.

If conscious introspection had been the only way of finding out what went on in the mind, we could never have gone far with investigating the unconscious. Even before Freud's discovery of free-association various techniques had been used to bridge the gulf between conscious and unconscious and so enable us to get a glimpse of parts of the mind of which we should not otherwise have known anything. The most important of these was hypnotism. With this method, in suitable cases, it is possible to recover memories and mental attitudes of which the patient is completely ignorant in his waking life. But by no means everyone can be hypnotised, and, furthermore, I believe that this method of investigation of the unconscious has disadvantages which Freud's psychoanalytic method avoids. The fundamental drawback to treatment by hypnosis is that it produces in the patient a state of dependence on the doctor and, indeed, relies for its success upon this dependence. The psychoanalytic method avoids this since it puts no pressure on the patient, being directed solely towards understanding him and enabling him to understand himself. This he cannot do while a part of him is cut off from consciousness. It is in order to get back into touch with this cut off or dissociated part that the patient is asked to make use of the technique of free-association, but he is in no way influenced as to the attitude he should take towards what he then discovers about himself.

There are, I believe, quite a number of misconceptions about how this free-association method is practised, and it is important to understand how it really works, because the greater part of the Freudian contribution to psychology depends upon the validity of free-association as a reliable technique for getting at the content of the unconscious. Some people think that it is a question of word-tests in which the analyst fires off a list of words to which the patient has to reply with the first word that comes into his head and then the analyst draws inferences and explains. Other people think it consists in the patient telling his dreams and getting them interpreted for him. Neither of these ideas is correct.

The analyst does not put questions or in any way direct the patient as to what he shall think about. All that he asks the patient is that he should let his thoughts and feelings go as they will, without trying to direct them at all, without selecting or suppressing any of them, and without rejecting whatever may come up. When consciousness thus abandons the direction of the stream of thought and feeling, the unconscious takes it over and controls what presents itself according to its own secret preoccupations, sometimes partly known to the person who is giving the association, sometimes quite outside his awareness, but in any case not recognised as being the real motive behind his apparently random ideas. Thus, when the patient appears to be thinking at random, he is really thinking in a fully determined way, but now the trend of his thoughts is guided by his unconscious rather than by his conscious feelings and desires. It is claimed that somewhere in this unconscious material the reasons for his illness will be found. These, just like a forgotten tune, defy all conscious efforts to recall them, but they are going on, nevertheless, working outside consciousness, carrying on, as it were, an endless train of thought or feeling not unlike the unconscious solution of problems already described. Certainly the more we try the less we seem able to get at them, but perhaps, if we stop trying, we shall be more likely to get on their track.

And, indeed, if we go about it in the right way, the task of getting at them is actually not so hopeless as it would seem, because, although it is true that we have to get round powerful resistances, there are also powerful forces helping us. The repressed impulses are on our side. These impulses never really submitted to repression and they are always trying to push back into consciousness—it is our task to make a bridge for them. This is what free-association tries to do. It sets going a process by which the dissociated material expresses itself, gradually becoming more and more clearly recognisable for what it is. Listening to an analysis is like watching a photograph developing in the dark room; at first it is a blank, then something dim is visible which gets clearer and clearer till at last one can make out the whole picture plainly. Or one may better compare it to a complicated piece of music at first unintelligible but gradually unfolding itself. This happens only, of course, in so far as patients are willing and able to relinquish conscious control, but as soon as they really do succeed in setting aside the voluntary direction and criticism of their ideas and feelings, the undertow of the unconscious at once reveals itself, sometimes with startling clarity even at the first attempt, sometimes less plainly, though even then, on looking back in the light of later knowledge, it can often be seen that, from the very beginning, the unconscious was proclaiming its secrets over and over in one disguised form after another. But for a long time, even after the analyst can perhaps see clearly what the unconscious is saying, realisation of what is hidden in the unconscious is still a long way from the patient's *own* consciousness. For the analyst to recognise it is not always easy, but much the hardest part is to get the patient to see it too.

The buried material consists of two parts, concrete ideas, and powerful emotions about them, and these, as a rule, begin to emerge separately. In this connection people seem to fall roughly into two classes. In one group the concrete ideas come up first, usually in the form of parables, dreams, parodies and other disguises; but the emotion which belongs to these ideas is much more strongly repressed and only comes through with the utmost difficulty. These are the people whose defence against the unconscious anxiety situation rests on dissociation of emotion rather than on forgetting the facts. In the other group it is the emotion which bursts its way through. It gets tapped suddenly by something which is actually associated with some unconscious preoccupation, though the connection is not recognised consciously, so that for a long time the patient has no idea what this emotion is all about. With these people it is the concrete ideas attached to the emotions which are deeply buried. Anyone who belongs to this group gets every now and then, in the course of his analysis, the curious experience of finding some apparently trivial idea suddenly letting loose a flood of emotion, and he may find himself in tears or in a panic without being able to understand what has upset him. It is not till both the emotions and the concrete ideas to which they are attached can make their way to the surface together that the patient begins to be relieved of his anxiety by beginning to realise the fantastic nature of his fears.

When I explained about free-association to one of my patients she was evidently relieved. She told me that she had always supposed that analysis was a game of *pounce*. The patient was got off his guard and then was betrayed into mentioning something like a snake or a Christmas tree, and then the analyst pounced on it and interpreted it as a phallic symbol, and that was how the treatment proceeded.

It is really very different from this. A good analyst, while, of course, he is bound to keep the results of his reading and experience in mind, should never feel sure of his patient's meaning till the *associations* tell him what it really is. If the patient can bring himself to let his thoughts go freely, they should together work out the concrete details of what the unconscious is occupied with; but in the end it must always be the patient who tells what they are both looking for, because only the patient holds the key to the secret beliefs and terrors and fantasies which are the cause of his illness. He really knows somewhere in himself, but what he knows is not accessible to consciousness. It is these unconscious parts of himself that give the key to the meaning of his symptoms. As the patient gradually gets back into touch with this part of his own mind, what it is trying to express or to hide by the illness at length emerges.

This gives the explanation of his symptoms. And the curious thing is that it also removes them. The reason seems to be that their usefulness has been destroyed. Psychogenic symptoms are created when powerful impulses which are being forcibly repressed from consciousness threaten to break through the barrier and become conscious. If this actually happens, the symptom is no longer any good. The symptoms served to disguise from consciousness what the unconscious was preoccupied with, but when once the disguise has been pulled off by the patient himself becoming aware of what the symptom means, it is no longer able to perform its function and is abandoned automatically.

I do not mean by this that it is enough just to find out what the patient unconsciously means by his symptoms and tell him. At first Freud hoped this was all that was needed, but he soon found out, to his disappointment, that it was by no means so simple as this. Merely being told, or even merely accepting intellectually what one is told, counts for very little. There is a big gap between knowing a thing intellectually and realising it. Everybody recognises this difference. In the first case what is known intellectually is just an isolated proposition, in the second it links up with the rest of experience, it fits in and its full meaning is felt, and when a patient knows the meaning of his symptom in this second more intimate sense, he cannot go on having that symptom even if he wants to. Sometimes, indeed, this remarkable fact—for it undoubtedly *is* a fact—leads to trouble. If an unwary doctor rashly attacks a symptom and succeeds in making the patient realise why he is producing it before he is ready with any better way of solving his difficulties, this patient's last state may be worse than his first.

Psychogenic symptoms, as has been said, are not produced just for fun, but only to meet a very real emergency. They are actually barriers against what the patient unconsciously regards as an intolerable situation, or safety valves for frustrated unconscious impulses when the tension threatens to become unbearable, and their function is to let off steam so as to keep down the pressure of undischarged energy.

If the defensive barrier is forcibly removed while the danger is still believed to be imminent, the patient will produce a new symptom or fall into agonising anxiety: or if the safety valve is stopped up without there being any other way of discharging the pressure, it simply means that the pressure goes on mounting, and again the patient must either protect himself by producing another symptom or else suffer an anxiety attack. So it is clear that a certain amount of judgment is needed about the advisability of taking people's symptoms away from them. Perhaps now and then the symptoms are the best adjustment to reality of which the patient is capable. Very often, however, this is certainly not true; he *is* capable of a better solution of his difficulties. I mention the possible dangers of removing symptoms recklessly only as a warning against wild psychotherapy, which attacks the isolated symptom without giving proper attention to the underlying anxiety which makes the symptom necessary.

This anxiety, though it feels very real to the patient, is not based on reality but arises because the patient is still unconsciously dominated by a fantastic picture of the world carried over from the early time when he could not distinguish between fact and imagination and was really helpless before the urgency of his own impulses. It rests on misconceptions which have remained fixed, like little hard pieces of insane delusion, in an otherwise sane personality, primitive beliefs and emotions which have not grown up along with the rest of him because they were met almost from the beginning by too severe repression, dissociated, and so never afterwards seen through and outgrown. Free-association is often able gradually to bring these fossilised remains to the surface. When they can be brought into consciousness and examined in the light of adult knowledge and experience, their terrors vanish and with them the anxiety and the need for symptoms. The right way to proceed, then, is always to pay attention to the supposed danger situation which makes the symptoms necessary, and if anxiety about this is successfully resolved the symptoms will disappear of their own accord.

SUMMARY

In this chapter I have put forward a very general preliminary outline of the Freudian theory of psychogenic illness. There is, of course, still a great deal to add. According to this theory, the symptoms of psychogenic illness all have a meaning, but this meaning can only be understood if we can find out the unconscious reasons for their production. It is claimed that psychogenic illness is a piece of behaviour as purposive as putting a hand up to ward off a blow. The purpose of this kind of illness is to prevent anxiety from developing. Anxiety is experienced when strong impulses are aroused which can find no means of discharge, and thus set up an intolerable condition of psychophysical tension. External privation alone might perhaps cause tension, with its accompanying anxiety, but in practice it is found that the anxiety of neurosis results from the internal frustration which is produced when strong contradictory impulses are aroused simultaneously and checkmate each other. When such a situation arises the resulting emotional tension may prove absolutely intolerable, and in that case it will be met by repression, that is by banishing from consciousness the conflicting impulses and whatever tends to arouse them. If such repression takes place, what is banished from consciousness continues to carry on a subterranean dissociated existence in the unconscious.

A condition is thus set up in which one part of the personality is fighting against the other, since the impulses which have been repressed never give up but go on and on always trying to break down the barrier and achieve satisfaction. A lifelong battle is thus begun between repressed and repressing forces, but, if repression is easily the stronger, consciousness may never know anything about it. If, however, repression threatens to break down, then this impending danger may begin to disturb consciousness by arousing anxiety.

Psychogenic illnesses are the ways in which the organism strives to prevent this morbid anxiety from developing. The symptoms, on this view, are produced for a very definite purpose, but this purpose is quite outside conscious awareness, and their production is involuntary and not under conscious control. They are really defences against the threat of the return of the repressed which, when repression weakens, begins to intrude upon ordinary consciousness.

Since this theory of psychogenic illness presupposes that the stream of consciousness and even the physiological functions can be interfered with by a dissociated and repressed part of the self of which the conscious personality is unconscious, I went on to give a few illustrations to show that, in some cases at any rate, such interference does undoubtedly occur, and I concluded by giving a brief account of the technique devised by Freud for getting in touch with this repressed part of the self which, according to the psychoanalytic hypothesis, produces and explains the symptoms of psychogenic illness.

CHAPTER II

In the preceding chapter I stated the fundamental assumption which underlies Freud's explanation of psychogenic illness and the free-association technique which he employs in its investigation and cure, the assumption that in psychogenic illness a part of the personality has been forcibly split off from the rest and is continually trying to push its way back to overt expression, so that whenever the repressing barrier weakens or conscious control is relaxed it tends to interfere with conscious thought and feeling and behaviour and to modify them in accordance with its own preoccupations.

It is not possible, here at the outset, to bring forward proof of such a sweeping assumption as this; its verification can only proceed gradually and must consist in showing how the apparent chaos of the material offered by psychogenic illness—which it is our business here to examine—can, if this assumption be granted, be reduced to order. Full verification would involve the study of the whole of psychoanalysis and cannot really be completed without first-hand experience, both of being analysed oneself and of analysing others.

In what follows I shall assume this hypothesis, entertaining it provisionally as if it were true, and then showing what can be made of it. If it throws light upon matters which otherwise would remain obscure, it will to that extent acquire a certain measure of probability.

Assuming, then, that parts of the self do get repressed, and that they really do lie *completely* outside consciousness, some way has to be found of getting in touch with them. As has been explained, experience shows that this can best be done by reversing the usual technique of conscious effort and concentration and just letting the mind drift.

According to the hypothesis we are assuming, it is claimed that the findings of this reversed technique reveal the causes of psychogenic illness; cure results from the readjustment of outlook which is made possible by their recovery in consciousness.

This free-association technique is like a dredging machine trying to release a ship's anchor which has fouled a snag. It delves down again and again bringing up the sea-bottom until at last the anchor comes away. When that is hauled to the surface the ship can go on her way.

In putting faith in free-association to reveal the preoccupations of the unconscious the analyst is of course assuming the validity of the hypothesis that the unconscious preoccupations really are there, and really always do take control when conscious control relapses; and perhaps in so doing he may be accused of arguing in a circle. But psychoanalysis, despite the exuberance of some of its converts, is, after all, not a Gospel, but an empirical science building up general laws on the material it observes. Perhaps there are exceptions to this rule on which the analyst relies. Perhaps not *every* association is relevant, nor *every* slip or dream or joke significant. Close observation, however, shows that at any rate these are often in some way related to the underlying preoccupation, far more often than anyone who has not investigated the question would imagine. All that is needed is that it should be sufficiently so for us to be able to reconstruct with fair certainty what the patient's deep unconscious emotional preoccupations are, if he will only carry out *his* part and say everything that occurs to him without selecting.

But now another objection may be raised. Free-association, it may be said, might give useful information about what lies in the unconscious if the patient were left to himself. But free-association as practised by the psychoanalysts is spoilt because the analyst interferes by putting all sorts of suggestions into the patient's head. Naturally, after he has got an influence over the patient, he hears back from the patient just what he *himself* has told him, and then he takes this as a confirmation of his theories! Of course his evidence grows apace!

This criticism is fundamental for psychoanalysis. To begin with, I will say that I think it *does* happen that the patient often tells the analyst what he thinks the analyst wants to hear. People who come with the idea that they have to recover infantile memories will sometimes search about for them dutifully; people who think they are going to be expected to talk about sex may begin by talking about nothing else. But these people are not free-associating. When free-association really gets under way the patient often does not know what he is telling. It comes in parables and disguises, the interpretation of which may require knowledge of the language of the unconscious.

Suppose it is now suggested to a patient that perhaps what he is really worrying about is not these disguised ideas but some other trouble which they stand for, he may agree or disagree, it does not greatly matter. The object of the analyst's interventions is not to get the patient to accept what he is told, but simply to help to get back into touch with a buried part of himself.

Bit by bit, as analysis advances, this buried unconscious becomes more accessible to consciousness; remarks which strike down to the unconscious help this, bad shots glance off. Interpretations are useful in analysis only in so far as they help to bridge the gulf between conscious and unconscious, and so enable the patient to get at fresh material. Obviously the analyst is not omniscient. When he is wrong the patient must correct him, and he will probably do so unwittingly in the next few free-associations which he produces. When the analyst's intervention is relevant the next association will confirm and amplify it, even though the patient may be intending, in consciousness, to contradict what has been suggested. The analysis is an exploration which the patient and the analyst are carrying out together into the obscure regions of the patient's unconscious. The patient knows the way, but he is blindfold; the analyst can see, but he does not know where to go. All that is necessary is that the patient should feel safe that whatever he suceeds in revealing will be received by the analyst simply as objective fact, in the same uncritical spirit as he himself is asked to adopt.

A number of further questions arise here, and I shall return to the problem of treatment in my final chapter.

But now there is just one more theoretical point I want to raise about the assumption on which the validity of free-association rests. In trying to explain why one train of thought calls up another, it is evident that I am assuming psychological determinism, namely, that even these apparently disconnected and senseless ramblings do not happen by chance, but follow some ascertainable general laws.

This question whether we should or should not accept psychological determinism has come up here in connection with the validity of free-association, but it has also a wider application. For psychological determinism assumes that, however disconnected they may appear superficially, mental events *always* happen in accordance with general laws, thus excluding the notion of chance from the field of psychology, as it has already for a long time been excluded from the physical universe. The assumption that general laws underlie the apparently disconnected ramblings of free-association is only one instance of this general position. It is assumed equally when we undertake to give causal explanation of other hitherto inexplicable phenomena such as psychogenic illness or minor everyday "accidental" errors or slips.

If we do not accept psychological determinism we must, I suppose, fall back on the notion of chance or accident to explain the order in which any of these various psychological phenomena present themselves, which amounts to giving up the attempt to find any explanation at all. This may be the only thing to do, since we should be foolish to waste time trying to find explanations where none exist: on the other hand, if they do exist, we should be foolish to give up trying to find them.

There are three possibilities: the sequences of mental events which we are considering may follow general laws which we can some day formulate; *or* they may follow general laws which contain so many variables that in practice their complication is impossibly great so that we never could in fact formulate them; *or* they may really happen by chance, in the sense that the events in question are not instances of the operation of *any* general laws, so that there is no sense in trying to explain them.

Perhaps enormous numbers of things are permanently inexplicable for one or other of these reasons; the question is whether it is or is not possible to explain these particular things we are discussing, first and foremost the symptoms of psychogenic illness, and in this connection such other deviations from our ordinary functioning as dreams, "accidental" slips and errors, or free-associations. Is it or is it not possible to link these things up by general laws, and if so, are those laws sufficiently simple to be ascertainable? Or are they each unique events, the result of a grouping of antecedents which may happen once perhaps and never again?

Obviously, nothing can be explicable unless it contains repetitions which can be classified. If each event were utterly new and entirely unlike any other, then explanation would be ruled out. But the psychological events we are concerned with are not obviously incapable of explanation in this sense. They can be thought of as series of events containing terms sufficiently like each other to fall into groups of similars which can be classified; they fall into recognisable patterns. Successful explanation would consist in discovering general laws about the relative changes of these classes of psychological events; the laws governing this pattern formation.

Whether we can in fact succeed in formulating such laws can only be decided by trying. In so trying we make the assumption that these relative changes really do follow some ascertainable general laws which it is our business to discover—that is, we assume the hypothesis of determinism. The physical world falls into patterns, too, and as physics has made its tremendous advances by working on this assumption, it will probably pay psychology to do the same.

All that this argument amounts to is simply this, that, although we cannot know for certain that there are general laws to be discovered in the subject-matter we are investigating, we do not know for certain that there are *not*, and the best way is to assume that there are, and try to find them out.

But assuming that there are laws to be discovered in this field, we still have several alternatives: are these laws bodily or are they mental? Or do mind and body mutually influence each other, or does only one influence the other? The considerations which should settle this question for us depend simply, I think, on what we can, in fact, find out. We have a certain amount of data of both kinds, we know something about our bodies and also something about our thoughts and feelings.

Some people seem greatly to prefer explanations in terms of

physical causes, and they would "explain" mental sequences by means of parallel bodily sequences and say that mental processes are simply products of physico-chemical changes which take place in the nervous tissues of the brain. They seem to feel somehow on safer ground in attributing what happens to the laws of physics or chemistry, as if there was somehow more real "causality" about material objects than about mere ideas. Indeed, I believe there are people who claim that only such explanations can really be "scientific" at all. This may be because they believe that explanations are truly scientific only when the laws of the relative change of classified groups are expressed in mathematical formulae; for certainly it is true, and perhaps will always remain true, that the subject-matter of physics and chemistry lends itself to mathematical formulation much better than the subject-matter of psychology. If this is all they mean, then it comes down to a mere matter of words—whether we wish to confine the meaning of the term scientific to explanation in strictly mathematical form, or whether we will widen it to include other kinds of explanation which are not capable of mathematical formulation.

But I believe it is more than a mere matter of the definition of the word "scientific". I believe there is also a metaphysical error underlying this preference for physical explanations which need not hamper anyone as soon as he sees through the assumptions on which it rests.

When we are explaining in physico-chemical terms we make use of such hypothetical entities as atoms, forces, electrical charges, etc. When we are explaining in psychological terms, the hypothetical entities we use are drawn on analogy with mental and not physical events. Here we explain the observed facts, not as the upshot of a cancelling out of physical forces pulling in various directions with various strengths, but of conflicts of instincts contradicting each other. The misleading assumption which makes people prefer the physico-chemical kind of explanation to the psychological is, I think, the supposition that such things as gravitation and acceleration are somehow more really existent than the impulsions of unconscious instincts.

What they have failed to grasp is the fictitious nature of *all* these hypothetical entities, gravitation and instincts alike. All that really exists is the data which are to be explained, the falling apple, or the nightmares or delusions. The terms in which the explaining general laws are expressed are all of them only hypothetical assumptions, not existent realities, and they are all in the same boat: one is no more "real" than another, all are equally justified if they do explain, and meaningless otherwise.

The observed facts we want to examine are mixed, some physical and some mental, but if our general laws explain, in the sense of reducing this material to order, we are surely at liberty to choose the terms in which we will state our laws in whatever way suits us best. The great thing to bear in mind is that these terms are all alike simply useful assumptions.

The hypothesis of unconscious thoughts and feelings and wishes is closely comparable to the hypothesis, for example, of unperceived atoms and forces: both are drawn on analogy from what is conscious and perceived, that is both are invented or constructed like round squares or chimeras, for a purpose. Their justification lies in the fact of the usefulness of the laws we formulate in terms of them. Unconscious mental states and unperceived atoms are exactly on a par, equally fictitious or real, as you please, equally justified if they can be used to make a working hypothesis.

What I want to make clear is just this, then, that to explain is simply to sum up sequences of classes of events which have been observed always to follow one another in the same order. We observe all kinds of sequences—physical following physical, as when clouds bring rain; physical following mental, as when grief brings tears; mental following physical, as when a blow arouses anger; mental following mental when, for instance, anger is followed by remorse. "Causality" does not belong to any one of these rather than to any other—the clouds do not "cause" rain in any more real sense than grief causes tears, a blow pain, or anger remorse. When we want to form general laws to explain what happens, we are free to select and classify our data in whatever way gives us the most comprehensive general laws, that is to say, wherever we can collect the most evidence.

Whether or no we are investigating scientifically depends on whether we are working to discover the general laws by observing the relative changes of classes of events: it does not depend in the least on the hypothetical terms in which we choose to state our general laws.

And I will now go further and say that not only are explanations in terms of hypotheses drawn on analogy with mental events no less "scientific" than those which are stated in terms drawn from physical events, but in dealing with the subject-matter we are discussing, namely, psychogenic illness, explanations in terms of these mental fictions are the best ones to choose, at any rate in the present state of our knowledge.

In this subject of psychogenic illness we have at present much more evidence about the sequence of classes of mental events than of any other sequences. We are very short of observed facts about the relation between bodily and mental changes. Although a great mass of interesting material has been collected in physiology and biochemistry, we still know very little about the physiological or biochemical modifications which go with changes of thought and feeling. We have not the least idea of what happens in the brain, for instance, in such an everyday psychological event as recognising a familiar object. We may talk about association tracts and lowered resistance at synapses, but we should be unable to describe correctly even the commonest mental phenomenon if we had to do it in physiological or biochemical terms. We simply have not got the necessary technique for observing concomitant sequences going on both mentally and also physiologically or biochemically, and that is the sort of thing we should need for physiology or biochemistry to be of much use in explaining psychogenic illness.

Perhaps some day we shall be able to fill this gap in our observable data, but at present we cannot do it, and to content ourselves with an act of faith about there being *some* causal relation between mental, physiological and biochemical changes —though very likely there is—gets us no further towards explaining why one mental event follows another or why a mental event follows a physical and *vice versa*.

If ever we do get necessary information, which we at present lack, for making a useful working hypothesis which will explain the symptoms of psychogenic illness in terms of physiological or biochemical laws, it will be all the better. There is no incompatibility between psychological and physiological or biochemical explanations: whatever explains, that is, brings order in the chaos of observed facts by reducing it to general laws, is justified, regardless of what the terms happen to be in which the laws are framed.

But we do not need to wait for physiology or biochemistry, since even now, on the mental side, we all know a great deal about the way feelings and thoughts connect with each other in conscious experience. Nobody seriously thinks of trying to explain our ordinary daily behaviour in physico-chemical terms: we explain it according to purely psychological laws which nobody questions. "He was angry because someone kicked him." "I ran because I was afraid." More or less by analogy with these psychological explanations of conscious mental sequences, we are beginning to be able to construct, bit by bit, a wider addition to this knowledge by finding out a little about the laws which govern *unconscious* mental events also, and about the relations between conscious and unconscious mental processes. We need be no more disturbed by the hypothesis that there are such things as unconscious mental processes than we are by the general assumption, always made in physics, of unperceived matter.

Of course the fact that in physics people can verify or repeat each other's experiments does make us more comfortable in relying on observed sequences of physical rather than of psychological events, and I think investigations about material phenomena certainly have in this respect a real advantage over investigations of psychological phenomena. Perhaps, however, we are inclined to over-estimate it: for even in repeating another physicist's experiments or observations there is always the subjective factor of the two observers to reckon with, so that in this field also it is impossible that the very same experiment should ever actually be repeated. But certainly groups of data are more easily isolated for observation, and the same situations are more nearly capable of being reproduced in physics or chemistry than in psychology.

This is a handicap that psychology has to recognise and put up with. But it does not necessarily invalidate all psychological conclusions. Undoubtedly we *do* collect evidence, and undoubtedly we do ultimately attain, if not to certainty in the general laws which emerge from our observation, at least to probability and even in some cases to a high degree of probability. But equally undoubtedly the method which our material forces us to employ is not "scientific" in the strict mathematical sense. The conditions under which we work make this inevitable: you simply cannot isolate and repeat a psychological experiment as you can a physical one.

Nevertheless, it would be pedantic to throw away the evidence which it is possible to collect simply because the investigation does not conform to the requirements of some other science whose methods and possibilities are quite different.

The *method* employed in psychoanalysis has one important point in common with other scientific procedures, and that is that it *is objective*. The material supplied by the patient is not weighed up by him but by the analyst who listens to him. This objectivity is all important and gives psychoanalysis the right to call itself a scientific study as compared with introspective psychology.

So far I have attempted to give an idea of the kind of approach which I want to make to psychogenic illness. I believe, as I have said, that it is produced to meet a situation which everyone has to face—namely, how to bear privation, or disappointment, or fear, and what to do about the mounting up of tension generated by emotional conflict and the anxiety which this inevitably arouses.

It is possible to meet this situation without falling ill, but undoubtedly the first experiences of disappointment and fear which happen in early childhood are critical. The way in which a child succeeds in dealing with these early situations of conflict sets the pattern for its later development. I believe that the foundations of psychogenic illness always date from the early conflicts between desire, disappointment and fear in childhood, even if the illness does not develop into a form which can be clearly recognised till much later. When we are more familiar with the childish manifestations of neurosis we shall recognise this illness much more often in its early stages; but at present so much of what is really neurosis in children is passed over as mere ordinary "naughtiness", or a phase which will be outgrown, that we do not give it the full weight it really deserves.

The fundamental point to be grasped is that what endangers mental health is the conflict which inevitably occurs to some extent in every child between its deepest instinctive cravings and the reaction of rage and fear which is aroused by disappointment of these.

It would seem that neurosis occurs when the rage and fear are so strong that they produce a deadlock which leads to the repression of the whole conflict. Constitutional inability to tolerate disappointment and delay may be a factor predisposing to neurosis.

This inability may be because of the violence of the conflicting emotions aroused, or because the conflict occurs prematurely before the rest of the personality is sufficiently developed to withstand it, or because of some inherent weakness, so that even a moderate amount of tension is too much for the child's make up. Any of these reasons may make the conflict intolerable and drive the child to deal with it in the neurotic way by repression.

Again, real experience of cruelty, either witnessed or endured, in connection with the people around whom the child's interest centres may arouse such strong fear or resentment that the resulting conflict is too acute to be tolerated: or, on the other hand, this excessive fear and resentment may not be based on real experiences but on fantasies whose origin lies in the child's own imagination.

The early pioneers in the study of the unconscious causes of mental illness laid great stress on the disruptive effects of painful or terrifying *real* experiences. They held that mental illness was produced by the repression of such experiences, and their therapeutic efforts were directed towards recovering memories of them.

Later psychoanalytic investigators have tended more and more to emphasise the importance, not only of real experiences, but also of the child's fantasies of injury which appear to be modelled on its own hostile impulses, aroused by disappointment, and which are often repressed just as the memory of the real experiences themselves may be repressed when they are too painful or terrifying. So now, besides the recovery of real repressed experiences, the psychoanalyst tries to recover the patient's repressed fantasies also.

But, since we have all suffered disappointments and reacted with hostility, and all dealt with the resulting fantasies of injury by some degree of repression, this repression alone cannot be held responsible for neurosis. What I am inclined to think is that repression leads to neurosis when rage and fear play an unusually strong part in the conflict which is being repressed, so that the need for repression is urgent and yet, on account of the strength of the instincts to be held in check, it is exceptionally difficult to maintain. At any rate it seems to be proved, clinically, that people who have, in fact, fallen ill of neurosis are all people who react to frustration with exceedingly powerful hostile emotions, though for the most part these hostile reactions are unconscious. It seems as if in the last analysis it was the violence of their own feelings, however provoked, which brought about their illness.

The effect of repression from consciousness is to break contact with reality. It is the conscious part of our whole mental make-up that seems to stand in closest touch with the outside world, and when any experience or instinct gets dissociated and so becomes unconscious, this means that it loses touch with real life. When this happens it stops developing, it can no longer continue to be modified by experience: and so, whatever has been dissociated does not grow up along with the rest of the personality which has maintained better contact with the outside world. It sets up what might be described as a delusional system inside the rest of the personality, cut off from the experiences which would normally modify it and dispel the delusion.

These repressed delusional systems are charged with the emotions which would be appropriate if they were real, and when repression is inadequate they tend to colour the person's outlook on reality, which is now interpreted unconsciously in terms of the delusions instead of being recognised for what it is. This means that reality is reacted to with emotions which would be appropriate if these delusions were indeed true, but which is quite inappropriate to the real state of affairs. This goes on until the delusions are either so successfully repressed that they do not interfere with real life, or else are dispelled by lifting the repression so that they may be known consciously and disproved by experience.

To give an illustration: suppose a child got the idea that when people tried to kiss him they meant to bite him or eat him up, and suppose that, on the strength of this delusion, he went through life kicking and struggling when anyone seemed likely to want to kiss him, hating them for it and wanting to revenge himself by biting them back. If they ever succeeded in kissing him, suppose he believed that they had bitten a piece off him or that he had managed to retaliate by biting a piece off them. It is easy to see what trouble this delusion would introduce into his emotional relations!

This picture is really much less fantastic than it seems. It is actually quite like what goes on unconsciously in many neurotics, and consciously in lunatics.

Abnormal people are chiefly to be distinguished from normal ones by the excessive power which these unconscious delusions exercise over their daily lives. I do not believe that even the most normal are quite free from this interference, and the difference between normal and abnormal can, from this point of view, be regarded as a matter of degree.

Another way of looking at the difference (which really amounts to the same thing) is that it depends on the extent to which the person is capable of coming into contact with reality and so correcting by actual experience the tendency to delusion which is latent in all imagination. Those who develop psychogenic illness are relatively deficient in sense of reality or impervious to the correction of imagination by experience. And this amounts again to saying that they are too much governed by their unconscious, they act in obedience to what *it* believes, rather than in the light of real experience.

It is from these unconscious delusions that the illness springs, delusions composed of fantasies which date from the early days when dissociation occurred and which have ever since remained quite out of touch with reality. The symptoms cannot be understood, therefore, unless we know what is being imagined and believed and wished and feared at this unconscious level.

The explanation of the symptoms of psychogenic illness will be in terms of the delusions which belong to the unconscious part of the patient's personality. This will become clearer if we take some typical illustrations of the sort of symptoms neurotic patients do actually develop, and then try to show, in concrete instances, just how they may be explained, working on the hypothesis that they are the expressions of dissociated impulses or early experiences or fantasies which in disguised form have broken through the barrier of repression.

I realise, however, that my explanations of the symptoms will not, after all, at first sight seem to make their meaning so very plain, and before we actually begin on the case illustrations I want to point out some of the main reasons why this must be so, otherwise what I say may simply be rejected as rubbish, without receiving the careful attention and hearing which it needs if it is to be understood. Inevitably the psychoanalytic explanations of symptoms which I shall offer will be bound to appear far-fetched and improbable; moreover, they may actually conflict with one another, since I shall sometimes have to offer several different and seemingly contradictory explanations of the same symptom.

The best defence I can make is that this would, after all, be what one would expect if the symptoms arise out of the conflict of incompatible impulses which are themselves foreign to our ordinary conscious ways of thinking and feeling.

It is perhaps this sense that the unconscious motives suggested are foreign to our conscious ideas, even more than the fact of their being contradictory, which makes us instinctively reject the explanations of psychogenic illness which psychoanalysis offers. The natural reaction to first acquaintance with these explanations seems universally to be one of repudiation on the ground that they are repugnant to common sense. Perhaps they are. But common sense is not the final court of appeal in scientific matters. There was a time when common sense energetically denied the suggestion that the earth is not flat and that the sun does not revolve round it. It was not common sense to suppose that human beings were the descendants of organisms resembling little lumps of jelly, or that our bodies consisted of millions of microscopic cells. And what could be more utterly repugnant to common sense than to believe with modern physicists that objects vary in size according to the rate at which they are travelling? The final decision in scientific theories depends, not on whether or no they conflict with the mass of accepted assumptions and prejudices which constitute the point of view of common sense, but on whether they are successful in reducing to order the facts which they set out to explain. "Common-sense" objections to new scientific theories, though they feel convincing at the moment, are apt to vanish with familiarity, providing these new theories turn out in practice to work successfully.

The objection raised by the apparent contradictoriness of psychoanalytic explanations will not cause trouble if it is recognised that what is to be explained is itself a contradictory state of mind, as, for instance, if what is wanted is to keep and at the same time to destroy the significant object, and that the symptom is often a compromise which attempts the doubly contradictory task of satisfying and at the same time preventing the satisfaction of conflicting impulses, indulging and at the same time denying and perhaps even punishing.

To explain the symptoms as the upshot of contradictory impulses is really no more paradoxical than to explain the motion of a billiard ball as the result of a parallelogram of forces which may be acting in opposite directions. But the explanations of psychogenic symptoms offered by psychoanalysis are liable at first sight to feel unconvincing, not only because they sometimes appear to outrage common sense and logic, but also for another reason, which is that the real meaning of these symptoms is not apparent on the surface, since, quite apart from any inherent strangeness or contradiction in the impulses to which they give expression, what is really wanted is usually not represented openly but only under a disguise. So long as repression holds, the impulses which are pushing up from the unconscious cannot achieve direct expression. Psychogenic symptoms are something half-way between the direct expression, which would arouse anxiety, and complete repression which is no longer possible. The unconscious impulses do get at least partially expressed in the symptoms, but only in a roundabout way: what is meant may perhaps only be hinted at or expressed in a kind of parable.

This is due, no doubt, in part to the veto which repression puts on direct expression, but I think the kind of mental operation which goes on in the unconscious would be found to differ considerably from conscious mental processes, even apart from any distortion which may be introduced by the need for concealment.

The forms of expression natural to the unconscious seem to be comparable to the language of dreams, in which wishes may be symbolically represented as having come true. For instance, to give an imaginary illustration, someone who was strongly patriotic, and preoccupied by the dread of a reduction in the Navy Estimates, might be supposed to dream of a woman dressed in red, white and blue, holding a trident. All is well, Britannia is still ruling the waves. This dream cartoon would bear a relation to the patriotic uneasiness very like the relation which I believe holds between unconscious repressed impulses and psychogenic symptoms. In fact, the parallel between psychogenic symptoms and dreams is very close.

Sleep seems to be a normally occurring disturbance of our consciousness which resembles psychogenic illness in that there is a temporary weakening of the barrier which in waking life shuts out the unconscious pretty effectively in healthy people. Even in the healthy the barrier is lowered normally during sleep, so that repressed impulses and unconscious wishes begin to speak out in the curious hallucinations of dreaming. Here what is trying to get expressed is frequently put in the form of a cartoon which is sometimes what we should call very ingenious if it had been done by someone who was awake. It is not exactly ingenious in a sleeper any more than neurotics are ingenious, or an absent-minded professor who makes "Spoonerisms"—this sort of oblique expression seems to be the natural way for the unconscious to slip through—for instance the two slips of the tongue I quoted in my previous chapter both availed themselves of a sort of punning: convict—convince, contract—contrast.

This tendency of unconscious meanings to be expressed in distorted and unfamiliar, and even what we might consider silly, ways helps to make it seem at first sight as if neurotic symptoms and similar things like dreams and slips had no intelligible meaning at all. But I hope to show that there is at least a possibility of making sense of all these apparently pointless human aberrations, and in particular of the symptoms of psychogenic illness with which this book is mainly concerned.

Obsessional symptoms are our best starting-point, because they are so clearly the result of some kind of mental activity cut off from the main consciousness and yet able to interfere with it. The sufferer sometimes feels as if he were compelled by some external influence, a feeling which becomes so strong in some forms of insanity that the patient is convinced that he is the victim of an external agency which has obtained a magical power over him. Obsessionals experience, in a lesser degree, just this same sense of being possessed by some force which is not their own will. They feel a tremendous impulse to do things which are apparently senseless, and yet they cannot be at peace till they have done them. Everyone has probably done a few mildly obsessional things, such as avoiding stepping on the cracks between paving-stones, or feeling impelled to touch some particular object, or not touch it, or touch it three times over. This sort of behaviour is just slightly obsessional. You do not really *have* to perform the silly action, but you feel a little uncomfortable if you do not. With the true obsessional all this is greatly magnified.

He may spend a large part of his life doing apparently silly things like avoiding cracks or touching special objects. He may even find himself compelled to carry out elaborate rituals occupying hours of his time every day. He feels what he is doing to be meaningless and yet he *must* do it. Or he may find himself compelled to think and think about some problem in which he feels no real interest. And yet he goes on thinking with a strained concentration which exhausts him. He worries and speculates against his own will as if it were a matter of life and death to him. If he is prevented from any of these compulsive actions he may become acutely miserable without understanding the reason. Now why do these people feel compelled to do all these apparently senseless things?

The explanation I offer is that these apparently meaningless actions have a very real and important meaning. Ultimately they may all be explained as defences against anxiety which have become necessary because the barrier of repression which normally holds down the contents of the unconscious is threatening to give way.

I explained in the preceding chapter that when this begins to happen it is necessary to take further defence measures, and these are the symptoms belonging to psychogenic illness. As we have already said, these symptoms may alleviate anxiety in one of two ways, either by reinforcing the repression or else by allowing the partially repressed impulses some kind of expression. When repression alone is not enough to allay anxiety, one way of reinforcing it is by over-emphasising the opposite of what has to be repressed. In effect it says: "How can I possibly want that? On the contrary, I want the very opposite". I have said that this way of reinforcing repression is called "over-compensation". It is a mechanism often used, and we are apt to see through it in other people, even though it feels very convincing when we use it ourselves.

When the partial failure of repression is dealt with in this way by over-compensation there is nothing of the original repressed impulse in the symptom. It is simply pushed farther back. Many obsessional symptoms can only be understood if we interpret them as defences in this sense of over-emphasising the opposite of some repressed impulse.

Thus over-compensation against a repressed death wish may take the form of an excessive anxiety about the health of the person concerned; conscious humility is often only the reverse side of unconscious arrogance. We all recognise that there is something suspicious about extreme politeness, which is indeed often an over-compensation against antipathy or contempt.

I have already mentioned another type of defence which consists in dissociating the emotion from the situation to which it belongs, so that the situation can be met without feeling anything about it. Here there is no positive symptom, only a negative one—a blank where some emotion would naturally be expected.

Obsessionals often make use of this type of defence. They may carry out their rituals without any conscious emotion, though these may indeed unconsciously represent something about which they feel passionately. The fact that what they are doing must have some deep significance for them is only betrayed by the intense anxiety which assails them if anything interferes.

When the difficulty is met not by more repression but by allowing the repressed impulses some expression, then there will be positive symptoms, though their meaning is usually not at first obvious, because the expression allowed the repressed impulses is disguised. What the obsessional patient does, avoiding cracks in the pavement, for instance, is not the actual thing his unconscious repressed impulses are urging him to do, but something else which only stands for it, as it were, symbolically, like Britannia flourishing a trident, or like a parable.

The sower went out to sow his seed, and it fell on barren ground, is just such a symbolic expression of an underlying meaning in which the *seed* stands for the *word of God* and the *ground* for *those who hear the word.* But, of course, in an ordinary parable we know what we mean by our symbols: the obsessional patient does not know. He would be in the position of someone who felt an apparently senseless compulsion to go about scattering seeds without in the least realising that what he really wanted was to preach the word of God.

In psychoanalysis the term symbol is used in this narrower sense and applied only to cases in which the identification between the symbol and that for which it stands is *unconscious.*

Symbolic expression is immensely widespread. As we go on I shall be able to give illustrations of symbolism in the strict psychoanalytic sense, which, from the nature of things, are bound to be unfamiliar to anyone who has not studied the ways in which unconscious preoccupations translate themselves into consciousness. Here, confining myself to the sort of things with which we are all familiar, I shall speak only of symbols whose interpretations we all recognise without difficulty.

Everyone makes use frequently of such symbols in poetry and slang; our own ceremonies and the magic rites of savages depend on substituting symbols for the things that really concern us. If anyone salutes the flag or stands up at "God Save the King", he is behaving symbolically, and so is the savage who burns a waxen image of his enemy—clearly the importance does not depend on the actual piece of bunting or the lump of melting wax, but on that for which they stand. By substituting symbols we can act out our meaning—pay homage to the king or country, or burn up an enemy. This is extremely like what the obsessional does—he acts out in his symptoms the meaning of something which he wants, or piles up the symptoms as a defence against something which he dreads, or represents the undoing of something which he regrets; only he does not himself recognise what he means by what he does.

It is characteristic of obsessional symptoms that the symbol representing the real underlying wish or dread is apt to seem to our conscious ideas very far-fetched; but if we knew what the apparently silly actions and speculations of obsessionals really meant, we should see that the effort which the patient puts into them is not out of place. It only *seems* out of place because it has been transferred from the original preoccupations, to which it was appropriate, on to a substituted symbol which in its own right might not have been interesting or significant at all. As I have said, there seems in this substituting of symbols to be an attempt to lessen anxiety. The patient goes on giving expression to a preoccupation which he has tried to repress, with only partial success so that he cannot entirely rid himself of it; but this expression, not being recognised consciously for what it really is, on account of the disguise, arouses less anxiety than if it were expressed quite baldly.

A doctor[1] in an asylum came across a very interesting case which showed such an obsessional symptom in the process of being created by transferring an idea which, in its original undisguised form, was too alarming, because too nearly intelligible, into something silly and harmless which could stand symbolically for it. A man of about thirty had for some time been

[1] Dr Adrian Stephen's case.

troubled with the insistent thought forming itself in his mind, "Cut it off, cut it off". This thought, about whose precise meaning he was doubtful, but which alarmed him, would not give him any peace till one day he decided to change it for himself. Whenever the alarming thought "cut it off" came into his mind, he quickly substituted the harmless and apparently silly phrase, "Sussex Gorse"—and he had already more or less succeeded in arranging matters so that it was now those words "Sussex Gorse" which forced themselves on his attention, instead of the original "cut it off". No one, seeing this patient a few years hence, will have the slightest idea that this curious obsession with the words "Sussex Gorse" has any sensible meaning at all.

In this case the patient actually consciously tried to substitute the senseless words "Sussex Gorse" for the other words "cut it off" which were too nearly intelligible and therefore too terrifying. If this suggestion kept on coming into his head undisguised he might one day really *cut it off*, whatever *it* was. But although the symbols may be substituted to avoid the anxiety which would be aroused by more direct expression, this substitution usually takes place quite involuntarily, and the person who is reacting to the symbol cannot himself tell you what more disturbing thing it stands for.

I will now quote a few of the symptoms of a typical obsessional case to illustrate the sort of things these people worry over, and then I will give the interpretation by which I should try to explain these symptoms.

I had an obsessional patient who was unable to pass a stone in the road without removing it. If she was in a hurry, she would shut her eyes and try not to see the road, but then she became dreadfully anxious and would often have to go back and examine the part of the road she had missed out, in case there might be a stone. The idea came to her that if she neglected to move a stone someone might stumble over it, fall under the traffic and be killed, and she would be responsible. She knew that it was nonsense, and yet she could not help herself. Again, if she touched anything with her hair, she would worry in case the hair had not been clean and she might have infected the object and somebody would catch the infection and die. These were only a few of her scruples, but they illustrate the sort of thing she worried over.

I should explain these symptoms as being *defences against an unconscious death wish*. They belong, I think, to the type of defence which reinforces the repression by emphasising the very opposite of the repressed impulse. What she dreaded consciously was that something she did or omitted to do might result in the death of some *stranger*. At times she was overcome with the feeling that either she or her mother must die, but she did not connect this with her illness.

I suggest that this feeling and her symptoms were closely connected. Her mother was terribly on her nerves, yet she felt she could not leave her. Living with her was spoiling her life; if only her mother were dead, she would be free to live a life of her own. I suggest that this patient had a very powerful wish for her mother's death which was in conflict with the rest of her rather exceptionally moral character and which had been dissociated because the strain of the conflict was unendurable. I suggest that this repressed wish was always struggling to get control of consciousness and action so as to carry itself out; it was held successfully in check, but only by a sort of exaggeration of the opposite as a make-weight, that is, by over-compensation to reinforce the insecure repression. In the symptom, as it actually appeared, there appeared no sign of the original repressed death wish. One could only infer the existence of such a wish from the fact that it was necessary to over-compensate so exaggeratedly in consciousness.

This patient's obsessional symptoms aimed, then, not at gratifying the unconscious murder impulse, but at reversing this wish so that she went out of her way to make quite sure that no harm should come.

Actually, in her symptoms, she was taking the most elaborate precautions to protect strangers from death, but this, it is suggested, sprang ultimately from the unconscious temptation to murder one who was very close to her. And although she repudiated this wish so strongly that her whole illness consisted in a symbolic contradiction of it, nevertheless, the fact that she had such a wish, even though it was strongly repressed, produced in her the most terrible sense of guilt whose real reason she did not understand. The aim of the symptoms was to alleviate her unconscious sense of guilt by reversing the murderous wish so that she was constantly taking precautions to make quite *sure* that no harm should come. Nevertheless the repressed impulse which underlay the illness and kept it going was murder.

But of course such an explanation is over-simplified; I am not satisfied that it is complete or deep enough. Behind the guilt and hostility which appear to account for the obsessional symptoms we shall, as we go on, be able to discover still deeper unconscious motives.

Trying to understand the unconscious motives of any human being is like trying to get at the middle of an onion, or digging through layer upon layer of geological strata. Each outer skin, or each geological layer, gives an explanation, which, so far as it goes, is not untrue, but there is always more beneath it.

If more details were known, the simple explanation in terms of unconscious murder impulses would turn out inadequate as an account of the force which was struggling against the barrier of repression, and such an account, even if it were complete, would only tell us half of what we need to know. For a proper understanding of the dynamics of the illness we need not only to know what impulses are being repressed, but also to understand what is repressing them, since the illness arises out of the conflict between these two opposed forces. Experience with neurotic patients in analysis reveals the driving force behind repression to be fear.

Fear seems to be the *traumatic* emotion, by which I mean that it is fear ultimately which is responsible for the dissociation of personality, or disturbance of the contact with reality, or repression into the unconscious, in which psychogenic illness originates.

In any case, in trying to discover what is "the true explanation" of any given symptom, it would be a mistake to suppose that one explanation necessarily excludes all others. There may be half a dozen or half a million explanations of any given mental event which may all be true at different levels and from different angles. I grant that it is very difficult to decide among all the possible explanations which are essential and which only contributory.

The fault lies partly in our imperfect knowledge. In the case of neurotic illnesses we know a mass of facts which are relevant and it is hard to decide which of them is actually causally dynamic. And, furthermore, the emphasis is continually shifting. We may find in a patient's mind a whole variety of longings and delusions which become stimulated from time to time by his circumstances. Now one and now another seems to be functioning actively at different times, like volcanoes continually forming new craters, the old ones sometimes erupting, sometimes quiescent or rumbling faintly. So we say that now one and now the other is mainly responsible for the illness at any particular time.

But such difficulties in arriving at a perfect diagnosis are not confined to psychogenic illness. In organic illness, too, there are usually many contributing factors of varying importance, and the treatment is successful in proportion to the skill in discovering and dealing with as many of these as possible, but good results can often be achieved even though all the facts have not come to light.

Similarly, in the case of psychogenic illness, considerable relief is sometimes given by bringing to consciousness even a few of the most important of the unconscious factors concerned in producing it, and one of these certainly often appears to be the unconscious impulse to murder. This motive seems to have been important in the case of the obsessional patient of whose illness I have just described, though from knowledge acquired in more radical analyses I feel sure that if this investigation had been carried further still, more deeply buried unconscious impulses would have been found underlying this murderous wish, so that, as it stands, this explanation of her illness is over-simplified.

SUMMARY

In the early part of this chapter I tried to meet a few of the objections which are likely to suggest themselves in connection with the assumptions made by psychoanalysts; the chief of these assumptions is that behind the symptoms of psychogenic illness lie repressed preoccupations which are prevented from becoming conscious; and, the second, that it is possible by means of free-association to lift the repression and get these preoccupations back into consciousness.

I instanced various experiences which prove that preoccupations do go on alongside of ordinary conscious thinking, quite distinct from it and quite unnoticed, but not so seriously repressed that we cannot now and then become aware of them.

As regards the way of getting into touch with parts of our own minds which lie outside consciousness, I drew attention to the common experience of how, in trying to recall something forgotten, it will often flash back into the mind just when all attempts to get at it by voluntary efforts have been given up.

Such analogies from things with which we are already familiar are not strict proof, but they make these psychoanalytic assumptions seem less improbable. They illustrate what is meant. Proof, as far as that is possible at all, can only come bit by bit to the extent to which the hypothesis really does seem to bring order into the chaos of the data presented by psychogenic illness.

I then went on to discuss a different criticism, namely, that psychoanalysts spoil their own experiment by not leaving the patient's associations free but continually biasing them by putting in suggestions. I answered this by explaining what is the purpose of the analyst's interpretations, and what effects they do, in fact, seem to have. I explained that the analyst's object is not to make the patient believe the interpretations which are made; all that he is concerned with is to help the patient to get into touch with the repressed material in his unconscious. The result of some interpretations is that, if he is really to carry out the analytic rule of saying exactly what comes into his head, the patient in his next associations produces fresh unconscious material which is somehow connected with the view on which the interpretation was based, though usually in ways which would not occur to anyone unfamiliar with psychoanalytic theory, and which could therefore only have been provoked by way of the patient's unconscious. If this happens, the analyst feels that his interpretation has been useful. If it does not produce some such release of unconscious material, he suspects that he has been off the track.

I next took up the question of the difference between normal and abnormal people, and suggested that this difference lay in the power to correct fantasy by coming into contact with reality. This contact is lost when a part of the personality becomes dissociated. The dissociated part does not get corrected by experience and therefore fails to grow up. It remains as a delusional system in the otherwise reality adapted, that is, sane personality.

Neurotics, on this view, would be people who have dissociated important parts of themselves so that they are left relatively deficient in reality sense, too much governed by repressed unconscious fantasy.

I devoted the last part of the chapter to a case illustration, but with the warning that the interpretations of symptoms which I should offer were hardly likely to seem convincing.

This is partly because what is trying to get expressed is foreign to our usual ways of thinking and conflicts with the ordinary bias of what we call common sense, and partly because it is itself full of self-contradiction, since what was originally repressed was not a single instinct but a conflict which had produced a deadlock. Furthermore, the emphasis is really shifting all the time, now one and now another of the patient's delusional ideas and his reactions to them being especially active in keeping up the illness.

And finally I explained that, on top of these other reasons, the interpretation of the unconscious meaning of psychogenic illness is bound to feel unconvincing because of the sort of language in which the unconscious seems naturally to express itself. It only gets through into consciousness in roundabout ways which appear unfamiliar and often silly—in parables, for instance, or parodies, or symbols, or even puns.

CHAPTER III

It is the fundamental hypothesis of psychoanalysis that neurotic symptoms have an unconscious meaning and are to be explained as resulting from the conflict of repressed impulses to which they give a disguised outlet.

I have so far discussed some of the intellectual difficulties which this hypothesis raises, and now we must consider a further set of difficulties, this time not intellectual but emotional, that stand in the way of our recognising the meaning of neurotic symptoms and arise out of the very nature of what is going on in the unconscious which understanding of the symptoms would reveal.

Freud's view is that the driving force behind neurotic symptoms is always a *wish*, but he would add that what is wished for is often something which we do not consciously regard as desirable, but rather as abhorrent. There is a conflict when a part of oneself desires what another part abhors, and this is solved, in the case of the neurotic, by dissociation of the whole conflict, so that the patient is actually not even sufficiently conscious of the longing to feel any need to repudiate it.

What lies behind the symptom may, then, be connected ultimately with a repressed wish, but it is a wish which has been dissociated so that the patient is not aware of entertaining it, *and* it is usually a wish which he would repudiate if he were to become conscious of it.

This is the first difficulty then; *the patient himself does not know of the underlying wish*, which really *is* unconscious, and he may laugh when anyone tries to show from his behaviour that, nevertheless, it must exist somewhere.

He may laugh, or may fly into a rage, and even exhibit moral indignation. But these reactions, too, may be symptomatic. They may really actually be defence-reactions against any lifting of the repression. When once anyone is in the grip of a conflict which has been solved by dissociation, it is hard, not only for anyone else, but even for himself, to know when he is really telling the truth.

And now there is another difficulty which is, perhaps, still more formidable, and that is that *we all have something in common with the neurotic.* The distinction between the normal and the abnormal, though it is real enough and all-important from a practical point of view, depends rather upon a difference in the balance of forces in the individual than on any actual difference in those forces themselves. It is more a matter of quantity and distribution than of any qualitative difference. In repressing conflicts, neurotics use defence mechanisms which are normal to all of us, though they are apt to apply them more extensively and less efficiently than the normal man does. But everyone has employed them, and we all use much of our energy in keeping out of consciousness wishes not so very dissimilar from those with which the neurotic is struggling. Since everybody is doing a certain amount of repressing, one may even say that the difference between health and neurosis is, in a sense, only a matter of degree, though, of course, actually, the difference of degree makes all the difference.

This is why the study of neurosis is so fascinating and at the same time so repellent. We all look to it consciously or unconsciously for a solution of our own difficulties. This also is why it is so hard to think about analytic theory in the cold abstract spirit of science, and why it is bound to arouse tremendous passions.

One of the striking differences between the neurotic and the rest of us is that we succeed so much better in our repressions. We really *do* repress so successfully that our lives are no longer disturbed by what we have thrust out of consciousness. This is probably due, in some cases, at least, to our having less to repress. Even if we must believe that there is hardly anyone so normal that he has not some potential anxiety to keep at bay, it is certainly true that the amount of this anxiety varies very considerably from person to person. In those who achieve a life which passes for normal, the pressure from the unconscious is not such a serious menace, because so much of them really grows up. A good part of their alarming infantile imaginings have come into contact with reality and been dispelled and they can repress successfully what is left. With the neurotic, since the drive from the unconscious is much more powerful, the repression is correspondingly less successful, and when it begins to fail he may compromise by throwing out symptoms. The more precarious the balance between repressing and repressed forces, the greater is the dread of anything that may stimulate the unconscious; but even the more or less normal among us do not really like to have our *modus vivendi* tampered with, lest our own repressions, too, should begin to give way. It must be that, without knowing it, we do really all dread many impulses which we are forcibly holding down in our unconscious, and this may account for the universal resistance which we all put up against recognising the meaning of the symptoms of neurotics.

This, then, is a second powerful reason why it is so difficult to understand the meaning of psychogenic symptoms. We are perhaps afraid to understand how others are defending themselves against what is in their unconscious, lest this understanding should weaken our defences against similar repressed impulses in ourselves. This explains why the longings which these symptoms attempt to satisfy are apt to appear to us so shocking, and at the same time so foreign.

The sense of unreality and moral indignation are two of the strongest weapons for keeping repressed material battened down in the unconscious, and it may be this feeling of unreality (which is, in fact, our instinctive defence against unwelcome or perhaps all too welcome, though repudiated, reality) that makes the longings claimed to be at the bottom of symptoms sometimes appear so unnatural.

All this obviously raises a very formidable difficulty when we want to estimate the value of any theory which attempts to explain what symptoms mean. If one has spent immense energy and made tremendous sacrifices over building up a defence against being conscious of impulses in oneself not very unlike those to which the neurotic's symptoms give expression, is it likely that one will readily believe it when one is told what these symptoms are about?

If incredulity is one of our natural weapons of defence, then our very incredulity may be evidence in favour of the thing we doubt! We can no longer trust now to common sense, for we are outside the realm where common sense applies, in the region where judgment is governed by emotion and not by reason.

As soon as anything seriously endangers our peace of mind, judgment tends to be swamped by emotion. This is striking when one tries to make up one's mind on the subject of the unconscious reasons for psychogenic illness, some of which apply to oneself as well as to the patient. Judgment may be biased in either direction, as much towards credulity as towards incredulity. It reaches colossal proportions, at times, in patients whose unconscious emotions are actually being explored. The patient may mask his deeper obstinate rejection of the truths which apply to his own case by an almost religiously uncritical acceptance of theory which is, however, purely intellectual; or, on the other hand, he may really develop a complete inability to take in the meaning of the explanation, behaving at times as if he were positively mentally deficient and incapable of putting two and two together. This is a mental equivalent of the actual psychogenic blindness or deafness to which I have already referred—an emotional stupidity.

Anyone who has undergone analysis will recognise from his personal experience this condition of temporary imbecility. But such emotionally inspired judgments are not to be relied upon; one could *almost*, in cases where something is particularly unwelcome, rely on the truth being the exact reverse of what it appears to oneself to be. But it is hard to be quite sure even of this. A correct conclusion is exceedingly difficult here. All that one can say is that one should not place much confidence in objections and criticisms which carry with them any marked charge of emotion, and the less it affects oneself personally the more likely one is to be able to judge dispassionately. Unfortunately, since we are all repressing unconscious material, none of us can achieve complete impartiality in the matter.

There are, then, two very formidable difficulties in understanding the reasons for falling ill: difficulties of an emotional rather than of a purely intellectual kind. The first is that these reasons are *unconscious* and the patient himself does not know anything about them, and not only does not know but does not *want* to know, and even falls ill "on purpose", one might say, in order *not* to know.

The second is that we, the investigators, do not want to know either, for reasons of our own; and we all of us, patients and investigators alike, have a remarkably good technique for remaining unaware of things which it would be painful for us to recognise, such things being apt to arouse in us the defences of incredulity, ridicule, rage or indignation.

And, besides these two emotional obstacles, a further very serious difficulty, to which I have already referred, lies in the fact that even if we had no personal reasons for not recognising the meaning of the symptoms, this meaning in itself is *really* not obvious but is disguised almost as if it were translated into some archaic language, not familiar to our consciousness, which we have to learn first before we can translate it back again in order to understand it.

Symbolic representation is a case in point. What is really preoccupying the patient does not here appear openly in the symptom; only a symbol of it appears, something which has been substituted for the really significant thing. The symptom may consist in saying "Sussex Gorse" when the real preoccupation is "cut it off".

Before what is being hinted at in these illnesses can be recognised, one has to have learnt, as it were, how to translate. Symbolic representation is only one of these disguises; there are a good many others which are even more unfamiliar to us. It may be that the symptoms adopt disguises partly in self-protection because the real underlying thoughts are too alarming to be faced; but, as I have explained, I believe translation would be necessary before we could understand any product of the unconscious, even if we had no reason to fear doing so. This, I think, is because the unconscious in expressing itself employs an altogether more *primitive type of mental operation* than those with which we are familiar in our ordinary waking life.

Instances of these more primitive methods of thought can be found in all sorts of other places besides neurotic symptoms, in myths, fairy stories, jokes, dreams, savage rites, ceremonies, children's thoughts and games. Reconstructing the forms of thought and expression from all these various bits of evidence is rather like reconstructing some lost language.

I shall go into these more primitive types of mental mechanism in a later chapter, and we shall then be in a better position to translate convincingly the meaning of the symptoms. From what has been said already it must be abundantly evident that great difficulties have to be overcome before the unconscious meaning of psychogenic symptoms can be recognised; but of them all, the greatest, I still think, is the fact that what those who produce the symptoms are trying to say, in the language of the unconscious, is just *what is not openly said—what none of us wish to hear*.

With all these formidable difficulties it is not surprising that the study of the unconscious is still in its infancy—one wonders how it ever even began! But fortunately there are forces on the other side too. Unconscious preoccupations, however vigorously repressed, still insist on trying to get a hearing and, in spite of all our reluctance, something in us all understands and responds. So gradually we can piece it out.

Now, for these things which we do not want to hear and are yet trying to say.

Some unconscious longings give greater offence than others. Most people seem to be fairly ready to entertain the idea that a man may have murderous instincts intolerable to consciousness against people whom he believes he loves. Murder is less disturbing than sexual desires. My difficulty is that, according to the psychoanalytical hypothesis which I am expounding, when we come to translate neurotic symptoms, somehow, even though perhaps only at the centre of the onion, we shall find that the wish which produces them is in some sense sexual. Even in provisionally putting down the symptoms of the obsessional case already quoted to a repressed murder impulse, it was suggested that murder was probably not the whole explanation.

"Neurotic symptoms", Freud says, "are substitutes for sexual gratification." And, furthermore, these gratifications are more often than not what is called "perverse"

This is a very sweeping statement and I cannot prove that it is true. The evidence for it is inductive and depends upon the whole mass of psychoanalytical research. But even if it should turn out later that it is not necessary in every case of neurosis to assume an underlying unconscious sexual wish, this does not affect the point that we are concerned with here, for in a great many cases the wish undoubtedly *is* both sexual and perverse. It is just this which makes it difficult to discuss cases, and it will cause many people to dislike, and perhaps therefore to reject, the theoretical explanations which will be offered.

We have already mentioned a few of the main difficulties which are going to interfere with the investigation of the unconscious reasons for falling ill. Being forewarned, we may be able to deal with them: we are prepared, at least, to find that the Freudian explanations of the meaning of the symptoms will *deal largely with sexuality and even with perversions.*

It is common knowledge that Freud says something of the kind, but it is not universally known what led him to say it. He did not say it merely to shock people, nor because of some peculiar unpleasantness in his own mind. It was the results of his clinical experience which finally brought him to make the surprising generalisation that *in neurotic diseases the unconscious impulses which cause the symptoms appear to be sexual, though not sexual in the ordinary sense.* It was on *clinical grounds* that he originally arrived at the idea that psychogenic symptoms were the result of unconscious mental forces, and he then proceeded to investigate these unconscious forces, first using the technique of hypnotism and later the free-association technique which he developed for himself. The discovery of this technique was one of his strokes of genius: that, along with his ability to adopt, while listening to free-associations, the same impartial uncritical attitude which he asked of the patient.

His other stroke of genius was the explanation which he hit upon after listening in this impartial way to the material which his patients put before him. He found that, in all the neurotic patients whose symptoms he was investigating, there was a disturbance in their love life and some degree of failure to maintain satisfactory sexual relations. A good many were actually more or less impotent or frigid, and none were getting complete sexual satisfaction, mental and physical combined. When he used his technique for investigating more exactly the nature of the unconscious impulses which were producing psychogenic symptoms in these patients, he found that these impulses seemed to have some of the qualities of sexual impulses, their urgent pleasure-seeking and tenacity, but that the gratifications which were actually being demanded were not the sort of thing in which normal sexual adults find their pleasure; they were, he found, more like the things from which the so-called "perverts" obtain their sexual gratification. It appeared that both these classes of people, perverts and neurotics, were often preoccupied with longings associated, not with the genitals and genital activity, but with other parts of the body and other activities—the mouth, excretory organs, seeing, touching, and even hurting and being hurt; the perverts consciously recognising their sexual pleasure in these things, the neurotics fighting against it, but still desiring it unconsciously. These were the clinical findings.

Freud's further stroke of genius was in the explanation which occurred to him of these strange facts. He suggested the reason why perverts, openly, and neurotics, unconsciously, seek sexual gratification in these seemingly unnatural ways. The theory he offered was that these satisfactions, which appear strange to normal adults, are really *the normal forms of infantile sexuality*. Perverts and neurotics are alike in this, that they have, for some reason, failed to achieve sexual maturity and are still preoccupied with infantile pleasures which normal adults have outgrown. This is the explanation of the meaning of psychogenic illness which I propose now to discuss. To many people it will not be readily acceptable, and some of the reasons why this must be so have already been suggested. But I think perhaps opposition to Freud's theory is often increased by what is really a misunderstanding, which has arisen out of the chronological order in which he himself arrived at his final position; and this misunderstanding, at least, can be cleared up.

Working originally with hysterical patients, the first thing that drew Freud's attention and laid the foundation of all his later work was this fact of the sexual nature of the repressed wishes from which the symptoms spring. It was only later that he was able to work out with equal thoroughness the other side of the picture, namely the nature of the forces which bring about the repression of these sexual wishes, although these are obviously equally important for his theory of the origin of psychogenic illness.

The objection so often raised by people whose knowledge of psychoanalytic theory is incomplete is that "Freud puts everything down to sex". These people have failed to grasp the real point of Freud's theory. If *everything* could be put down to sex there would obviously be no conflict and no repression. It would be much nearer the truth to say that Freud puts down all psychogenic illness to the deadlock which arises out of the conflict between infantile sexuality and fear or aggression or rage.

But even restated in this more accurate way I am not imagining that everyone will immediately agree that Freud is right, nor see at once how valuable this idea is for the understanding of psychogenic illness. If this explanation of psychogenic illness is in fact correct, the meaning of the symptoms is bound to be hard to recognise, and it does not seem that anything short of years of experience of the material offered by patients themselves, and, more important still, by one's own personal analysis, would suffice to carry any real conviction.

We can now begin to see yet another reason why the meaning of neurotic symptoms is bound to be hard to recognise. Even if the symptoms do, in fact, spring from unconscious preoccupations struggling for expression against a barrier of repression, these preoccupations are not anything like the things which grown-up people ever think about in consciousness. They are, fundamentally, the impulses and terrors appropriate, not to adults, but to infants and young children, impulses from which the sexual urge has either not developed away, remaining "fixated" to an immature level, or to which it has "regressed" again after having once reached a more adult level. We shall find both fixation and regression complicating our discussion of cases, and of the two it is the regression which seems to be the most important factor, since it pours into infantile preoccupations the full urge of adult sexual desire.

I tried in my first chapter to show that people may be influenced by unconscious preoccupations, and that if, owing to painful conflict, these preoccupations suffer repression into the unconscious, they may later give rise to psychogenic illness.

Now I want to show that the unconscious preoccupations which lead to psychogenic illness concern *infantile sexual interests*, and that they become powerful in interfering with consciousness when *adult sexual urges* regress and reanimate these stages of development which are normally outgrown.

Objections may be raised to either of these points. The reality of this infantile sexuality may itself be doubted, or the occurrence of fixation and regression to it may be disputed.

With regard to sexual fixation and regression, there is the evidence of perversion to show that the sexual urge *can* entirely abandon normal aims and attach itself to activities not usually thought of as sexual, but which constitute the pervert's whole sexual life. If now these "perverse" activities can be shown to resemble the normal pleasure-seeking of infants, quite a strong case for either sexual fixation or regression will have been made out. It will then be appropriate to say that the sexual urge has for some reason failed to reach, or has abandoned, the usual adult interests and has attached itself to infantile pleasures instead, reinforcing them by regression. As we go on I shall be drawing parallels between the pleasures of infants and the sexual aims of perverts, in order to show that perversion is a form either of fixation or regression. In the same way, I shall draw parallels between infantile pleasures and the unconscious preoccupations of neurotics and the insane.

On the other question of infantile sexuality itself I shall have a great deal to say. The one of Freud's statements which has aroused the greatest storm is the claim that young children have a sexual life, and I want to try and explain what he means by saying this. No one, I suppose, will dispute the fact that babies get pleasure from sense stimulation: the question is whether this kind of "sensual" pleasure should properly be called "sexual". Certainly it would be great folly to think of the sensual pleasures of infancy and the sexual experiences of adult life as being identical; nevertheless, if we compare them, although they differ in the bodily organs concerned and in the biological purposes involved, they seem to be sufficiently alike in the special quality of pleasantness to justify us in saying that they all satisfy a single pleasure instinct.

To begin with, the baby's life centres round the alimentary and respiratory processes of feeding and excreting and breathing. If these activities failed the baby would not live, and this keeping alive is their biological function. But these activities seem, even from the beginning, to have a value, not simply for utility, but also for pleasure. One may therefore justly think of the baby as actuated by two fundamental instincts, to live and to enjoy. The need to live causes it, for instance, to crave nourishment, and the need to enjoy causes it to seek sense stimulation. Both these fundamental instincts find satisfaction, to begin with, in the activity of suckling.

This double satisfaction of instincts, one biological and the other for pleasure, is paralleled later in the two values of adult sexuality which fulfils, not only a biological function—this time reproduction—but over and above this has its sensual pleasure value which can be sought independently.

Now although the biological significance is different, the quality of sensual pleasure attached from the beginning to other important early physiological functions, nutrition, excretion, respiration and so on, seems to have remarkably much in common with the sensual pleasure which, in adults, is attached to the activities concerned with reproduction. Both pleasure-cravings have the same sort of urgency, so that frustration feels almost, or quite, unbearable, and in both the experience of satisfaction, when the craving has been intense, is felt as a revelation of magical power giving rise to love for the stimulating and satisfying object.

But there is a difference in the love-objects of infancy and adult life. While, for the adult, the object of love is the whole person of the beloved, for the baby the objects are those things which stimulate the senses, the nipple or the milk which stimulate its lips and throat and smell and taste, the urine which passes over its urethal mucous membranes and the faeces which excite pleasure sensations; and it is not incorrect, however grotesque it may at first sound, to call these the baby's first love-objects.

It is true that this applies only to the early beginnings of pleasure-craving and satisfaction; later on the child begins to feel love, not simply for the parts of its mother and itself which produce its satisfactions, but for the whole person. Even then, however, its feelings remain closely associated with the bodily organs around which its pleasure-craving centres, and it still seeks pleasure in connection with the people it cares for in terms of the sense-stimulation of these parts of its own body. It gives physical expression to its feelings of love and hate by sucking, biting, licking, swallowing, vomiting, spitting, wetting, messing, breathing and smelling, or holding up its bladder or bowel products, or its breath.

So far we have only mentioned the sense-stimulation which belongs to the alimentary and excretory and respiratory functions, and in fact these seem to overshadow the other senses in early life because of their overwhelming biological importance. But even the other senses also show this same double functioning, being at one and the same time the organs of biological utility and also of pleasure-craving which, when satisfied, arouses love. And, just as the child uses its alimentary and excretory functions as vehicles for its love and hate impulses, as well as for bodily nutrition, so also it uses many other functions—touch, sight and hearing, these all having a sensual pleasure value as well as biological use.

After puberty, when the reproductive functions have come to equal or actually to supersede in urgency even nutrition and respiration, the genital organs which carry out these functions concentrate on themselves a large part of the pleasure-craving which in childhood was more generally diffused over the other senses, so that the adult seeks sensual pleasure and loves and hates in genital terms.

It is true that even in adults pregenital sense-pleasures, such as the mouth pleasure of kissing, the skin pleasures of touching, the pleasures of sight, hearing and quite often of smell, usually still retain considerable pleasure value, and the similarity of the pleasure quality of such pregenital and frankly genital sense-pleasures is a matter of ordinary experience. More rarely, but still quite commonly, the pleasure of sucking, licking, biting or passing urine and faeces, is still recognisably erotic in adult life, and there can be no doubt that the pleasure which children experience in all these acts has this same peculiar but unmistakable quality.

It seems to follow from all this that human beings have in them, even from their earliest years, besides their biological needs, a pleasure instinct which is satisfied by the sense-stimulation of their bodies, and that, even in infancy and childhood, such sense-stimulation has much in common with the sense-pleasure which in adult life is called sexual, and which appears, developmentally, to be simply the end-point of a continuous progress of the pleasure instinct towards maturity.

The capacity for sense-pleasure depends upon the special excitability of the parts of the body which are closely connected with important biological functions; in adults these are the genital organs of reproduction, but in earlier life the excitability is found in other parts of the body associated with other biological functions.

It was mainly because of his discovery that the pleasure instinct appears in early life to go through a continuous process of development, concerning itself first with pregenital and later with genital pleasures, that Freud considered himself justified in classifying pregenital with genital pleasure-seekings as manifestations of a single instinct, and calling them all "sexual". The similarity between the actual sensations experienced when, even in adult life, pregenital and genital zones are stimulated by a loved person, added a further reason for classing these pleasures together.

One important quality which belongs to satisfaction of the pleasure instinct, whatever the bodily organs involved, is its overwhelmingness and the sense of being taken up on the tide of feeling which can no longer be regulated or controlled, and, indeed, seems to come from outside, almost like a possession by spirits. With this comes a great sense of power when there is no need to resist, but a terrible sense of danger when attempts are made to struggle against the tide in vain. Patients in analysis experience this fear when their unconscious impulses are pushing hard against the barrier of repression, and in such cases the dreaded breakdown of control may be represented in consciousness as fear of orgasm itself, or, interchangeably, as fear of soiling, or wetting, or exploding, or having a fit, all of which often represent orgasms in the unconscious.

This fear often appears in patients' dreams. About half-way through the analysis, when some of the repressions had already been lightened, but while he was still in dread of his own sexuality, Mr L., who had come to be analysed on account of impotence, dreamt that a woman, who appeared on investigation to stand for the analyst, was trying to light a gas fire. She fumbled with a sort of plug which she failed to put into the wall. He tried to light the fire himself but also failed. He was in great anxiety lest both their attempts should produce an explosion.

Now, in Mr L.'s case the administration of an enema in childhood by a woman had produced a violent and unfortunate emotional reaction, arousing strong sensation, which, though painful, was erotically coloured, so that there persisted in his unconscious a mixed dread of, and craving for, the repetition of the experience. The putting in of the plug by the woman in order to kindle the fire represented symbolically the administration of the enema, and the arousing of the erotic sensation. The explosion seemed to represent the emotional reactions to the situation in which intense physical feeling resembling orgasm was combined with fear, rage and repudiation.

At a corresponding stage in her analysis, Mrs D., who was frigid, dreamt that her husband, about whom she had strong conflicting emotions, was pouring petrol into a tin through a funnel, with a lighted pipe in his mouth. She shouted to him to throw away his pipe as there would be an explosion. The pouring of the petrol into the tin seemed to be a symbolic representation of intercourse, which, in this patient's unconscious, was pictured pregenitally in terms of urination and was regarded as highly dangerous on account of her own explosive emotional reactions to it. Her frigidity was a defence against this, and her character was organised mainly along the lines of defence against loss of control of her strong and conflicting repressed sexual feelings.

Fear of the power of such repressed feelings and the attempt to struggle against them may lead to a loss not only of sexual potency, but also to a much wider impoverishment. To lose this pregenital sort of potency of the physiological functions, to exchange pleasure and acquiescence in them for dread and struggling against them, is to suffer a sort of castration of one's humanity. For the physical side of this pleasure-seeking instinct, which consists in the special sensitivity of appropriate parts of the body, appears to be the foundation of very important emotional capacities. It seems, indeed, to underlie not only the feeling of love in a narrow sense but actually of the capacity to care for anything. On its successful growth depends not only all human relations but all other interests too, and when it is arrested, or seriously impeded, the development of interest in other people and also in the whole outside world suffers more or less severely. I shall have more to say about all this later on. Here we are concerned with getting clear as to what Freud means by sexuality, and I have explained that Freud classes as sexual all satisfactions in the stimulation of the bodily senses which have the peculiar erotic quality experienced by normal people in genital love, whether the organs from which this pleasure is obtained are the genitals or other sensitive parts of the body, and whatever the age of the person who experiences the pleasure.

The relevance of all this to our present investigation is that, if we think of emotional development in terms of the stages through which the capacity for sexual pleasure passes on the way from infancy to adult sexuality and of the different excitable bodily areas and exciting objects appropriate to the various stages, a flood of light is thrown on a number of abnormalities of mind and body which were formerly inexplicable. These can now be recognised as the effects of abnormalities in the growth of the sexual instinct which has somehow failed to become established at the adult level, either because it never reached it and still remains fixed at some earlier developmental stage, or because it has regressed back to some previous stage, from a maturity which, though actually achieved temporarily, had, for some reason, to be abandoned again.

Freud maintains that the stage at which the sexual instinct is functioning, the bodily regions which crave stimulation and the objects by means of which this stimulation is obtained explain the form taken by many psychogenic symptoms and by the perversions. I hardly expect, however, that his views on the developmental history of sexuality, on which this hypothesis depends, will be taken on faith. I propose, therefore, to devote the next three chapters to a description of the stages through which, according to Freud, the sensual pleasure-seeking of infants and young children passes on the way to full-blown adult sexuality. I shall give in each chapter such evidence as I can find for supposing that the stages which I shall describe really occur in the course of development, and also I shall quote cases of psychogenic illness in which the motive behind the symptom appears to be a still persisting unconscious preoccupation with these early interests, and I shall draw parallels between these infantile interests and neurotic symptoms, on the one hand, and, on the other, recognised perversions whose sexual intention nobody doubts.

On the hypothesis by means of which it is proposed to explain the unconscious reasons for neurotic illness, neurosis may be described as the equivalent of perversion, in that the type of sexuality is the same in both; but there is this difference, that whereas in the case of perversion the total personality has more or less accepted this type of sexual desire, enough at least to tolerate it in consciousness, in the case of neurosis this same type of sexual desire, though present, is repudiated and repressed from consciousness.

In both cases, this sexuality which is called perverse might, with equal justice, be called infantile, since it is a regression to the craving for kinds of sense-stimulation or for stimulating objects normal in the course of childish development and only becoming out of place in adult life.

But of course regression does not simply re-establish the original state. This pouring of an adult urge back into infantile forms is very much a case of filling old bottles with new wine.

In spite of the close similarity between the type of physical satisfaction sought in infancy and in perversions (consciously) or neurotic symptoms (unconsciously), there are also striking differences between the "perverseness" of the normal baby and the pathological perverseness of the neurotic child or adult.

What really makes sensual desire pathological at any age, as distinguished from normal love, is the fact that this morbid kind of love is mixed with hostile emotions, and it would perhaps be proper to alter our attitude towards so-called "perversions" in the light of this fact, distinguishing normal sexuality, whether adult and genital, or immature and concerned with other pleasure organs, from that other kind of sexuality which really is abnormal and morbid, the sexuality in which love has been infected by hostility. When this mixture of emotions exists, the acts, which in health would arouse physical pleasure leading to love for the object and later for the whole person who is the source of this pleasure, accompanied by a desire to give pleasure back, now arouse a complex sensation composed of a mixture of pleasure and pain, leading to anger and contempt for the object or whole person concerned, accompanied by a desire to degrade or inflict pain and punishment. In pathological sensuality stimulation of the parts in which desire has been aroused causes the patient to *hate* rather than to love the object or person concerned.

The parts of the body in which sensual desire may be aroused are, as we have seen, different at different stages of development; in early childhood, the organs belonging to the functions of nutrition, excretion and respiration, the mouth and throat, anus and urethra and lungs, together with the organs of smell, sight, touch and hearing: later, the genital organs. These organs, as we have seen, have a double value, serving both our two fundamental instincts at once. On the one hand they are the sensual pleasure or "sexual" organs by way of which emotional relations with the outside world are established—these emotions in health being love in pathological conditions and a mixture of love-hate. On the other hand, however, they also have quite other functions, serving the primary biological instincts also—nutrition, respiration, excretion, reproduction, and so on.

In health this creates no disturbance; the addition of pleasure and love to the biological functions simply makes them worth while. As long as the pleasure instinct is healthy, life is worth living and the bodily organs through which this instinct finds its satisfaction carry on their biological functions healthily. But when this pleasure instinct is diseased, life loses its savour and the biological functions very often show a parallel disturbance.

If, for instance, mouth pleasure is disturbed by conflict between acceptance and repudiation, satisfaction and frustration, sucking and biting, fondness and revenge, disturbances of appetite may result. If smelling pleasure is similarly upset by contradictory responses to the desired stimuli, respiration may be affected, and so on with the other organs which simultaneously satisfy pleasure and biological needs.

It follows from this that the healthy development of the sexual or sense-pleasure instinct is extremely important, not only for happiness, but for bodily health also.

Now as to the things that upset this sense-pleasure instinct. The instinct is founded, as we have seen, on the craving of certain parts of the body for sense-stimulation leading to a discharge in some appropriate activity of the tension produced by the craving, such discharge being followed by rest. This craving is from the beginning of life one of the urgent needs of the organism, but it is one which meets with constant disappointment.

The disappointment, producing as it does a mounting up of undischarged tension, sets up a state of uneasiness, soon experienced as fear, leading to a reaction of rage. The rage if explosive may do what is required by relieving the accumulated tension, and thus peace may be restored, though without resulting in fondness for any outside object, since the wished for pleasure was not experienced. But if the tension is not relieved by pleasure, and if, further, the rage set up by the fear of tension is also checked by more fear, so that relief is not obtained, then a more pathological situation will arise.

The psychological tension of unsatisfied sense-craving which fails to find discharge either through pleasure or through rage may become intolerable and may then be dealt with by the neurotic solution of repression in which primitive sensual craving and the reactions of rage and fear are all banished together from consciousness. Situations liable to reawaken the old conflict henceforth tend to arouse anxiety, and are avoided, and sexual development is thus arrested, with fixation at a primitive level.

What persists in the unconscious is a mixed condition of primitive sense-craving, rage and fear: situations which in a normal person would arouse sexual pleasure tend now to provoke this mixed emotional reaction instead.

The pleasure zones are transformed by disappointment into *dis*pleasure zones, the emotions expressed through them are hate as well as love, and stimulation of them is resented as an insult and dreaded as a danger, as well as welcomed. In this way aggression, rage and suffering become themselves tinged with sexual feeling or pleasure-craving.

Usually, however, the sexuality which gets thus entangled with fear and rage and pain is not the adult emotion to which the name sex is usually given. It has in it a large element of the earlier sort of pregenital sensual pleasure-craving of which we have just been speaking—the craving, for instance, of the mouth to suck the breast, or some other stage in the developmental history of the sexual instinct (for instance, in the case of Mr L., whose dream has just been quoted, the craving appeared to be anal). The early pleasure and love have been turned by disappointment into *dis*pleasure and hate, sucking has been transformed into biting, anal pleasure into pain, nevertheless the whole situation remains sexual, and just as normal stimulation of the pleasure zones leads to being in love, so you may say that stimulation of these same parts, when they have turned to *dis*pleasure zones, leads to being "in hate". Many people who are supposed to be in love are really in hate with each other. For them pain and hate have been sexualised.

There is, I think, a biological value in rage and hate. If one considers that the sense-pleasure obtained from the pleasure organs is what, to begin with, makes life worth living and gives the zest to the biological functions which is needed to make the child fight to carry on its existence, it seems to follow that when, owing to disappointment, pleasure organs turn into organs of *dis*pleasure, life is endangered. These very sensations which were to have introduced the organism to love are now a source of pain; and while this is so they must be regarded by the organism as something hostile. The disappointed pleasure zones of its own body are the first "enemy" to its well-being of which the organism becomes aware, antedating all outside enemies. This is perhaps the origin of the turning of rage against the self which is such a striking characteristic of those who suffer from psychogenic illness.

The *dis*pleasure experienced in its own pleasure zones is probably the first object of the baby's fear, constituting an enemy from within, and the attempt to exterminate this enemy brings with it the danger of emotional suicide. To avoid this, hostility, which primarily turns inwards against the *dis*pleasure zones themselves, is deflected and turned outwards against the sources in the outside world from which disappointment comes. These now replace the *dis*pleasure zones as "the enemy", and so the organism is protected from emotional suicide. Hate is healthier than despair, both are reactions to the same *dis*pleasure which follows disappointment.

In the deep analysis of some patients, both male and female, one comes sooner or later upon a dread, which often appears in the form of fear of death; and sometimes it seems correct to interpret this as fear of the loss of the power to care, an extinction of the pleasure instinct itself—the emotional death of which we have just spoken. This reaction to disappointment is what I mean by despair, and it is regarded by the organism as the supreme danger. It might perhaps be compared to what happens to the instinct of hunger, which, if long unsatisfied, first is felt as pain and then disappears, so that food is no longer desired and even provokes vomiting if it is taken.

A similar extinction of the pleasure-hunger brought about by disappointment seems to be what is most deeply dreaded of all. Any fate, however painful, is felt to be preferable to this, and it is striking how patients whose fear of this "aphanasis" (as Dr Ernest Jones calls it) is strong, will work up misery and inflict actual bodily suffering on themselves rather than wither away altogether.

It may be that something like emotional death is the real explanation of the deterioration which occurs in some cases of *dementia praecox*, and melancholia comes near to it, though some feeling is kept alive by suffering.

In the case of neurotics, however, though the dread which they occasionally experience may relate in part to this earliest of all the dangers which disappointment creates, interest has in fact always been securely enough anchored to the outside world for a total withdrawal to be now out of the question. Their pleasure zones have *not* given up hope; they have successfully escaped emotional suicide, and the death anxiety which they have to face is essentially anxiety concerning the consequences of their own aggression against the disappointing world which has now become "the enemy", the attack having been successfully deflected away from the original "internal enemy", the displeasure zones themselves.

I am afraid in this digression into the biological value of rage and hate, and the meaning of the pathological fear of death, I have trespassed on ground too difficult and controversial to interest everyone, but we can now get back to our main theme.

The point of fundamental importance which I am anxious here to emphasise is that what upsets the smooth functioning of the pleasure instinct, and leads to all the psychogenic abnormalities which we are trying to investigate, is *disappointment*. According to what a child does about this, he grows up mentally healthy or ill. This fundamental problem of how to deal with disappointment runs right through the history of the child's gradually developing relations to external reality and especially its emotional relations connected with these early sensual pleasures of which I have just spoken and which I am proposing to regard as constituting the immature stages in the developmental history of sexuality. These pleasure-cravings of childhood are intense: but since it is hardly possible, even under the most favourable conditions, to enjoy nothing but unbroken satisfaction, bitter disappointment is a situation which every baby meets almost from the very beginning of its existence.

At this time its power of tolerating any state of tension, with the accompanying anxiety and fear, is very weak; real self-control is not within its power, and it has at its disposal only three alternatives, despair or rage or repression. Despair means the extinction of pleasure—emotional death. But undisguised rage lays the child open to all the terrors that must beset any small creature which attempts to rear itself up against a huge and powerful enemy. And for the human child there are further complications, one being the conflict which is set up by its rage at being disappointed and its already existing love for the ones who disappoint it, and the other being its utter dependence on these very ones against whom its rage is directed. If it bites the hand or breast that feeds it, the food is withdrawn. The child seems commonly to regard disappointment as punishment for its own attacks and in this way it loses courage.

Repression evades this difficult situation by dissociating pleasure-hunger without destroying it. Thus it avoids conscious *dis*pleasure and the open rage which at first accompanies this: it simply evades the immediate danger by shutting off the entire conflict just as it stands, so that the whole emotional complex—craving, love, rage and fear—are all excluded from consciousness, thus behaving towards mental pain in a way comparable to the escape from excessive physical pain by fainting. This is in the long run a bad solution, however, because it provides no discharge for the craving, and while the conflict remains unresolved the craving will go on, though now entirely outside consciousness, so long at least as repression is successfully maintained.

This was the situation in which Freud found that many of his patients were, even though years had passed since the original disappointments occurred. They had not got over them. They were still unconsciously living in the old infantile situation in which their early disappointments befell them, still craving the infantile satisfactions and still torn by the old conflicts between love on this early infantile model and rage and fear. Freud considered that these early situations had become as it were embalmed and preserved in this way right on into adult life, because in early childhood the problem of how to deal with disappointment had not been well solved. At that time it was met by not admitting reality, by pretending all was well when it was not, and dissociating into the unconscious the wishes and fancies which, openly recognised, would have aroused an active conflict between love, rage and fear.

Neurosis, it thus appears, is really a flight from the pain of facing reality at some point. When the child finds it cannot or dare not satisfy some desire, it may refuse to admit this reality and repress the desire, all the while clinging to it obstinately in the unconscious, though perhaps being quite unaware in consciousness of any disappointment.

The mere fact of having dealt with disappointment by repression is, however, not enough to distinguish the neurotic from the normal person, since this reaction is, to some extent, universal in all human beings. Normally, however, the unavoidable repression of early childhood seems to be more or less outgrown. Desires which were, perhaps, repressed at their first appearance get modified in the ordinary course of development and reappear in more acceptable forms, putting up substitute outlets which are more attainable. Fears which were realities in childhood are ultimately seen through and discarded, wishes appropriate only to infancy are really outgrown.

With the neurotic things turn out otherwise. The original disappointment is never accepted, and the primitive demands of instinct are retained in their original form, unmodified. One patient said to me, half in joke, half in anger, "The Constant Nymph simply isn't in it with me!" On another occasion she compared herself with the famous Pears' Soap cartoon of the baby in the bath howling for the lost soap, underneath which is written, "He won't be happy till he gets it". This is indeed the neurotic situation—they simply *will not* take any substitute for the original pleasures which were denied them. Their primitive instinctive cravings continue unchanged. Time does not alter them, they do not mature, and experience seems unable to touch them. They remain embedded in the unconscious like fossils, shut off from the air, retaining their old form. The early infantile wishes and fears which were originally repressed remain infantile ever after, little foreign bodies like splinters in the otherwise developing and maturing character. And just as these infantile wishes, though unconscious, are still dynamic, so also are the infantile fears. These, too, have never been seen through and outgrown. If now at some time or other the repression weakens, those repressed infantile wishes, and the fears which are bound up with them, may force their way back and gain some kind of indirect expression in the form of symptoms, and these symptoms will therefore be about *infantile* preoccupations in some sense, either representing a gratification of wishes or, when fear or remorse prevail in the conflict, a denial, or a punishment, or a restitution, or a combination of all these. Similarly, the fears which conflict with the wish for satisfaction will also be infantile. The point I want to make here is that if the original dissociation happened in infancy and the dissociated wishes and terrors have remained marking time in a state of repression ever since, then we should naturally expect any symptoms which these repressed wishes and terrors ultimately succeed in producing still to be about infantile preoccupations, no matter what the actual present-day age of the patient may happen to be.

If this is true, then we cannot properly understand the meaning of the psychogenic symptoms unless we know something about immature sexuality, that is, about the kind of gratifications which infants and children seek before they have reached the capacity for adult love relations, since it is just these wishes which, meeting with early disappointment, are liable to get repressed, and later may reappear again in symptoms. What will then reappear will be what was originally repressed—a conflicting emotional state consisting of infantile sexuality and sexualised rage and fear which together produce sexualised hate.

But psychoanalysis is not content to leave the matter there. The hate is not ultimate. It sprang originally from desperation: it began as the reaction to an intolerable situation of frustrated longing, and so it does not seem to be so fundamental as the original longing itself. It is true that once the two have become entangled and have set up the internal contradiction which makes satisfaction impossible, it may be an extremely difficult task to separate them enough for desire ever to get satisfaction. The difficulty is that the hate itself, or the cruelty which springs from it, has become sexualised, and is now itself a real sexual aim, and may even be unconsciously preferred to relations of real love.

But the whole illness is a vicious circle, and this vicious circle can be broken. The neurotic might be compared to some starving animal which, owing to its hunger, has become ferocious. When food is at last offered, it feels impelled to devour not only the meat but the person who offers it also, mistaking him perhaps for someone who formerly withheld food from it and imagining that it cannot otherwise satisfy its hunger. But this animal does not dare to carry out its wish because it reads the outside world in terms of its own impulses and so believes that this person who is offering the meat is as ferocious as itself. It expects to be attacked, or turns against the meat itself. So it rejects all food and only grows more hungry and more ferocious. This vicious circle is based on a mistake. Whatever may have been true in the past, it is an error to suppose now that it cannot eat without destroying those who feed it, or that they will respond to demonstrations of ravenousness with attack, or that the meat they offer is bad. In time the animal may be sufficiently reassured to be persuaded to taste a morsel of food, and if no harm comes of this experiment it will soon be eating its fill. With the appeasement of hunger the ferocity will abate, and the hatred of those who offer meat will be replaced by the love which satisfaction engenders. So the vicious circle is broken.

This breaking of the vicious circle is how neurosis is cured, but the cure is not a simple matter and the obstacles may perhaps be illustrated by continuing our parable of the hungry and ferocious animal, even though the picture we shall draw of it is not true of any animal that ever was actually seen. Our difficulty would be represented by saying that the animal does not any longer want meat, nor anything which it can now have, or even could have had in the real world. It has a craving, born of long fasting and dreaming, for impossible meals. Moreover, it is full of moral scruples about eating, which it regards as disgusting, and it is ashamed to live by food like other beasts. It regards offers of meat as temptations and insults. And finally it has learnt to take a pleasure in starvation and also believes that by refusing food it can prevent everyone else from eating, and this gives it a bitter pleasure which may compare in intensity even with the pleasure of satisfying its own hunger.

You see that it is not so easy to persuade our perverted animal to try food; nevertheless, all its objections go back in the end to the conviction that its own disappointment is inevitable, and they will be dispelled gradually if the possibility of real satisfaction for itself comes home to it at last.

Now that we have made a beginning in the direction of a deep psychoanalytic understanding of the meaning of psychogenic illness as arising out of the conflict between pleasure-craving and fear and rage, repressed early in life so that the pleasure zones and pleasure objects are of an infantile rather than of an adult type, it may make things clearer if I describe, by way of illustration, the symptoms and treatment of an actual case of psychogenic illness.

This case was a patient of my own, an unmarried woman of thirty. She told me how she had suffered all her life from the idea that she was like Cain, the murderer of Abel. She hated to read his story. She was four years old when she was christened, and remembered that when the clergyman made a cross with the water on her forehead she was terrified lest it should never disappear, and everyone would see it and she would be branded before the whole world. She used to say that *never* must she allow herself to feel jealous of anyone.

Here you have some of the symptoms; strong over-compensation against jealousy, and the fear of being branded with the cross of Cain on her forehead.

This was her history: when she was nearly four her mother had another baby and she, as the elder child, was turned out of her cot in the parents' bedroom by its arrival. The day after the new baby was born she was allowed to go in and see her mother, and asked if she might hold the baby, but in a few moments she begged the nurse to take it from her because she felt sure she was going to drop it. Next day the baby died. This did not seem to her a mere coincidence: she appears to have believed that she was in some way responsible. It was undoubtedly true that she had wished the new baby might be removed, and now, when it did, in fact, die, she felt as if the wish had *brought this about.*

She got back her cot in her parents' bedroom and remembers feeling glad but guilty at being there again. She said she tried to believe what they told her, that it was the fault of the nurse who had let the baby get a chill, but she knew she had been frightfully jealous, and the idea haunted her that somehow her jealousy had killed it. Her own christening came about half a year later, and she struggled against being christened at all because a teacher had said that if you died unchristened you went to Hell. She thought this would mean that the baby had gone to Hell and she refused to believe what the teacher said about christening.

Four years after the death of this baby her mother had another one, which once again turned the elder child out of her cot in her parents' room. She remembers being in the top room with her doll, and first trying to kiss it and be fond of it, then getting angry with it and pushing its eyes in. She was frightened when she had done that, and tried to get the eyes back again, but she could not. Finally she slid the doll to the edge of the bed and succeeded in having it fall out on the floor without *exactly* having pushed it.

It broke to pieces, and then she was frightened again and set up a great crying, so that her grandfather came and comforted her. She felt a terrible hypocrite because she knew she had meant the doll to fall and be broken. At other times she pushed in the eyes of other dolls or pulled their heads off.

I suggest that this child could not resist repeating, in this symbolic way, the destruction of the usurper which she felt had been so successful on the first occasion, but that she had by this time developed the neurotic's capacity for doing things "accidentally on purpose", as we used to call it when we were children, so that the deed was carried out, the doll fell and was smashed, but she could still remain uncertain whether *she* was responsible. Later, when she had to wheel out the new baby in the pram, she contrived, in spite of strict warnings to avoid pavements, that the wheels mounted on the curb crookedly, the pram overturned, and the baby fell into the road. This time, fortunately, the baby did not die.

She had never connected her terrible feelings of being like

Cain and her overpowering dread of jealousy with these episodes.

There is little doubt that this patient, when she was turned out of her cot by the first new baby, had indeed hated it and wished it away. It then died and was really taken away. This is the sort of situation which might well lead to repression on account of the strain of conflict between satisfaction at the fulfilment of her jealous wishes, and fear and remorse. She did, in fact, repress jealousy after that, and on the surface tried to pretend, and nearly all the time persuaded herself that she loved the new baby brother who was born later. But the jealousy came out in her actions, symbolically, in voluntary injury to her doll when she pushed in its eyes and let it get broken, and again "accidentally" in actually endangering the baby's life when she tipped the pram over. She remembered other similar "accidents". Once her brother fell out of the window and would have been killed but for a lucky chance. She was *not sure* whether she had pushed him or not.

In consciousness she was impelled to over-compensate against her hostile wishes, but all the same the repressed hostility due to jealousy managed to get a disguised expression in play and "accidental" behaviour.

Two features especially marked in this patient were her timid, innocent voice and manner and her submissiveness to her mother up to the time of her breakdown. This I am sure was not her original character. I should judge that by nature she had been a lively aggressive child. I think the far-reaching change in her character leading to meekness and self-sacrifice originated, among other things, in this incident of the baby's death, and was largely the effect of remorse and fear, though, like all neurotic symptoms, it was probably complex and contradictory in its origins, and contained also the gratification of deeply repressed infantile wishes.

She remembered having consciously felt deep resentment that her mother should have had a baby when she had not got one herself, and she seems to have believed that she had robbed her mother of this baby who died. She felt at the time that the baby ought to have been her own, and she was furious with her dolls for not being real live babies. She had ideas of actually stealing her baby sister, and other babies too. As she grew up she seems to have made tremendous efforts at restitution. After the baby's funeral she remembered that her mother was lying ill on the bed, looking utterly miserable, and she climbed on the bed beside her with the thought, "I will make up to her for it. I will be the baby instead of the other one". And her mother turned her face away. This made a deep impression *because of her guilt*. I think that she felt she had lost her mother's love by robbing her of the baby. As she grew up, she played the part of a self-sacrificing daughter. She was continually making her mother presents, she took over much of the housework while her sister studied and won prizes at school. She took great care of her mother's health, and when she grew up and began to earn money she gave it to her mother. All the time she was full of resentment. She was jealous of her sister's success, felt tied to her home, and bitterly resented the inner compulsion which obliged her to sacrifice herself. She ended by having a breakdown, and then she swung round suddenly into hating her mother and blaming her for having ruined her life.

As in the case I quoted earlier, so here, also, we can trace back at least a part of this patient's illness to a repressed murder impulse, the motive for which was jealousy.

But in this second case the analysis was carried further, so that, below the jealousy and murder wishes, still deeper buried motives were reached which explained the jealousy and murder and also the whole wealth of symptoms which came to light on a closer investigation of her life. Her most striking symptom during her breakdown, the one that finally brought her to treatment, was severe abdominal pain. The pain was so bad that she screamed and said it would drive her mad. She was examined repeatedly and nothing very definite could be found. There was obstinate constipation, over which the patient showed abnormal anxiety, and there was some visceroptosis. In the end a surgeon decided to operate on the chance of finding appendicitis. I understand that the report was "a fibrous appendix" which does not sound as if there had been enough found to explain the severe pain. Emotionally the patient was definitely worse after the operation. In the hospital she had suffered agonies of fear and hatred and thought she would go mad lying in her bed in the ward. It was after this experience that her compensation broke down and she swung round to open hatred of her mother. After the operation the pain continued the same as before, and the constipation was as obstinate as ever; the patient was entirely incapacitated by suffering, and some years later they operated again and removed a cystic ovary, which again is not always incompatible with good health, and again the pain remained as before. She then became suicidal and was for a time under restraint.

I will give you the interpretation of this patient's physical symptoms which I arrived at in the course of a great many hours of analysis. It was built up, bit by bit, from her associations. As we go on it will become clearer how a diagnosis of the unconscious meaning of an illness is arrived at during psycho-analysis, and on what kind of evidence it rests. Here I am only summarising my findings: later I will give samples of the evidence on which they were based. The constipation appeared to stand for pregnancy and the severe abdominal pains appeared to symbolise intercourse and labour, represented consciously as pain, for guilt reasons, to combine punishment with her unconscious pleasure and thereby excuse it, as if she were saying, "surely, since I am so miserable I cannot be blamed, it isn't as if I enjoyed it". There is no doubt that human beings are capable of getting intense unconscious pleasure under the disguise of pain in consciousness.

This would explain the curious change that came over the symptom at times during the treatment. Originally the sensation was described as severe pain, but as the analysis went on it changed its quality till the patient herself recognised it as being a pleasurable sexual feeling. From babyhood she had slept in her parents' bedroom and knew that something happened between them at night. This aroused in her a mixture of excitement and jealousy, and it was this emotional conflict which underlay her abdominal pains. These then, represented sexual excitement, labour and birth all together. The fantasy had a deep sexual thrill, but it had been necessary to transform this pleasure into pain because of the guilt concerning her rivalry with her mother. But at the same time she was filled with a deep terror of the very pleasures which she desired, which were represented in her fantasy as frightful tortures leading inevitably to death. The reasons for this intensely sadistic-masochistic view of sexuality, which is common in neurotics, we shall go into when we are discussing the development of infantile sexuality. I think ultimately it can be traced back to jealousy and disappointment, and represents a fantasy of revenge on the rival and on the disappointing love-object, but in her case it was strengthened by the real facts of her home life.

The pain of all this conflict caused it to be dissociated, leaving her emotions unconsciously fixated at a primitive level of development.

Her disappointment at not getting the longed-for physical pleasure and the baby from her father led to revengeful impulses against him which took the form of fantasies of genital injury. She had a dream in which a nurse said to her, "What did you want to do to your daddy?" and she replied, "I wanted to kill him underneath and in his throat". This fantasy of revenge brought with it fears of revenge in kind, which expressed themselves in her belief, persisting on into adult life, that intercourse and a yielding to sexual pleasure meant death to herself and to her lover. When such fantasies came near to consciousness she felt giddy and twice had actually fainted. Her abdominal symptoms she described as a sense of having been crushed and mutilated and the sharp pain which made her scream felt like a dog gnawing at her vitals.

These sensations represented the fulfilment of the deeply repressed wish, dating from her early childish love, that she really should have had done to her the things which she imagined her father did to her mother. But the cruel form which this wish fulfilment took was the result of her own hatred towards the parents who had disappointed her.

This turned the fantasy of intercourse into a delusion of being doped and poisoned, and changed her abdominal sensations from pleasure into pain. The gnawing inside was the equivalent of her repressed wish to attack with her teeth.

The jealousy which, together with fear, lay at the root of the whole conflict and forced its dissociation was twofold, directed against her mother and also against the baby who stole her coveted position. The guilt over it all was greatly enhanced by the actual death of this baby, and I think she had the unconscious belief that because of this she had forfeited the right ever to have a baby of her own. Her hatred of women as rivals led to great subservience to them, and to the idea that she must sacrifice herself to her mother.

Along with all this, there was a strong desire for restitution; she would have given anything to have been able to put back the doll's eyes which she pushed in, and to restore their heads. And one component of her urgent longing to have a baby herself was really to give it back to her mother, partly to lessen her guilt and partly because, in spite of everything, her love for her mother was real and deep.

By her abdominal pains therefore she combined a number of wish fulfilments. Partly I think she was symbolically taking the place of her mother of whom she was jealous, having the sexual thrill and the baby herself instead of her mother, partly she was restoring the dead baby to her mother again, partly she was suffering symbolically the revenge which, on account of her disappointment, she wished to take upon her parents, partly she was punishing herself by pain and by giving up her own intense wish to have a child, since all this illness made real marriage and pregnancy impossible. This is one of the most important things about neurotic symptoms, that they give unconscious gratification in fancy while they exclude the possibility of conscious gratification in reality. They give only the shadow, not the substance.

Here then, when we begin to carry our attempts to interpret the meaning of a psychogenic illness rather farther below the surface, the superficiality of the simple murder explanation becomes apparent. The deeper the interpretation is carried the more complicated it becomes, the more full of contradictions, since it is always trying to satisfy conflicting impulses. It is true that in the last analysis it can be reduced to something simple involving the fundamental passions of humanity—love, disappointment, jealousy, rage, revenge and fear—but these forces, conflicting and turning back on each other, can produce in the living human being an emotional tangle almost infinitely complicated and only to be unravelled with much expenditure of time and patient investigation.

That the resulting description should be involved is inevitable, but I am unwilling to give, by over-simplifying, a false picture of the unconscious reasons which underlie psychogenic symptoms. It can hardly be expected that anyone who is not familiar with the analysis of patients will immediately accept the explanation of Miss M.'s hysterical symptoms which I have just summarised. I myself am satisfied that it is in the main correct, because of the immense wealth of corroborating material which came out in the course of a long treatment. As we go on I shall refer back to her case, from time to time, giving samples of this evidence, and perhaps, in the end, the interpretation I have given of her illness may begin to appear more plausible.

What emerges when free-association brings out material from deeply repressed unconscious levels is a curious mixture of memories of real early experiences interwoven closely with primitive fantasies which have given these experiences their terrific significance to the child. Incidents, not necessarily remarkable in themselves, may be interpreted fantastically by the child in terms of its own wishes, intentions and deeds. Being held up to be kissed by an old grandmother may have meant to the child a meeting with Red Riding Hood's wolf (three of my patients remember having been terrified of being kissed by old grandmothers, believing they meant to bite or devour them); a real death may have seemed to it to be the magical outcome of its own hostile wishes; the administration of an enema may have appeared as a dangerous attack; a careless joke may have been believed in dead earnest. It is often difficult, in this tangle of fact and fantasy, to sort out what was real and what was supplied by the child's imagination; and Freud, during the earlier years of his work, was led for this reason to believe that much of what he learnt from his patients was real experience which afterwards turned out to have been pure fantasy, or, even when it had some real basis, was so woven round with fantasy as to give a significance out of all proportion to the facts, these being in themselves sometimes, though of course not always, of quite an everyday description.

It has now become clear to psychoanalysts that much of what appears to the patients as memory must be viewed with caution, but this does not make any very material difference to the importance of what they are telling, since for them, as children, fantasies may have been just as capable of setting up intolerable tension as real experiences, and it was how things *seemed* to them, rather than how they really *were*, that mattered. It may be that in the obsessional case I quoted earlier—the one who was afraid of causing the death of strangers—further analysis would have revealed important real early events behind her exaggerated sense of guilt, like this unfortunate death of the baby of whom my other patient had been so jealous. Such real events do terribly accentuate guilt in a child already prone to it. But the basis of the guilt lies in its *own hostile wishes* and, deepest buried of all, perhaps, in the secret feeling of triumph over the belief that these have succeeded. That alone, without any dramatic outside confirmation, may be enough to make a patient ill. In the case of this obsessional, we cannot be sure whether her guilt was about fantasy or reality, because she was a hospital patient and I had not the opportunity to carry through a thorough analysis.

In what follows I am proposing to illustrate important points as they come up from the analyses of two patients, this woman with the abdominal pains, whom I have called Miss M., whose analysis lasted three years, and a man who can be Mr J. whom I treated for about a year, at the end of which he was obliged to discontinue because of the great difficulty and expense of coming daily from his distant home. Both these cases were severe, the patients being very seriously incapacitated in their daily lives.

But I realise that I cannot expect evidence drawn from just one or two isolated cases to carry much weight. I shall amplify with further examples as we go on. But in going over cases in my mind I realise that it is not easy to find suitable illustrations. The analysis of any given case necessarily lasts over hundreds of hours of free-association. Each bit of light thrown on the deep meaning of the illness is, taken by itself, quite unconvincing, and proof, in so far as that is possible, rests on the cumulative evidence which is gradually piled up by enormous masses of hints, symbols, emotional reactions, dreams and so on. Here I cannot do more than just pick out samples of dreams or symptoms or associations as they occur to me from cases which I have analysed or which others have already published, to illustrate the theoretical explanation of the meaning of psychogenic illness which I am trying to establish.[1]

I hope, however, that even the illustrations which I have been able to give so far will have been satisfactory at least on this preliminary but fundamental point, that symptoms may be reactions to the threat of a *return to consciousness of repressed impulses*, and further that what actually appears in the symptoms may be explained with reference to these impulses, either as reactions against them or disguised and partial outlets for them, comparable to what sometimes happens in "accidental" behaviour. But I hope it is also clear that to regard the symptoms merely as expressions of forbidden wishes would be too simple. The actual situation is more complicated than this, for, since the symptoms probably express contradictory urges, they may, very likely, besides being gratifications, also be exaggerated defences against the possibility of gratification, and perhaps also punishments for having indulged in it, or restitutions for the supposed harm done by it.

SUMMARY

At the beginning of this chapter I explained why I think we are all bound, for personal reasons, to find it hard to recognise the meaning of neurotic symptoms. It is, I believe, because we all share, to some extent, the danger from which the neurotic seeks to escape by way of his illness. We are none of us quite secure against the internal menace which comes from our own repressed impulses, and so we all resist insight which might threaten our own repressions.

[1] I fully realise how far from satisfactory this is, and I hope some day to publish some complete analyses in fuller detail which may perhaps be more convincing.

From the patient we meet with the strongest resistance, because, from the nature of the case, he is unconsciously afraid to admit the existence of these repressed impulses which his whole illness was designed to keep out of sight, and he often defends himself by non-comprehension: and even we ourselves, for our own reasons, share his reluctance to bring them to light.

In so far as we are in better contact with reality than he is, or relatively immune from his anxiety, we have less need to shut our eyes. Moreover, both he and we do, somewhere in ourselves, recognise what the unconscious is trying to express, and the unconscious allies itself with our efforts to bring this to light. So the task, though difficult, is not impossible.

The other obstacle to understanding the meaning of psychogenic symptoms lies in the form of expression which they naturally adopt. I explained that the reason why the unconscious impulses which underlie psychogenic illness appear only in disguised forms may partly be the need to hide their real meaning from consciousness, but I added that I think this is not the whole explanation. The unconscious, which is itself primitive, having been dissociated at an early age, seems to find it natural to express itself in a primitive sort of language, of plays on words, for instance, or parables or other symbols.

In the last part of this chapter I explained Freud's theory about the nature of the repressed impulses which underlie psychogenic illness.

His view, based upon an immense amount of clinical evidence, is that psychogenic illness depends on the presence of conflicting impulses which have been dissociated from consciousness and are being held in a state of forcible repression. On the evidence with which his patients supplied him he came to the conclusion that emotional conflict only reaches the pitch of intolerable tension at which dissociation occurs when one of the instincts involved is the sexual one. On this view, therefore, psychogenic illness is always based on a repressed conflict between the sexual instinct and some other very powerful instinct such as jealousy or rage or fear.

The last point I made was that, according to Freud, the form taken by this sexual instinct, which gets involved in conflict, and repressed, differs in some important respect from what we usually mean by sexuality. The dissociations which lead to psychogenic illness occur early in life, and the type of sexuality involved is a type appropriate to the age at which the dissociation occurred. Since the dissociation arrests further development, sexuality does not mature, so that what these patients still crave, unconsciously, are the gratifications of childhood rather than those of adult life, though now reinforced with the strength of adult sexual power, and, furthermore, entangled with the various other conflicting primitive instincts which led originally to the dissociation.

It is these immature and primitive cravings, together often with repudiations of, or punishments for them, which reappear in disguised forms in the symptoms of psychogenic illness, and therefore we cannot understand these symptoms unless we are familiar with the developmental history of the sexual instinct.

I ended this chapter by giving a more complicated case history, in which I tried to show that, although the repressed wish to murder did explain the illness, up to a point, the symbolic meaning of the most important symptoms could not be understood without going deeper. The patient's chief symptom, abdominal pain, was, I suggested, the outcome of a conflict between early sexual excitement and jealousy and fear. This "sexual" excitement must have been associated with cravings at the pregenital stages of mouth and bowel pleasure, the repudiation of this pleasure, owing to conflicts over jealousy and fear, leading in turn to parallel disturbances in the biological functions of these organs and to the changing of pleasure into pain.

CHAPTER IV

In my previous chapter I spoke of Freud's stroke of genius, the theory he hit upon for explaining the strange discovery which emerged from his insight into the unconscious preoccupations of his patients. What Freud found was that the unconscious preoccupations which came to light during the investigation of psychogenic symptoms appeared to be concerned with sexual pleasure, although not ordinary adult sexual pleasure. As he sat day after day listening to what his patients told him, it dawned upon Freud that what they were unconsciously aiming at was a kind of gratification closely resembling the sexual pleasures of perverts, being sexual in quality and yet concerned, not necessarily with the genitals and genital activities, but with other parts of the body and other activities.

His stroke of genius was in recognising that these gratifications which perverts, consciously, and neurotics, unconsciously, desire are identical with the sense-pleasures of infancy and early childhood. He therefore formulated the hypothesis that what has happened, both in the case of perversion and of neurosis, is that sexual desire—the craving for sense-pleasure—has failed to reach maturity, remaining arrested ("fixated") at an earlier stage, or having reached maturity, has for some reason regressed again.

On this hypothesis the symptoms of psychogenic illness are explained as being expressions of a conflict between immature sexual pleasure-seeking and repressing forces which prevent this pleasure-seeking from becoming conscious and deny it direct satisfaction.

In order to understand psychogenic illness, therefore, it will be necessary to be acquainted with the developmental history of the sexual instinct so as to be familiar with its immature as well as with its adult forms.

As already said, some people dispute the view that there is any sexual life before puberty, but no one who has observed children without interfering could long doubt that they have interests in their own and other people's bodies, and are capable of deriving pleasures from them which are comparable to, though rather different from, what adults experience in their sexual life. They are certainly capable of experiencing jealousy even at a very early age, and jealousy, though it poisons love, still presupposes love's existence.

I am going to begin by giving as simple a statement as I can of the psychoanalytical view about the immature sexuality of children. I cannot do more to start with than state simply a theoretical reconstruction of the child's emotional development. Later, I will give illustrations from actual cases of psychogenic illness, to show to what extent this hypothesis of fixation and regression is useful in explaining the meaning of symptoms. This is all I can give in the way of support for the hypothesis, and it does not amount to much more than illustration of its possible applications. But the hypothesis, however far-fetched it may seem, has this much to be said for it: that it has not been arrived at *a priori*, but has been built up on a very large number of clinical observations. Also, it is the only existing theory which even begins to bring order into a whole mass of strange and hitherto inexplicable human abnormalities. It is not claimed that, as it stands, it explains everything. Much of what happens in the minds of neurotic patients and in the insane is still obscure. This is true, of course, also in physical medicine with regard to what is happening in the body. The discoveries Freud has made about the unconscious with the help of the free-association technique might be compared with the early advances in bacteriology which followed the discovery of the microscope. In both cases a new field of research has been opened up and a small part of it has, tentatively, been reduced to order. We have at last some guiding lines to work upon, but we are not able as yet to understand anything like the whole of the material presented to us. All we can say is that we have made a beginning, incomplete, as yet, but at least enough to enable us to see some indication of the causal pattern into which the hitherto chaotic mass of our material seems to fall.

Before, we had not even this; from now on, we are in a position to observe with some hope of advancing gradually further and further in the reduction of the chaos to order. This in itself makes the Freudian hypothesis worth studying.

But there is also another point in its favour, and that is that it would seem to throw light on problems other than those of neurotic illness which it was originally intended to explain, such as perversions, primitive customs, folk-lore, mythology, fairy stories, dreams and even a considerable amount of normal behaviour, including much that is of great value in human achievement and character formation. In this respect it resembles the theory of evolution, which was very quickly seen to apply to much more than the original pigeons and tortoises from whose study it arose. For the sake of clarity I propose to state the hypothesis dogmatically, without constantly putting in "Freud says" or "Psychoanalysis holds". Let it be understood that I am simply *stating a case*, and that I do not imagine I am *proving* anything.

We have grown accustomed to the idea that the most fundamental of all the instincts is the instinct to survive, and we are inclined to think of babies as actuated mainly by this need. We explain their sucking, breathing, kicking, screaming as expressions of their survival instinct, and no doubt this is correct, as a partial explanation of their behaviour. But the need to keep alive is not the only need that babies have. In addition to trying to survive, living beings also try to get pleasure.

The first part of the body which stands out in consciousness as a source of pleasurable sensation must be the mouth. Through this the baby not only gets nourishment which is needed for existence, but through it also it obtains its chief enjoyment in life. The act of suckling is thus not only the expression of the baby's self-preservation instinct but also its first great physical pleasure. Any interference with this pleasure will thus cause disappointment.

The pain of what we call disappointment which is produced by failure to find satisfaction for an urgent craving seems to consist in the resulting state of pent-up emotional tension. The organism does not easily tolerate this tension, and tends to fall ill it if cannot find a way of discharging it. In the case of hunger for nourishment, lack of satisfaction soon leads to death;

but in the case of that other hunger for pleasurable sense-stimulation, which later develops into sexual desire, the organism continues to live, but suffers until it can find some way of discharging the pent-up emotion which constitutes its disappointment. One way of obtaining relief, employed in infancy, and even much later in life, is to give this emotional tension a bodily discharge in a burst of tears or rage. Another way is to look for some object which will do to satisfy the craving if what was originally wanted cannot be had. A starving man who could find no food might chew up his boot leather. Similarly, the baby who wants the mouth pleasure of sucking and cannot get the breast, casts about for a substitute, and sooner or later discovers some part of its own body—thumb, tongue or toes—and sucks that instead, getting a certain amount of satisfaction.

But there is more in suckling than mere nourishment or sense-pleasure. The baby's first emotional relationship with another living being rests on this mouth contact and the feelings of satisfaction or distress which it arouses.

It is impossible, of course, for us to have any real appreciation of what the state of mind of a baby a few weeks old can be like, and when we attempt to reconstruct it we are bound to be much too anthropomorphic. We all know, however, that with us glamour falls on whatever satisfies the craving for sense-pleasure, and this is no doubt equally true in infancy. In adult life it is the pleasure obtained in physical relations which causes lovers to deify each other, and we can be sure that the same holds good of the pregenital sense-pleasures, and that they too cast a glamour over whatever ministers to them. Bodily contact with another human being must be the starting-point of human love: and this comes first to the baby in terms of its mouth sensations and activities in its contact with its mother's breast. The breast must therefore be the first object in the external world which the baby may perhaps be said, for want of a better word, to love, though exception may well be taken to speaking of love at all in such a primitive connection.

So, when disappointment breaks this relationship and the baby is driven to turn away from the outside world on to itself for satisfaction, it may be said, even if only in a very rudimentary sense, to have transferred its love from its mother to itself, and so to have begun to be auto-erotic. The high value which satisfaction of the craving for pleasure confers on whatever brings that satisfaction about—what Freud, rather discouragingly, calls "sexual over-estimation"—is now transferred from the mother's breast to itself.

This transferring of disappointed pleasure-craving from the outer world back on to the self may be resorted to again later on, when the child has developed from the sucking stage of infancy to more nearly adult love needs, and so a habit of seeking comfort in masturbation in one form or another becomes established.

But it is not only that love is transferred to the self in the auto-erotism which follows on disappointment, but that disappointment makes a change in the original love itself. The change occurred while the object of the baby's pleasure-seeking was still the mother's breast. When the baby has experienced the loss of the nipple and fears a repetition of this unpleasant experience, the original impulse to suck may change into an impulse to bite, thus introducing a conflict at the very outset of its relations with the external world.

The setting up of this sort of self-contradiction in a vital physiological function as a result of thwarting may indeed be regarded as the earliest starting-point of neurosis, and may supply the key to the explanation of later disturbances of physiological functions. Suckling, however, is not the only function in which such conflicts occur. Equal in importance in infancy to feeding is breathing, and here, too, it seems that contradictory impulses may be aroused simultaneously, as when the baby's screams or tears interfere with its normal breathing. This may later be re-enacted as a symptom in the form of some disturbance of respiration or speech. A similar state of self-contradiction may occur a little later in the physiological functions of the bowels and bladder. The body behaves as if it was in conflict with itself, and was trying to react in two contradictory ways at the same moment. Smooth functioning becomes disorganised, the motor discharge of the instinct is interfered with and a state of tension results.

To say that the baby is thrown into an emotional conflict between desire, on the one hand, and rage, aggression and fear on the other, all directed to the same object—the breast for instance—is, of course, to interpret the situation in terms which are borrowed from later life and are no doubt inappropriate to the baby's stage of development. I do not know how this mis-statement is to be avoided, since we have no better terms in which to describe the early stages of mental life which precede even the distinctions introduced by the knowledge of words. How appropriate such a description would be even in the case of adult emotional conflicts may be questioned. But if we are to speak at all of emotional events we must put up with the imperfections of language, and, when we are speaking of the mental life of babies, we must make even further allowances for the inevitable inaccuracy of our descriptions. Such terms as pleasure, desire, love, rage, aggression, retaliation, fear, despair, call up in our minds the ideas of emotions as we know them in later life; but these emotions certainly do not suddenly spring into being when we reach maturity, they must be developments from primitive feelings, the germs of which at least are probably present even in infancy. It would involve an impossible clumsiness of language to speak continually of the baby's emotions as "the primitive prototypes" of adult emotions with which we are familiar.

All babies, then, may be described in this necessarily inaccurate fashion as reacting to early disappointment by some emotional conflict between desire and rudimentary love on the one hand, and fear, or withdrawal, or rage, on the other, both sorts of conflicting emotion being directed towards the same object, to begin with the mother's breast, and being expressed, on the physiological level, by coexisting tendencies to contradictory bodily reactions, as, for instance, sucking and biting or swallowing and vomiting.

The disappointed baby withdraws its interest on to itself and takes to sucking or biting its own thumb, but still treats this new object as if it were the original one, the breast, loving and hating it simultaneously. Later, as fresh disappointments occur, the child may again fall back on its own body for relief, but here again the emotion which it transfers on to itself from the disappointing outside world will not be pure love alone but a conflict in which love and hate are both included.

Auto-erotic activities are, generally speaking, much more than mere attempts to obtain sense-pleasure. They are often, in part at least, acts of cruelty or revenge in which the person's own body is being treated as if it were the body of someone else, displacing on to it emotions which originally were directed to that other person's body, simultaneously loving it and also symbolically destroying or mutilating it; and I believe that the widespread condemnation of auto-erotism, and the guilt which people feel about it, arises mainly from the unconscious recognition and condemnation of the hostility originally directed towards the earliest love-objects, which is here acted out on the self. This would explain the sense of ruin and self-degradation which so often follows upon the act of masturbation. Masturbation springing simply from feelings of love does not have this devastating sequel. The more destructive the fantasies consciously or unconsciously connected with the activity, the more violent the grief, shame and fear of consequences; nevertheless the component of love, which is never entirely absent, produces at the same time a preoccupation with the self which has in it something of the "over-estimation" of a lover's feelings.

In learning how to make external love relations, there is always this alternative of loving oneself instead, and in most neurotics we find that preoccupation with the self has been abnormally accentuated at the expense of objective love directed to other people. It may indeed be that the pull towards self-love is stronger in some temperaments, the need to make outside attachments stronger in others. With repetitions again and again in later life in the face of new difficulties in making contacts with others, this tendency to give up and fall back on self for comfort may become a deeply rooted character trait.

This auto-erotic falling back on the self is sometimes the explanation of the psychogenic bodily symptom one finds in hysteria. A part of the patient's own body, or a bodily function, has become, as it were, unconsciously sexualised, and preoccupation with it takes the place of preoccupation with outside love objects. These preoccupations may blend love and hate in any proportions, the amount of suffering and shame which the symptom causes depending on the strength of the hate component. In so far, however, as the symptom represents an acting out on the self of a desired sense-stimulation, it will, at some level of the mind, be desired, and this explains what Charcot called the "*belle indifférence*" of the hysteric to his physical disabilities. It is more than indifference, it is, unconsciously, deep satisfaction, which explains why he clings so tenaciously to his symptoms.

This deep pleasure significance of hysterical pain came out strikingly in the course of Miss M.'s treatment. From time to time, when the pressure of her hatred was temporarily alleviated, the pains suddenly transformed themselves into conscious erotic pleasure. She recognised that the actual sensations were the same, but instead of causing her suffering, they were a source of exquisite delight. The translation of what is unconsciously an auto-erotic gratification into a conscious pain or disability happens if the pleasure is too guilty to be enjoyed openly and has to be combined with self-punishment to excuse it, as it were. But however painful it may be in consciousness, a hysterical symptom is, I believe, always a profound auto-erotic gratification in the unconscious.

The child who falls back on its own body for gratification, either in the form of recognised auto-erotism or of hysterical bodily symptoms, clings to its early sense-pleasure, refusing to pass on or accept substitutes and so remaining fixated and failing to mature.

This clinging to the original demands for pleasure is the neurotic reaction to disappointment. It occurs equally in cases where there is an open attempt to gratify the disappointed wishes auto-erotically by some kind of self-manipulation or when the wishes are repressed, since this does no more than transfer them to the unconscious where they still persist and still clamour for satisfaction.

The essential factor which brings about this neurotic arrest of development seems to be the fear aroused in the child by its own violent emotional reaction to interference with its pleasure-seeking or sexual instinct. In those who develop psychogenic illness one always finds that interference with pleasure has been reacted to with intense hostility. This hostility itself, however, seems to be an attempt to deal with the excessive tension brought about by the damming up of the instinct which is denied its outlet.

What makes tension excessive is probably often a matter of individual constitution. We are not yet in a position to be dogmatic on this subject, but it certainly seems that intensely strong pleasure capacity at an early age is often a predisposing factor, since this intensifies the pain of disappointment so that any thwarting will be reacted to by violent paroxysms of rage or by withdrawal into despair. Such children would be especially vulnerable psychologically, the very intensity of their power to enjoy making renunciation harder and thus creating in them a predisposition to fixation. The innate strength or the premature awakening of the pleasure capacity may be one factor in the development of neurosis, but no doubt actual experiences often play a part of greater or less importance in precipitating the illness. In some cases where the predisposition is marked quite a small amount of frustration is too much to be borne, while in others whose resistance is greater, healthy development would be disturbed only by unusually trying experiences. Any existing tendency to the fixation at childish levels of sexuality which produces neurosis is accentuated by repeated frustrations and also by violent interruptions, so that these might turn the scales in favour of neurosis even in the case of a child healthy enough to tolerate ordinary strains. Violent interruption with sudden fright seems to have a "traumatic" or splitting, dissociating, effect upon the personality. Thus, if a child who is indulging in some auto-erotic pleasure, such as thumb sucking, or other more definite genital excitation of its body, is suddenly confronted by a furious parent or nurse, who forcibly cuts the pleasure short and perhaps inflicts some alarming and bewildering punishment, the tendency to fixation, conscious or unconscious, on that pleasure will be greatly increased.

Again it would seem that such experiences become most "traumatic" when the child is already "guilty" and vulnerable on account of its own hostile feelings. Neurosis is thus best looked on as the result of a combination of causes, some internal or constitutional, some external, whose relative importance varies from individual to individual.

Fixation, however brought about, consists in clinging to the early forms of pleasure and still being preoccupied with them, consciously or unconsciously, when a normal person would have outgrown them. But this does not necessarily mean that, in the case, for instance, of a mouth fixation, the person will always go on sucking. The arrested emotions which become fixated to the originally denied pleasure are, not simple desire, but a conflict between desire and repudiation, love and hate, and the resulting behaviour depends upon which of these two is the more powerful. Even at the suckling stage a baby who has suffered disappointment or pain in connection with feeding may turn away from the breast and obstinately refuse to suck; and, later, the adult may actually refuse mouth activities, even, in some cases of insanity, to the extent of dying of starvation.

Analysis would suggest that the reason for this extreme repudiation is, once again, the entanglement of the early pleasure hunger with the destructive rage provoked by thwarting. To begin with, perhaps, the conflict itself produces an almost mechanical blockage of the sucking instinct, which one might compare with the experimentally induced disappearance of a normal reflex which has been associated artificially with pain. I have already explained how a similar confusion may be introduced into other physiological functions, such as digesting, excreting, breathing or speaking.

But even more important is the change in the child's picture of the outside world which follows this awakening of hostility. The baby expresses the hostility aroused by disappointment of its pleasure-craving with the part of the body which feels the craving. It loves by sucking and it also hates by biting. For quite a long time the small child continues to use its teeth for attack and revenge, and when it begins to be able to form ideas of what to expect from other people it can do nothing but interpret them in terms of itself, so that it dimly expects love and hate to be expressed by them also in mouth terms.

That this happens is, of course, only an inference which we draw from evidence which comes much later in life. The baby does not make any such logical deductions as "I want to bite, therefore I shall be bitten". Probably it does not at first make any clear distinction between what is itself and what is not. But certainly it must in general be true of all of us that as we gradually advance towards this distinction we must form our conception of what the outside world is like on the pattern of what we are like ourselves. In primitive races even adults remain anthropomorphic and egocentric all their lives, reading the whole of the natural world in terms of their own instincts. In so far as babies, who live in terms of their mouths, form any sort of conception of an outside world as distinguished from themselves, it must be a mouth world, and thus, for the angry baby who wants to bite, the outside world, in so far as it is apprehended at all, is probably a biting world.

To the extent, therefore, that hostility is awakened, the whole world changes from a safe to a dangerous place. Again and again in patients with unconscious biting fantasies one comes upon the same terrors, such as the wolf grandmother in Red Riding Hood, or the witch who fattened Hansel to eat him, or the seven little kids whom the wolf ate up, etc. Similarly, where there are fantasies of voracious sucking and draining, one comes on a horror of vampires or of spiders which catch flies and suck them dry.

Mr J., just after saying that his wife forced him into all sorts of unnecessary *expenditure*, had the fantasy that his mother might really have been a terrible and depraved person who had sucked like a vampire first his father and then his three elder brothers, and who might also suck him dry. He had the fantasy that she would suck his penis away from him. A great impression had been made on him by a story he heard, or believed he heard, of the great suction power of women's genitals and the fearful strength of their thighs. This exactly fitted in with his own secret dread, and was embodied in his unconscious image of his mother.

The day he produced this fantasy he had spent half an hour telling me that analysis had drained him of all initiative and enterprise and had ruined his health. He admitted that his wife said he was better, but his own feeling was that he was utterly incapacitated and might barely get away with his life. I explained the meaning of these fears.

He was feeling about me now in a way which was quite out of touch with the real situation, but was appropriate to the fantastic picture of the dangerous vampire woman which he had kept in his unconscious from the time when he had repressed it at an early age. This vampire woman was even then not a real person, his own mother, for instance, but a fantastic travesty of her, distorted by his own voracious hostile reactions towards her when she disappointed him, perhaps at the time of his weaning. Unconsciously I meant to him emotionally this frightful fantastic creature, no matter how little he believed all these horrors about me with his adult intelligence—and of course he did not believe them, for he was not mad—all the same he believed them emotionally because he feared me in just the way any of us would quite rightly fear a vampire monster if such a creature really existed.

This fantasy of draining which belongs primarily to the mouth stage may be carried over later to the genital relation in so far as the penis is regarded unconsciously as the equivalent of the nipple. One patient, who was repressing very violent fantasies of draining the loved-hated object, dreamt of a man who was impotent, so that, in order to get from him what she wanted sexually, she was driven to syphon a fluid from his penis which appeared to be a mixture of blood and water.

People who have these unconscious draining impulses fear the consequences of their own aggressive attitude: they expect that others will rob and deplete them and they also fear the effects on themselves of what they have wished to take by force. The persistence of this draining reaction to suckling disappointment explains certain kinds of character formations such as the need some people have always to make use of others, to get things out of them, to take hospitality, meals or money, which is often accompanied by an uneasy sense of obligation and need to placate those who have been used. It also explains the fear often expressed by patients that they will be poisoned or infected, or that they already have inside them something bad which will harm themselves or other people. A person who has this unconscious idea may worry over such a thing as a pimple or a septic spot, taking it as an indication that this internal poison is beginning to work to the surface. One patient had the idea of eating something which would go bad and then send up poisoned bubbles to her brain. The exaggerated fear of any smell from the body or breath depends also upon this unconscious fantasy of there being something bad and dangerous inside. By transposition of fears connected with the mouth downwards to the genitals sexual contact may be feared as poisonous. This is the explanation of exaggerated dread of sexual infection.

Such illustrations show how a person may react to life in what might be called starvation terms, in which the need to feed on other people is paramount but is accompanied by fear of the dangerous effects of such feeding.

But in explaining this starvation attitude to life it would be wrong to put too much emphasis on real mouth deprivation or hunger in infancy. In such cases the starvation from which the patient suffers, though it takes a mouth pattern, is essentially a starvation of love which may be expressed in cravings belonging to any of the bodily zones from which sense-pleasure can be derived, and usually contains a considerable element of desire which was originally genital but has been transferred by regression to the earlier mouth pleasure zone.

I can discuss this better by and by, when we are considering the later stages of emotional development.

The fact that a symptom takes an infantile or pregenital form must not blind us to its more adult meanings which are often disguised by regression. On the other hand disappointment of infantile pleasure-craving undoubtedly predisposes to further emotional trouble at later stages, each reinforcing the other and contributing to the final illness.

The important thing to be noticed at this point is not so much regression as the fact that in the fantasies of these patients with fixation on, or regression to, the mouth level of sensual pleasure-seeking, the mixture of hostility in their own attitude has transformed their outlook on the world so that what they take inside them is regarded as poisonous or infectious. This is because, like the child, the unconscious of the adult still reads the outside world in terms of itself, and therefore when it itself becomes hostile, it feels as if the external world had also been transformed into an enemy, and it expects a retaliation proportional and similar to the hostile attacks which it itself is impelled to make. For the baby to whom reality presents itself mainly in mouth terms, and whose hostility expresses itself in biting, this retaliation will be fantasied in terms of being bitten or devoured. (By this, of course, I do not mean that the baby makes conscious inferences from its own behaviour to the behaviour of others.)

This early mouth preoccupation is the origin of many childish terrors. I have a friend who remembers believing as a child that he was being fattened for the table. When kind people pressed food upon him he mistrusted their motives and was half afraid to eat it (he has grown up unusually lean). I have already said how deeply such stories as Hansel and Gretel, Red Riding Hood, and The Seven Little Kids seem to affect some children. It may be objected that this child copied the fairy stories, but why did that particular theme of being eaten impress him enough to distort so amazingly his perception of his parents' real attitude? I suggest that this particular child happened to be vulnerable because of his own biting fantasies. And why are such stories as these to be found so constantly in fairy tales and folk-lore? Why does Cronos devour his children?

It would seem that these primitive tales and fables spring from the preoccupations which we have all shared in infancy and which still to some extent persist in all of us, even though with advancing years the emphasis of interest has shifted. Sometimes, however, it happens, as we have seen, that the focus does not shift, so that interest in these early mouth preoccupations is abnormally prolonged into later life, when it may give rise to psychogenic symptoms.

This abnormal preoccupation with immature or, as it is technically called, "pregenital" sexual pleasure-seeking may come about for two reasons. Fixation we have already discussed. The other reason is regression, to which some reference has also already been made. By regression, as I have just pointed out, infantile activities which have originally a considerable charge of sensual pleasure attached to them may become sexualised also in a more adult way. The urge which normally goes into an adult love may be dammed back for various reasons so that the normal outlet becomes impossible. Then the whole driving force of adult sexuality may regress to these infantile sensual pleasures, and other organs of the body may now, consciously or unconsciously, come to represent the genitals from the point of view of sexual pleasure. A doubly strong craving for stimulation is thus set up in these organs—a craving which would, in any case, have belonged to them in their own right as pregenital pleasure zones, and also the added craving which they acquire by regression as genital substitutes. When both these urges converge on one bodily part, as, for instance, the mouth, this may set up a very insistent need. Such a mixture of pregenital pleasure-seeking, together with regression from later more adult genital sexual desires, is the explanation which psychoanalysis offers for the perversions, and it is possible also to explain many symptoms of psychogenic illness if we assume that there lie behind these, in the unconscious, fancies about pregenital pleasure zones similar to those which perverts express openly in their sexual life.

In such fancies the pregenital pleasure zones are substituted for the genitals, so that ideas of intercourse, impregnation and birth are now thought of in connection, not with the genitals themselves, but with the mouth, for instance, or the anus, and the impregnating fluid is imagined to be, not semen, but saliva, urine or faeces.

The psychoanalytic hypothesis, as has been explained, is that psychogenic symptoms can be understood if we think of them as expressions of repressed unconscious sexual wishes cast in a pregenital form. If once this hypothesis is assumed, the dreams and fantasies, conscious and unconscious, of neurotic patients at once become intelligible.

Direct evidence of the reality of pregenital sexuality can be obtained by anyone who cares to listen to the conversation and play of children themselves. Children all seem to pass through a period when they speculate about intercourse, birth and impregnation, and they produce their own theories as to the ways in which these things happen. At what age such speculations first begin may depend on the child's circumstances and what happens to excite its interest in these questions. Often the witnessing of sexual scenes or the birth of other children first sets the child wondering, or it may be in connection with the birth of animals, such as kittens or puppies, or the hatching of eggs. There is usually something that happens in the first three or four years of a child's life to set it thinking. The explanations it invents are naturally coloured by its own experiences and preoccupations. Even if it has outgrown the suckling stage, the mouth is still a centre of great preoccupation; it may still be indulging in thumb-sucking, or may be undergoing the experiences of teething. So, even apart from regression, it would be likely that in a good many of the explanations which little children invent for themselves of how babies get in and out of the body the mouth would figure importantly. They find out very soon that the baby is actually for a time inside the mother. How does it get there? One common theory is that she eats or drinks something and then it grows inside. What she eats or drinks is the problem. Some think it may be seeds or fruits, but after all why should the result then be not a plant, but a baby? More often the child comes to the conclusion that what is eaten is something produced by the body, milk, or saliva (taken from the earliest stage of preoccupation), but also perhaps excretions or blood (if the child's interests are concerned with later stages).

At a very early age children find nothing to dislike in such ideas, and there is plenty of evidence that they even find them highly attractive. It is only later that they banish them from consciousness with very great severity and feel them to be disgusting. These early theories of impregnation reappear, however, as elements in symptom-formation.

In analysing patients who happen to have good memories for their childish ideas, or who in the course of treatment regain such memories, the analyst hears all sorts of childish sexual theories in which other parts of the body have been substituted for the genitals, or other bodily fluids for the impregnating material. We are here concerned with such theories in so far as they belong to the mouth level of preoccupation. Frequently one hears of the mouth, lips, tongue, saliva and breath having been given a sexual significance in these early fantasies, and they often assume this significance unmistakably in the bodily symptoms and fantasies of psychogenic illness.

I have already referred to the patient who, having successfully repressed the fear of genital injury, which was an unconscious factor in her neurosis, showed instead a morbid dislike of the lips, breath and saliva. For a long time she simply could not mention these things, though she tolerated intercourse itself. Her fear of genital relations had been displaced on to the earlier pregenital ideas connected with the mouth.

Miss M., who suffered from only partially suppressed fears concerning rape and childbirth, remembered that as a child she had been very much worried at being kissed by a grandfather, whose moustache was dirty, for fear that something from the moustache had got into her mouth and would grow inside her. She had a dream in which after running away in panic she was forced to come out of her hiding-place and kiss her father, and some magical fluid passed from his mouth into hers. She remembered wondering whether she could get a baby on purpose by eating something, and she thought that when dogs investigated excreta in the street they were looking for something which would make puppies. Once or twice secretly and with a great sense of guilt she tasted her own excretions, hoping that in this way she would get a baby of her own. Then she began to fear she was poisoned.

Similarly, children seem to believe in birth by the mouth. Miss M. had a dream of lying across her mother's lap with blood pouring from her mouth and her vagina. Then something blocked her mouth so that she could not speak. The associations to this dream pointed to menstruation and birth. In several other dreams her mouth was blocked by a sticky substance which reminded her of fluid excretion, thus symbolising a fantasy of anal birth transferred to the mouth.

Even when patients do not remember their very early fancies, their symptoms often show unmistakably that pregenital pleasure organs are being invested with genital significance.

Mr J. spoke of a very alarming tongue sensation from which he had suffered from time to time all his life, in which his tongue seemed to be growing too big for his mouth, or, again, seemed to be paralysed. Occasionally, too, he was unable to swallow. This patient, though not actually impotent, had a great deal of anxiety about intercourse. Considerable evidence came up during the course of treatment to show that in these mouth symptoms the tongue was a substitute for the penis, while swallowing had a female significance.

Such proof of the sexual significance which attaches to the pregenital pleasure organs, supplied directly by children themselves or by neurotic patients, could be piled up indefinitely, but perhaps the most striking evidence of all is given by the insane, who sometimes express quite openly what is in their unconscious.

Since for the present we are concerned with the mouth preoccupations of infancy, I shall here quote cases illustrating this first stage of infantile sexuality. In all these cases the effect of their own mouth hostility in transforming mouth pleasures into crimes and dangers comes out strikingly.

While I was at a mental hospital in America I was brought into contact with a great many patients who would not eat, by having for some months to do all the artificial feeding on the women's side. Some of them told me that they were too unworthy to eat, some that it was useless because they had no insides. But the majority of them gave as their reason that they were being poisoned. These patients, if not artificially fed, would have carried their refusal of food to the point of dying of starvation.

It is possible to understand their attitude towards eating if we think of it as due to fixation or regression to infantile preoccupations with the mouth, together with terrific conflict over the desires thus aroused. The symptoms may often be explained as repudiations of certain mouth wishes which at once attract and disgust or terrify the patient. I believe that the very common insane delusion of being poisoned has its origin in unconscious fantasies of dirty or destructive mouth impregnation, based on infantile mouth wishes but enormously reinforced by regression which carries back on to the original pregenital mouth preoccupations a good deal of a more adult genital significance, translated into mouth terms.

The emotional tone of these sexual fancies is transferred from the pleasure originally belonging to them into pain and horror in proportion to the strength of these patients' own unconscious hostile destructive impulses which have become entangled with their sexuality.

When such patients refused to eat, from the fear of being poisoned, they would then really be repudiating some fancy of disgusting or even sometimes murderous impregnation by mouth, which, notwithstanding the fear and horror which it arouses, has, nevertheless, a dreadful fascination for them because, in spite of its terrible transformation, it still attracts them sexually.

One of my patients in the mental hospital, a girl of twenty-three, who in most ways would have struck one as perfectly sane, assured me solemnly that while she was in another hospital during a previous attack of insanity the doctors had made her drink urine. This delusion represents one of the infantile notions of impregnation which are held by children at first without any disgust at all, but which are later repudiated with abhorrence. As it happened, this patient could remember having really believed in impregnation by urine when a child. She told me that when she was quite small a little girl friend had told her, as a great secret, that that was how babies were made. Though she was revolted, she had believed it, and had gone on doing so for years, telling nobody.

A male patient of whom I saw a good deal in the asylum refused to swallow anything, even his own saliva, which he was continually spitting out. He kept this up night and day for weeks on end till he was exhausted. I think that it is highly probable that some idea of being poisoned was at the back of it, and that this had the meaning of destructive impregnation for him too, which he repudiated with all his strength. There is also another possible interpretation of this symptom, and both may well be true, though, in a way, they are contradictory. This patient, displacing from the genitals upward to the mouth, may have given a sexual significance to his saliva and unconsciously or possibly even consciously looked upon spitting as a sort of ejaculation. It is curious that we actually do use the same word for a form of mouth expression and for a genital activity.

This interpretation is suggested by a similar case of Dr Abraham's, a neurotic this time, who had a curious tendency to excessive salivation. This symptom the patient himself, without having heard of any of these theories, described as "mouth pollution", and gave a sexual signification to it spontaneously.

In the case of this asylum patient, it will be seen that I am suggesting that a male patient may be preoccupied with the theory of *being* impregnated as well as of impregnating. I shall also give cases of women patients whose unconscious preoccupation dealt with impregnating, and this may sound curious. But one of the striking things about these patients is the bisexuality of their unconscious. They do not seem to have been able to make up their minds which sex they want to be. They are attracted by both and afraid of either. One of my friends told me of a case of a male asylum patient who actually believed he was pregnant and was extremely proud of it, and took the greatest care of himself on account of his "condition".

I had a woman patient who had one finger thickened and deformed. When she was in an acute phase of her insanity she attacked another woman and thrust this finger down her throat so far that she injured the larynx. Several times she also thrust it down her own throat. When she was partly recovered and able to converse intelligibly she told me that this finger strongly reminded her of a penis and that it belonged to the devil. She had a horror of it. It was in fact the finger with which she had masturbated in childhood. In this case, the symptom substituted the finger for the penis and the mouth for the vagina. The patient took a male sadistic attitude in her attack on the other woman, while, in relation to herself, she played the parts of both male and female. This sort of evidence is not confined to insane patients only. I have already quoted cases of neurotic patients whose unconscious preoccupations seemed to be about the mouth as a substitute for the genitals.

In another case which I have permission to quote the person was not even obviously ill at all. She was a very intelligent young doctor, a friend, not a patient, of my own, who was going over to me, for interest, some of the important points in her own training analysis, which had recently been successfully completed. This young doctor told me of some strange dreams she had had at a crisis in the analysis. She had gone to be analysed, among other things, on account of migraine which always came on just before her periods. It was a fairly typical migraine, with one-sided headache and vomiting. She was just expecting her period again at the time, and woke in the night with the headache and nausea. Then she went to sleep and had a vivid dream that she was drinking urine and menstrual blood. She woke and vomited with feelings of the most intense disgust. Then she fell asleep again and dreamt that she saw her parents in bed together, and was overwhelmed with violent feelings of rage against her father.

She and her father were, in fact, devoted, and she had never till then realised the existence of her repressed hostility to him, which appears to have been based on a childish theory of intercourse as a disgusting mouth relationship. After gaining this insight into the meaning of her migraine and nausea, her attitude towards men changed noticeably, and she was much easier and happier in their company. She also ceased to have nausea and vomiting at her periods.

On another occasion in her analysis, also connected with her attitude towards men, she dreamt that she was eating excrement, and woke with a disgusting bitter taste in her mouth which she could not get rid of for some days. The unconscious fancies here seem, in the main, to have been sexual ones transposed from the genitals to the mouth and so given, as it were, a pregenital setting, at the same time being changed from pleasure to horror, but still remaining sexual, although love had disappeared and was replaced by repulsion and disgust.

These cases which I have quoted so far have been mainly illustrations of symptoms which represent sexual fantasies displaced by regression on to the mouth, the real interest being still genital. It would seem to be this reinforcement of adult sexuality which makes patients often defend themselves so desperately against their mouth fantasies.

There is nothing sinister in a baby's impulse to bite its mother: it is simply hungry or else angry at having the nipple taken away, or perhaps playing, and it bites—that is all. But if the whole force of the adult sexual desire regresses to this infantile situation, and reanimates it, and if the mixed emotion involved contains a high proportion of hostility or fear, the case is far different. The rage and devouring are not on a simple baby scale any longer; while they remain unconscious they are perhaps really cannibalistic. That, I believe, is why patients fear them so.

On the other hand it would be a mistake to regard even devouring as altogether hostile. The original biological purpose of the mouth relation *was*, in a sense, devouring—getting milk was the purpose of sucking. At the infantile level the devouring impulse may be looked on as the baby's attempt to keep the source of milk and pleasure, not to let it ever be taken away.

The prognosis for the patient seems to depend on the balance between the components of the conflict in his individual case. The more aversion, fear, destruction and hate preponderate the worse is the outlook, but even in the most hopeless cases there seems to be some love and some attempt to save, alongside of all the obvious efforts to destroy. Unless the doctor understands this he cannot help the patient much.

One of my patients in the asylum, a young woman who refused to eat anything and had to be fed artificially, begged me not to do this because she said she knew that what we were giving her was the chopped up remains of her ancestors. The two-sidedness of her attitude about this cannibalistic fancy was well illustrated by her symptoms. She told me that since she had been in hospital she had grown a second complete new set of teeth, in addition to the usual ones, so that now she had twice as many teeth as other people. May not the explanation of this bizarre fantasy perhaps be something like: "All the better to eat you with, my dear!"

But she said she heard these teeth telling her *not* to eat, and indeed her repudiation of the wish was strong enough for her to have consented to die by starvation rather than gratify it.

The patient's otherwise inexplicable symptoms become intelligible if one thinks of them as the outcome of an unconscious cannibalistic fancy over which there was terrific conflict.

Another patient who was not in the least insane had a sort of waking dream one morning while waiting for his breakfast, in which something was served up which seemed to be burned brown on top. Association led to biting fantasies aroused by the sight of a woman's breast and other fantasies of mincing people up. More repressed but still unconsciously active were early childish interests in faeces and ideas of eating them.

This patient had all his life had the habit of tickling his mouth with the rough hairiness of his blanket, at the same time sucking his thumb. For him, unconsciously, the mouth, besides its pleasure value in its own right as the organ of sucking, also represented the female genital. One day in the course of his analysis he suddenly realised the meaning of his sucking symptom as a symbolic way of representing intercourse, translating it into its childish antecedents from which the perversions are all in fact derived. The discovery made him happy because it released him from considerable unconscious guilt by explaining his "perversity", of which he was afraid, as a survival of his normal childish sucking needs.

Evidently his early discoveries about sexuality had come at a time when he was still strongly dominated by his mouth cravings. He identified the breast and the penis, describing the woman's body as one with two penises above and none in the right place.

After discovering for himself the meaning of his thumb-sucking, this patient developed a sore throat which he recognised as also having psychological significance. The analysis on the day he spoke of this symptom ranged round many themes which had symbolic reference to the meaning of his symptom, including cows' udders which combined for him the ideas of breast and penis.

The light thrown on such cases as these is the sort of evidence on which psychoanalysis bases its theory that certain kinds of psychogenic symptoms really are the result of fixation or regression of sexual preoccupation to an infantile level, when the mouth and its activities are all important, both for love and hate.

But to understand this is not enough. Merely to be able to translate the language of the symptoms is of little or no use. The thing that matters most is to understand how the fixation and regression *came about originally*, what it was that made the early situation of frustration so intolerable that repression was the only way out and development was arrested. I have explained that I believe the root of psychogenic illness lies in disappointment leading to a conflict between desire and fear or hostility. The baby whose pleasure-craving is not satisfied normally tends to react violently against the pain of dissatisfaction with aggressive impulses, and this puts it in a dilemma. If it does not discharge its pent-up emotion, tension threatens to become unendurable. But if it discharges it, this must take the form of attack either on its own self or on those very people on whom it depends for satisfaction. I have suggested that the child's first reaction to the pain of the unsatisfied craving of the sense-pleasure organs is to turn against them. *Dis*pleasure in its own pleasure zones, which have been transformed by disappointment into an internal enemy, leads to a turning against these parts of its own self which make life worth living. The danger is that too great success along this line of defence would result in emotional death. This danger is avoided by projection of the source of pain and therefore of the object to be destroyed, "the enemy", from the disappointed pleasure zones themselves on to the outside world. Rage and destruction are now directed outwards and self-destruction becomes turned into aggression upon the outside world. But here again new fears arise. There is fear of the reaction itself, the explosion of aggressive rage. The baby may well terrify itself by its own crying and screaming and the holding of its breath which threatens to suffocate. Furthermore, the external object now attacked may retaliate, and the baby reading the world in terms of itself now dreads the retaliation, tooth for tooth, bite for bite. This may produce yet another reversal of object so that the attack is redirected back from the outside objects on to the self again. This is the origin of self-punishment or conscience which I shall discuss in much greater detail later on.

Of course I am not pretending that all these fears are

consciously formulated. No doubt the small child's reactions to disappointment are hardly more than blind struggles to avoid pain and danger, almost on a level with the behaviour of a rabbit chased by a dog. What I have tried to bring out is that, in these struggles, the child is torn by conflicting fears which may land it in a deadlock from which every way out is blocked. The rabbit bolting away from the dog and then finding its way suddenly barred by running into a wire netting will perhaps end by simply crouching there motionless, apparently half dead. The child, finding that some fresh terror blocks every way of escape from the pain of an intolerable situation of disappointment, dissociates and represses the wishes whose disappointment led to the trouble. It is as if, just like the burnt child who fears the fire, those who have suffered by frustration have learnt never again to permit themselves to risk feeling and *wanting*. But since it is impossible entirely to smother powerful instincts, a characteristic neurotic compromise is reached, in which these instincts which met with intolerable disappointment are excluded from consciousness, but nevertheless persist in the unconscious, still retaining much of their infantile setting. On account of their loss of contact with reality they have failed to mature, and it is this failure which distinguishes the unconscious sexual desire of neurotics from the conscious wishes of normal people.

To say that the emotional life of the neurotic is paralysed by excessive fear is at any rate one way of putting the difference between neurotic and normal life: or looking at it from a stage farther back, neurosis could perhaps be regarded as the result of an overwhelmingly vivid imagination of danger or suffering which gives rise to this excessive fear.

To say, alternatively, that neurosis results from an over-tender conscience is much the same as this, for what sharpens the prick of conscience is fear based on a vivid imagination of the consequences of transgression. Another way of regarding the difference between neurotic and normal would be to say that the child who cares most passionately at an early age is most in danger of neurosis, because its disappointment is proportionately severe and may be unbearable.

Still another way of putting it would be to say that the neurotic, tolerating disappointment less readily than the normal person, reacts to it with greater rage. His fear of retaliation may then be regarded as a secondary consequence of this rage. The child who is most headlong and ferocious in his fantasies of attack and revenge on others, reading these others in terms of himself, might be expected to have correspondingly appalling fantasies of the retaliations to be dreaded from them. And belief in this retaliation will in turn provoke further fantasies of attack, and a reaction of self-punishment, working up in a vicious circle. The beginning of this vicious circle is hard to determine—who can tell whether the child or the outside world was the original aggressor? In any case I think we may say broadly that early rage and early terrors will be found to be complementary to one another, though in the course of subsequent repression and over-compensation the outlines of the original emotional make-up of the child may get covered over and be hard to recognise in the adult. The furious baby may have become in adult conscious life a meek saint; the child who used to lie awake listening in agony to the footsteps of bears coming upstairs to devour him may have developed into an intrepid big game hunter.

However one likes to picture the origins of the difference between normal and neurotic, whether the excess in early childhood be of love or fear or imagination or rage, the upshot, at any rate, is repression and arrest of emotional development, so that, at least with part of his energy, the neurotic continues, though unconsciously, to be preoccupied with immature longings and terrors which the normal person has successfully outgrown.

It would be worth while for everyone who intends to practise medicine to bear in mind the possible psychological meaning which the illnesses he is called upon to treat may have for the patient, and which may be co-operating with organic factors to keep the illness going, or may even, sometimes, be the whole cause of it.

I should like to say just a word about the sort of symptoms in which it might be worth while to keep in mind this idea of unconscious mouth preoccupations as a possible explanation, even if I can do no more than just suggest a bare list of them. Vomiting is important, especially perhaps the vomiting of pregnancy. Unconscious fantasies may also be a factor in anaesthetic sickness, and sea-sickness, even when they are not the whole cause. Anorexia (loss of appetite) may be wholly or partly psychogenic. So also with oddities in the choice of foods (this occurs especially in pregnancy, when there is now and then a tendency to eat dirt). Again, there are aberrations of the appetite leading to excessive hunger, especially at night, in which satisfaction of the food appetite may be substituted for the satisfying of sexual hunger.

Psychogenic causes should always be kept in mind in chronic alcoholism and dipsomania, also in drug habits.

Some kinds of pain, especially dental neuralgia, are, I think, occasionally psychogenic and connected with fantasies in which there has been displacement upwards from the vagina or from the anus to the mouth and teeth. Spasm of the oesophagus and some cases of cough or throat-clearing may refer to unconscious mouth impregnation fantasies. I have myself had two cases in which severe inflammation of the mouth was unconsciously produced by the patients themselves by constant picking, the unconscious motive being auto-erotic; and in two other cases I was strongly tempted to believe that their septic throats were psychogenic, the irritation being unconsciously displaced from the vagina.

Respiration is only second in importance to nutrition and, like eating, spitting, swallowing and excreting, so also breathing is used to express love and hate as well as to carry on life. This has very important clinical implications. Voice disturbances, aphonia, stammering and mutism may arise from conflict between love and hate expressed in terms of breathing or speech.

The unconscious fancies behind these throat and speech symptoms seem to be concerned partly with biting and swallowing and partly with respiratory attacks taking such forms as overpowering by air, assaulting, as it were, with words and breath. These must be the fantasies which in everyday life inspire those bores who are determined to talk one to death, or, at the opposite extreme, those people who unconsciously so fear the destructive power of their breath that they never dare speak above a whisper. In medicine they should be borne in mind in investigating asthma and many other less well-defined disturbances of air entry into the lungs. There is great need for more investigation as to how far psychogenic interference with proper air intake may be a predisposing cause in tuberculosis.

Flatus is unconsciously employed by a great many patients as a vehicle for expressing hate and destructive impulses. Organically this belongs to the group of symptoms connected with the digestive system, but psychogenically it seems to have affinities with breath and connects up with the sense of smell. It is taken symbolically as a very specially hostile kind of overpowering and is equated unconsciously with terrific explosions which will blow the enemy into a thousand pieces.

But I should like to repeat that overpowering need not be thought of as all destructive. Overpowering may be an act of love as well as of hate. It is very important to remember how close together these two lie and how constantly the same act or symptom expresses, not simply one or the other of a contradictory pair of emotions, but both simultaneously.

I have mentioned a few of the more obvious common symptoms which may be connected with unconscious mouth, tongue, throat, eating and breathing fantasies. It would be impossible here to give an exhaustive list of them, and the task of producing convincing evidence from clinical cases is indeed beyond the power of a single individual. What I hope is that when the psychological attitude towards illness becomes as familiar to doctors as the organic point of view already is, evidence will be collected of a sufficiently wide nature to be of real value in deciding the relative importance of these two factors in the causation of the actual phenomena of illness which are the subject-matter of medicine.

No doubt both psychogenic and organic abnormalities will be found to be present simultaneously in a large number of cases and then the diagnostic problem is a delicate one. It is necessary to decide whether both, though present, are dynamically important in causing the malfunctioning of which the patient complains. I have explained that practically everyone would, on investigation, be found to be holding down some disappointed pregenital pleasure-seeking impulses repressed in the unconscious; it does not follow from this that every digestive or respiratory disturbance is psychogenic in its origin. Similarly we all have various organic defects, but it is not certain that the particular symptoms we may be complaining of are produced by them.

Because a patient complains, for instance, of abdominal pain and backache, and on physical examination also turns out to have a movable kidney or visceroptosis, this does not mean that the pain is necessarily the result of the physical condition or that it would disappear if this were put right. On the other hand it is just as important to avoid the opposite mistake of diagnosing some symptom as psychogenic and treating it as such when really all the while it is organic. It may happen that a patient who has been undergoing analysis, say for headaches supposed to be psychogenic, develops choked optic discs and dies of brain tumour. Mistakes undoubtedly happen in both these directions occasionally. One simply has to be always on the look-out and try to decide what is the dynamic factor in each case.

A new field of medical research of the very highest importance will be opened up when the doctors who treat organic diseases and those who have learnt to understand psychogenic illness begin to co-operate. At present it too often happens that the surgeon for instance who is called in, let us say, in a case of abdominal pain, diagnoses appendicitis or duodenal ulcer, without having in his mind the possibility that the pain may be neurotic in origin. This may lead to unnecessary operation, leaving the patient no better than before. For some patients the very fact of being operated upon has symbolic meaning which causes them to seek operation and unconsciously to produce symptoms which will deceive the surgeon into thinking operation called for, when, in fact, there is nothing organic the matter.

In the hospital where I was a student a hysterical woman patient, who must, I think, have been of this type, came complaining of abdominal pain and, on examination, was found to have eleven operation scars on her abdomen. All these operations had failed to alleviate the pains from which she suffered, and there is small doubt that their origin was psychogenic. Fortunately it was decided not to add a twelfth scar, but the patient was turned away without help. The case of Miss M. was similar, but she had got off with only two unnecessary operations.

A differential diagnosis between organic and psychogenic is sometimes not at all easy, and it is further complicated by the way in which organic and psychogenic factors play into each other's hands to create a vicious circle of illness. The best hope of correct understanding and treatment of difficult cases, however, undoubtedly lies in closer co-operation between these two branches of medicine, and I believe that it will be out of such co-operation that the next important advances in medical science will come.

SUMMARY

In this chapter I began my account of the developmental history of sexual life as it emerges from its early beginnings in the sensual needs and pleasures of infancy.

This development may be arrested in some cases, perhaps, because of a constitutional defect or as a result of bodily injury, such as also occurs sometimes in physical development; but in the case of neurosis, which on the Freudian view is also to be regarded as an arrest of development, this appears to be due to the dissociation and repression of a part of the personality which comes about as a reaction to early frustration. This results in the disappearance of the disappointed impulses so far as consciousness is concerned, but an unconscious preoccupation with them which is not outgrown.

Development may proceed normally in other respects, but this preoccupation remains in the unconscious just as it was, unmodified by subsequent experience.

If the dissociation occurred at the time in infancy when the mouth was the focus of the greatest interest, then the preoccupation which persists in the unconscious will still concern the mouth and all the primitive fantasies of love or hate which were at that time associated with it.

The arrest of sexual development may be absolute, but more usually it is partial only, so that some degree of normal emotional growing up takes place alongside of the dissociated fragment. This, however, remains as a potential source of anxiety. It does not submit to repression without a struggle, and it is always trying to get back to consciousness and seeking satisfaction. It still forms a part of the sexual life, and whenever the remaining conscious part of this is stimulated this repressed part also tends to be aroused, leading to difficulties in the love life and even in other relationships which are not overtly sexual. In some cases *all* contacts become, to some extent, dangerous and guilty, through their unconscious linking up with repressed forbidden impulses.

If later on there comes a check to the more adult forms of sexuality, there is a tendency for the sexual urge to regress from this later acquired stage of development back to the earlier stages, thus strengthening the repressed impulses and intensifying the internal struggle.

It is often not till some such situation arises, reinforcing the repressed infantile preoccupations with adult sexual energy, that an outbreak of symptoms actually occurs.

In the last part of the chapter I quoted a number of cases in which the underlying repressed preoccupation seemed to be with the mouth and mouth functions. It appeared that the patients' sexual interest had partly undergone fixation at the early infantile level of sucking and biting, connected with the nursing period, but that in addition the sexual drive had regressed from the adult genital level so that the mouth, tongue and throat and their functions stood symbolically for the genital organs and genital activities.

In my next chapter I shall go on with the Freudian account of psychosexual development.

CHAPTER V

In order to be able to understand the meaning of psychogenic symptoms we have begun to investigate the developmental history of the sexual pleasure-seeking instinct. In the preceding chapter we were concerned with the first stage in which preoccupation centres round the mouth, through which both the primary instincts for nutrition and for sense-pleasure obtain their satisfaction, and by which the infant makes its first love contact.

The other physiological function complementary to nutrition is excretion, and unbiased observation leaves no room for doubt that the bodily organs associated with excretion—the anus and the urethra—share the capacity for sensual pleasure which belongs to those parts of the body technically called "erotogenic". Preoccupation with these bodily organs constitutes the second stage in the developmental history of the sexual pleasure-seeking instinct.

Undoubtedly there is sensual gratification to be had in the stimulation of the anal and urethral mucous membranes during the acts of excretion, and in the relief experienced in evacuation; and here again, just as with the mouth, we have the perversions to show how highly charged with sexual pleasure this stimulation may be.

A very large number of symptoms and dreams and the memories and fantasies of patients and the games of uninhibited children bear witness to the fact that human beings normally pass through an excretory stage in the course of their emotional development, in which faeces and urine are regarded as important substances, of high value, and not in the least repulsive, though always perhaps a little dangerous, because so potent.

At first hearing it may seem surprising and even shocking that it should be taken for granted that every child is so disgusting in its taste. Even if it appears, from the things remembered by patients in analysis, and from a few children's games, and the behaviour of the insane, that some people do take a pleasure in evacuation and its products, it may be felt that these are just isolated cases, people with diseased minds. Yet I am sure this would be wrong.

Observation of children leaves no doubt about the occurrence of a stage, even in the most normal development, at which the buttocks, the acts of excretion, urine and faeces are the objects of delighted preoccupation. At a school run on modern non-interference lines for small children of two and three the little pupils devoted a whole morning to making up a chant about their behinds, which was a paean of triumph. Anyone who reads *The Arabian Nights* will observe that even with adults, at any rate in the East, this preoccupation with the buttocks may focus considerable sexual interest. This is a puzzle to our Western point of view, but it is difficult to say which way to set our problem, whether to be surprised that Eastern adults admire, or that Western adults repudiate, the buttocks. In the East it would seem that the childish high valuation of this part of the body persists, while with us the early preoccupation is now denied, though it is not thereby abolished, and the persistence of a highly ambivalent interest still reveals itself in the form of more or less derogatory joking, which is apt to pass beyond joking and become insult.

The reason for swinging over from pleasure to pain, pride to shame, delight to disgust, tenderness to insult, is the hostility which becomes entangled with the original pleasure. Just as we saw earlier, in the case of mouth pleasure which is transformed into aggression, so that love-sucking becomes rage-biting, so again at the excretory stage we have to reckon with the conflict and possible deadlock between two contradictory urges; of love when pleasure is obtained, but of rage, aggression and disappointment together producing hate and contempt when it is reprobated or interfered with; and love and hate will now be expressed in excretory terms, both originally, when the child is actually passing through this stage of its development, and also again later if it regresses back to this stage.

This, I believe, is the explanation of the paradoxical fact that just those very sense-pleasures which in early life must have aroused such extremely strong feeling are apt to be reacted against with especial violence later.

Some adults, it is true, still remember their childish excretory pleasure, and some still continue to experience pleasure in excretory activities which amounts, at times, actually to orgasm, but they are usually deeply ashamed of these sensations. Most adults have ceased to feel them and even entirely replaced them, so far as consciousness goes, by disgust.

From all this, a general principle emerges which serves to explain the curiously severe attitude we seem so often to adopt towards out bodily functions.

I am quite sure that whenever anything is rejected with particular violence, especially if it is condemned morally or, as is more fashionable, aesthetically, there is some defence behind this repudiation. The things which are repudiated in this particular way are things whose attraction needs to be guarded against: they belong to the class of forbidden pleasures. The conventional adult attitude towards excretion and the buttocks fits well with this general thesis. These things were once objects of great interest, pleasure and curiosity, but at an early age it was just over these matters that some of the first interferences, reproofs and frustrations were encountered, with the result that what was once desired is often transformed into an object of aversion.

But there is more to be said about this question of disgust at the excretory functions themselves. Much of the disgust heaped upon these functions would seem to belong, originally, to sexuality and not to excretion. It appears to be transferred to excretory activities either by regression, because the child takes flight from the genitals and refuses to pay attention to them, falling back instead upon its earlier interests, or else because the child, interpreting sexual activities in terms of its own best known pleasures, does actually picture sexual relations in excretory terms at a time when it itself is greatly preoccupied with its own excretory functions and products. The disgust, then, is about the excretory organs in so far as those are really thought of as the organs, *not of excretory, but of sexual activity*, in so far as that is hated and despised.

The evidence that the contempt is often felt in the unconscious for sexuality is immense, and it is striking how often this contempt finds expression in picturing these activities in excretory terms. An insane patient spoke of the sun, which in her case seemed to stand symbolically for her father, as having been turned into an old watering can for which she expressed contempt. I think this watering can was a parody of the penis urinating. This patient, in one of her lucid intervals, in speaking of her childish memories, volunteered the fact that as a child she had occasionally seen her father urinating, and the sight, for a number of fantasy reasons, which will be more intelligible later, had been charged with such violent emotion that she had not been able to deal with it and had been driven to dissociate the emotion.

What gives the edge to this belittling attitude is primarily jealousy at the parents' mutual preoccupation, from which the child is shut out, and fear of them when they are united. One gets the picture from the child's point of view of the parents banded together against it.

I am told that in primitive communities where there is no feeling against the children being present when the parents have intercourse, little children often attempt actually to pull the parents apart. The idea that these two are against the child when they are united seems thus to be a projection of the child's own jealousy, and behind it lies the child's wish to keep them separate, and behind this is the disappointed love which would like to keep possession of the parent and resents a rival.

But there are also two contributing factors to the child's aversion from the parents' sexuality, and so to excretion in general, in so far as that is taken to represent what the parents do together. One of these is the result of the parents' interference with the child's own early sense-pleasures: the child pictures sexuality in terms of its own pleasures and it resents what it regards as the parents' hypocrisy in pretending to be so moral by day and then going off at night to do these very things which they try to persuade the child are so wicked and disgusting, and which the child itself is strictly forbidden to do.

The other factor which enters into the child's aversion from the parents' sexual relations is on a really genital level, at least to begin with, and in speaking of it at this point I am anticipating a subject which I shall discuss fully in the next chapter when we deal with the last stages of childish sexuality in which preoccupation passes from the pregenital pleasure zones and is focused on the genitals. I want, however, to say a word here about the child's fears concerning genital sexual activity, because these fears are often important in bringing about regression of sexual preoccupation from the genitals themselves to the pregenital pleasure zones, especially those connected with excretion, and so tend strongly to reinforce the disgust with which these come to be regarded.

Fear of the effects on the mother of sexuality in so far as that is connected with menstruation and childbirth may indeed have some basis in reality, but this is slight compared with the contribution from fantasy. The truth seems to be that the child who is resentful or jealous secretly longs for revenge on those who have made it suffer, and is thus predisposed to interpret what it observes as a sign that its hostile wishes towards its parents are being fulfilled. One patient, whose early conflict of love as against sexual rivalry with her mother had been intense, remembered how she used to walk about crying when her mother was out of her sight, imagining her trampled to death by horses. At night she used to creep to her parents' bedroom door to listen for her mother's breathing, fearing she would die in the night. This state of abnormal fear for her mother's safety arose out of her intense wish for her death, struggling against an equally strong need for her, which made the idea of the success of the hostile wish unendurable. Genital sexuality was for a long time repugnant to her. She developed a vaginal spasm when she attempted it. At the same time the mouth became invested, by regression, with abnormal significance, her horror of the genitals being displaced on to the lips, tongue, breath and saliva.

In other cases blood and childbirth sometimes become degraded by regression to faeces and evacuations. Whatever there may have been in the way of an eary taboo put upon infantile excretory pleasure in the course of nursery training is now greatly intensified, and any aversion which may have tended, at the genital level, to be twisted round into contempt will now add a further contribution of contempt to the attitude taken toward the excretory processes which have been substituted for the genital ones. This is striking in obscene language and jokes, whose purpose is very often a sexual insult couched in excretory terms of abuse.

It has already been explained that excessive disgust at dirt and exaggerated reactions of cleanliness may often be over-compensations against an unconscious preoccupation with these excretory pleasures, and this need to over-compensate is increased in cases where the repudiation, which has for some reason become attached to the genital level of development, has been carried over to this slightly more tolerable, but still repudiated, substitute. The sensual pleasure of the excretory functions, thus secondarily sexualised by regression, is now converted in consciousness into exaggerated disgust.

Similarly the physical sensations connected with the excretory functions which were originally intensely pleasurable, and still remain so at some deep unconscious level, may be transformed by over-compensation, at least as far as consciousness goes, into suffering. And this transformation from pleasure into pain may again be greatly accentuated by regression when the pregenital excretory pleasures are made to stand symbolically for the repudiated pleasures of genital sexuality. It was this reinforcement by regression that caused such acute conflict in Miss M. over her bowel functioning. The conflict which in consciousness was acted out over her bowel functioning really derived most of its intensity from the much more important conflict over genital sexual ideas of intercourse and childbirth which had been transposed by regression into bowel terms and smothered in the disgust which originated, in the first instance, in her jealousy, fear and rage about her parents' sexual life. Her dreams showed clearly the genital significance which she attached to the anus, and the confusion which she had made, on account of her regression, between back and front.

One night she dreamt that she was in bed with a doctor who

was *behind* her. He said, "Now you know what the position is", and did something to her from behind. Here there was obviously a confusion between the genitals and the anus similar to that which we have already seen in the case of the mouth. And again we can draw the obvious parallel with the perversions.

Another time, she dreamt that her brother—with whom she had had sexual play—was pinching her behind, and she asked her mother, "Why can't he do it in front?"

Certain facts in her childish history may explain her asking her mother this question in her dream. When she was quite little her mother discovered her indulging in genital masturbation, and gave her a very severe fright about it, and forbade her ever to let anyone touch her there but a doctor. The result was that, although she still went on with the practice, it was with the greatest secrecy and dread, and she was haunted with the idea that she was injuring herself, while she also made a very considerable regression to the earlier level of anal interests which she had begun to outgrow, now developing the constipation from which she suffered for the rest of her life, and unconsciously transposing on to this constipation much of the anxiety which really belonged to her forbidden genital activities. Her secret dread was that these had injured her genital functions, but she could not face this idea and so repressed it, experiencing anxiety in consciousness over to her excretory functions instead. She was in agonies of fear that something terrible was wrong with her if her bowels would not work. To her unconscious the failure of her bowels to work appeared to be a punishment for her jealousy of her mother's pregnancy which had originally driven her to masturbation, and which was now represented as having rebounded on herself like a boomerang and damaged her own sexual power represented regressively in terms of bowel functioning.

In connection with this sexualisation of the infantile anal interests by regression, Dr Karl Abraham points out how, if the urge of adult sexuality had been displaced from the genital to the anal zone, patients may deplore the inhibition of the bowel function just as though it were "genital impotence". In thinking of the person who is hypochondriacal about his motions, he says, "One is tempted to speak of an 'intestinal impotence'!" Miss M. worried herself in a similar way. I have already said that she developed abdominal pain which she described as agonising and on account of which she was twice operated on, the appendix being removed the first time, and one ovary the second, without any improvement resulting. She had the most vivid fancies of the appendix growing into the ovary, which, after a period of analysis, she recognised as fancies transposed from a highly sadistic theory of intercourse. She had the idea that something was stuck inside her, which she *must* get rid of, even if they had to cut it out with a knife. Towards the end of her analysis, when her fantasies about this something stuck inside her were very near to consciousness, she dreamt that she was lying ill and she heard someone say, "She must have it cut out of her with a knife or she will die". This same something stuck inside her was often represented by her faeces.

The repressed wish behind such fantasies as we have been describing in Miss M.'s case and the symptoms to which they give rise comes from the last stage of emotional development which will be discussed more fully in the next chapter, the stage at which the capacity for sense-pleasure at length becomes focused on the genital organs themselves and the wish for genital contact begins to be felt. Disappointment of this wish tends to produce the reactions with which we are familiar—that is, anger, regression and a flight to compensatory fantasy satisfaction in which the child pretends it really has the things it wants and cannot get. But we have seen further how disappointment changes the original love wish into a different attitude in which love and hate are combined so that the fantasies which represent its satisfaction become guilty, painful and terrifying. What is now fantasied as being stuck in the body may thus be regarded with fear and horror instead of with pleasure: nevertheless it is still the object of sexual desire and so felt, in spite of everything, to be thrilling and precious. The resulting attitude is ambivalent.

In one of her attacks of pain Miss M. screamed for a knife to cut it out herself, and she was constantly trying to get doctors to operate on her. At the same time she was unconsciously unwilling to let go the faeces which she kept inside her by obstinate constipation. She was obviously in great conflict as to whether to hold or to repudiate what she fancied as being inside her, which was represented by what caused the pain and by her faeces. Her symptom was a typical neurotic compromise attempting to satisfy both sides of the conflict, resulting in holding on obstinately, and at the same time experiencing no pleasure but, on the contrary, agonies of pain and anxiety.

I have mentioned already how during treatment this translation of pleasure into pain was actually reversed. When she first came to analysis, she described the abdominal sensations she suffered as *agonising*, so that she did not know what to do with herself, and feared she would go mad with pain; but, as time went on, and the sexual fancies behind the pain became clearer, the character of the sensation itself appeared to alter. Instead of pain it took on more and more the character of sexual excitement, which at times was so frankly pleasurable that she admitted that she did not wish to be without it. At one stage in the treatment, when she was becoming conscious of her bitter hostility to and resentment at sexuality (the deep root of which was disappointed jealousy), she was again seized with excruciating intestinal pains. At this time some of her jealousy and hatred were transferred on to the analyst and she took pleasure in fantasies of my suffering similar agonies. I think her own pains, though by regression they were referred to her bowels, were, actually, a physically acted fantasy of the pain into which, by reason of her jealousy, she had translated her ideas of her mother's sexual experiences. With the lessening of her hatred and jealousy as a result of the lifting of them nearer to consciousness and a beginning of insight into their origins, the pain again subsided and began, intermittently, to be replaced by recognisably sexual pleasure.

As we are concerned in this chapter with the excretory level, I am emphasising this aspect of Miss M.'s case, but actually the same fantasies were acted out just as strikingly also on the mouth and throat level. Corresponding to the fancy of something stuck in her bowels, which amounted at one time almost to hallucination and was acted out in her constipation, she had also the fantasy, more deeply hidden, of something stuck in her mouth which she described as being like sticky pudding She had a series of vivid and terrible dreams of assault by rough men in which she was unable to speak because her mouth was stuffed with this substance. Again and again she dreamt of having something stuck in her throat. Quite near the end of her analysis she dreamt that a doctor stood by her bedside and said, "I can cure you but I must choke you to do it!" It seemed that, for her unconscious, the genitals, the anus and the throat were treated as being equivalent and interchangeable, so that the genital sexual desires represented by something stuck in the vagina, which often appeared in her dreams openly, could also be represented symbolically in the form of things stuck either in the bowel or in the throat.

The same change from pleasure to pain which occurred during analysis in her bowel sensations also happened over a bitter taste which she was apt to get in her mouth when she was anxious. When she had analysed the meaning of her mouth preoccupation, this taste suddenly turned from bitter to sweet. She said that it felt like a miracle and that she would be afraid to tell anybody because they would laugh at her.

She also frequently suffered from septic throats, and here too, though I cannot prove it, I suspect that there were psychogenic as well as organic factors at work. She herself noticed that during her treatment her attacks of tonsilitis coincided with renewed attacks of constipation, and that both these physical symptoms flared up when she was in a mood of hatred, and suffering from nightmares of attack by wild uncontrolled men. These moods alternated with other states in which she was unresentful and happy; at such times she had pleasant and often frankly erotic dreams, and then her bowels acted freely and her throat was quite well.

Another patient produced transitory symptoms of sore mouth and haemorrhoids simultaneously, both of which disappeared almost overnight after an interpretation of their symbolic sexual significance.

Whatever one may think about the real origions of these mouth, throat and bowel symptoms, it was clearly established that they were strongly influenced by psychogenic factors and came and went with the recurrent attacks of hatred from which these patients suffered, and when they achieved insight into the unconscious sources of this hatred and so were relieved of it, the physical symptoms vanished.

It is an interesting fact that the illnesses which Miss M. developed should have led to repeated examinations by doctors of the vagina, rectum and throat, when one remembers her mother's warning that she was never to let anyone touch her genitals but a doctor. The patient was certainly sexually excited by these examinations, though for guilt reasons she actually experienced pain rather than pleasure during them. Of course she was quite unaware of the curious way in which she was still achieving her object, while with the greatest literalness obeying her mother's commands.

So far we have been able to recognise this patient's anal symptoms and interests as the result of fixation on primary infantile sensual pleasure, to which a secondary importance had been transferred by regression from the genital sexual desires when these became too guilty or alarming to be enjoyed.

In considering the sexual significance with which the infantile pregenital activities may become invested by regression, however, we must not think only of the sensual pleasure side. These pregenital activities which concern the mouth, for instance, or the excretory functions, are not only confused with genital ones as sources of pleasure, they are also very commonly regarded by the child as the *means of reproduction*. It links on to what has already been said about eating unconsciously standing for impregnation. Over and above the equation of sensual pleasure zones, the importance of the excretory activities seems to be greatly enhanced by a further question which preoccupies the child while it is still very young—the question where babies come from. Over this question, just as over the question of genital sensation, what lies behind the child's curiosity is its own awakening sexual wishes. With the focusing of its pleasure-seeking impulses upon the genitals it begins itself to *want* both sexual pleasure and also a baby of its own. Sometimes this wish comes to consciousness in connection with the actual birth of a new baby brother or sister, suddenly appearing in the night while the mother is ill, and taking everybody's attention. Sometimes this event has not actually occurred, but it is dreaded, a threat hanging over the child's head. The problem also arises remarkably early in connection with the child itself, whether boy or girl. Shall I have a baby? How? When? How shall I come by it? How should I know when I had one coming? Should I be ill, or die? Perhaps I can't have one..., perhaps I have got to..., and so on. Behind all such questions lies the *wish* to have one.

In trying to puzzle out the answer, the solution which seems to occur almost regularly to the small child is that there is some connection between babies and faeces. Patients again and again show unmistakably that they unconsciously regard defaecation as an act of birth, and the product as equivalent to a baby. I overheard some children of six or seven amusing themselves by cooking up a concoction of slimy brownish paint which they called "tut tut". This "tut tut" was moulded into a paste and then there was a lot of laughing and whispering. Finally they explained that they intended to make a man out of it. They had the interesting idea, which was never investigated, that only men and not women were made of "tut tut".

Similarly, Mr J. remembered hoping, when he was little, that his faeces would come alive. This patient had considerable envy of women on account of their capacity for sexuality. He considered that sexuality was allowed women but forbidden to men. He also greatly envied women their power of bearing children. His symptoms included violent attacks of diarrhoea, with terrible anxiety about not being in time to reach a lavatory, and fear of soiling himself. He himself interpreted this diarrhoea as at least partly a symbolic miscarriage, and a normal motion, of which he was always proud, as a successful birth; but the explanation of the symptom was certainly not a simple one.

In the course of being repressed, such ideas, no longer accepted quite naturally, are often looked upon as comic. The same children who made the "tut tut", when they were just on the threshold of the period of repression of pregenital interests, made endless jokes about chocolate puddings, going into roars of laughter which strongly suggested an "improper" meaning. Here again there is a combination of mouth and excretory fantasies, this time in the slightly repressed form of a joke.

The curious fancies about reproduction to which I have referred here may seem strange and unfamiliar to our adult ways of thought—and repulsive too—but it must be remembered that our adult attitude towards the excretory functions is a product of careful training, and vigorous repression, reinforced by regression from unacceptable genital sexual fantasies, while the child's early attitude, in so far as it remains free from hostility, is entirely different. It thinks it quite natural and agreeable that birth should take place by the bowel and that bowel products should perhaps even turn into babies, and it sees no reason why eating any of the body's products might not be a good way of starting a baby growing inside it. In that case what could be more natural than that by and by they should be born by way of the bowel? But if for any reason there are strong feelings of guilt about this idea of having a baby, then this will attach itself to the infantile equivalent, the faeces, and this will then become a guilty idea too. If there is a secret guilty unconscious wish to keep the baby, and to hide it, then there may be, for instance, constipation, so that the faeces are not parted with either. If there is unconscious anxiety about this hidden baby, there may be transferred conscious anxiety about the faeces which are not passed, or what is inside the body may be hastily got rid of by diarrhoea or vomiting.

The other equation which is brought about by regression is perhaps even more startling—an equation between faeces and penis. There are certain affinities between the pregenital and genital pleasure zones which seem to favour such equations of the different parts. The stimulation of the oral mucous membrane in suckling is the first sense-pleasure, while the other great sense-pleasure of infancy comes from the stimulation of the anal and urethral mucous membranes. In adult female sexuality pleasure again depends on stimulation of mucous membrane, this time of the vagina. As was illustrated in Miss M.'s case these various kinds of pleasure from stimulation of mucous membranes may become equated, and any of them may become the physical goal of sexual desire of the feminine type. And so whatever stimulated any of these openings by going in may come, consciously or unconsciously, to be equated with the penis, and whatever comes out with the baby.

In neurotic symptoms the transpositions between mouth, anus and vagina on the one hand, and nipple, penis and faeces on the other, are almost infinitely complicated, and any one of them or a symbol representing it is apt to arouse a variety of emotions connecting up with all three. That it is possible to make this sort of transposition between genitals and mouth and anus is shown without disguise in the perversions, and the same thing is happening all the time, though less obviously, both in sublimations and also in what we are here concerned with, neurotic symptoms.

Fantasies of the feminine type of sexuality referring to the penis as well as to childbirth may be found either in consciousness or in the unconscious in men as well as women, and when, in either sex, there has been conflict over taking up the feminine rôle in childhood, the form of these fantasies is apt to be transposed into one or other of the pregenital equivalents.

Mr J., who remembered hoping his faeces would come alive as babies, also had a frightful nightmare in which the whole room was full of faeces turned into snakes, which I think here represented penises rather than babies. Fantasies like Miss M.'s of having something concealed inside the body occur in male patients with homosexual tendencies, and in their case also what is unconsciously fantasied as being inside the body appears sometimes to be a baby and sometimes the penis of the person with whom the patient is sexually preoccupied, but this again may be represented symbolically in terms of faeces. This fantasy may become conscious in insanity. In paranoia, the form of insanity which is more popularly known as "persecution mania", which has for some time been recognised to have close connection with homosexuality, the patient believes people are pursuing him, or wronging him or plotting against him. Male patients suffering from paranoia often actually have the delusion that what is persecuting them in this way is actually inside their own bodies. In the unconscious this persecutor seems to be identified with the father or his penis, and sometimes this persecutor is actually thought of as stuck in the bowels or anus and is identified with the faeces.

In Miss M.'s case, besides the equation which we have already seen between faeces and baby, there seemed also to be this equation of faeces and penis. In her unconscious the holding back of the faeces, when she was constipated, appears to have represented both the possession inside her of a fantasy baby, and also the retention of a fantasy penis. Not only childbirth but also intercourse fantasies were expressed by this patient in double language, both with intense conflict, at the excretory level in terms of retained faeces which she could not get rid of, and alongside of this, at a rather more genital but still highly sadistic level, in the fantasy of the appendix growing into the ovary till they were inseparable and the ovary was destroyed.

The attitude towards this hidden possession is usually ambivalent, containing both joy and also remorse and the fear of injury and punishment. In moods in which the prevailing emotional attitude is love, it is regarded as a welcome present. Miss M. had a dream of three Christmas trees. One of these touched her, but one she had to avoid touching because it belonged to her father and mother. Then the third one touched her and she got a huge present. The hugeness of the present seemed to refer to its being very splendid, but also to dread about the relative size of her own body and the sexual gift she wanted.

In moods in which the prevailing attitude is jealousy and fear the possession is regarded as a horrible disease. When she was stealing jam from a cupboard as a child, the chair broke and Miss M. fell down and a splinter went into her groin and made it bleed. Twenty years later when her breakdown occurred she believed that this splinter which had penetrated her body had started a cancer growing inside her and that this was the cause of all her pain. About the same time she also had what was practically a delusion to the effect that this something which had gone inside her and made her ill was now beginning to push its way out of her in front.

In the case of a certain type of woman patient, there emerges on analysis with surprising regularity a fantasy of having something inside which is *dead*. This was actually in consciousness in Miss M.'s case during the breakdown over her abdominal pains which led first to her unsuccessful operations and later on to her being taken to a Mental Hospital. She really believed when they X-rayed her, and again when they made a vaginal examination under chloroform, that they would discover the remains of a dead child inside her body.

This fantasy appears, once again, to have its origins in the child's early sexualised destructive impulses. If its hostility to the parents was great, it may transfer its fear and hatred of them on to this thing of theirs which is believed to be inside itself, and wish to kill it and from that go on to believe that it has killed it. Here the vagina, or its pregenital equivalents, are being regarded as castrating weapons. This is one origin of the unconscious belief of having something bad or dead inside the body. The faeces inside the body often stand symbolically for this dead thing.

These fantasies which underlie psychogenic symptoms, whether they are expressed in genital terms or regressively in terms of pregenital equivalents, have behind them the dynamic force of adult sexuality. For this reason the patient clings to them and resists the acceptance of reality which cure would involve. In spite of all the disgust and fear and conflict, the patient's whole sexual interest has become centred round these fantasies, and he feels, without of course recognising it clearly in consciousness, that the doctor in trying to clear up his misunderstandings is attempting to rob him of all sexual pleasure.

But these fantasies to which the neurotic clings so tenaciously can never satisfy him. They are only fantasies and cannot give the satisfaction which comes from real living, and besides this they deal for the most part with infantile wishes which are unattainable and would, in any case, be unacceptable to the patients themselves now that they have grown up. But even this is not the greatest trouble. In so far as fantasies are inspired simply by love without conflict, they do no harm. But the instincts which find expression in these fantasies are by no means pure love, but a mixture of sexual pleasure-seeking and *hostility*, and the conflict thus produced is one of the great sources of psychogenic illness. What was originally intensely strong pleasure-seeking seems to have been transformed into intense hostility and manifests itself in an attitude towards the objects originally loved and desired which might best be described as passionate cruelty. This passionate cruelty is a reaction to disappointment not confined to any particular stage of sexual development. At the genital level it manifests itself in impulses of bloodshed and murder which sometimes find open expression in the perversion of sadism. Often, however, the horror inspired by such impulses leads to regression to the earlier mouth or excretory levels of pleasure-seeking. It is as if pregenital activities or organs or products get substituted for genital ones because they are less alarming, less dangerous and less forbidden than the original genital love-hate fantasies of sexualized cruelty which concern mutilation and bloodshed; and since it appears that hostile reactions of especial strength are apt originally to be provoked by thwarting and interference with anal pleasures, it is in anal symbolism that hate and destruction seem most often to find their expression.

In the neuroses the same sexualised destructive genital or pregenital fantasies as appear in the sadistic and masochistic perversions are often present in the unconscious, but they are opposed by strong resistances, and the symptoms they produce take the compromise form of passionate cruelty impulses combined with repudiations and defences against their being actually carried into effect, together with restitution and self-punishment.

Miss M.'s regression to constipation, flatulence and abdominal pain amounting to torture was a flight from her underlying fantasies in terms of blood connected with genital injuries. Sometimes when these terrifying fantasies were pushing against the barrier of her repression they would appear in consciousness in a sort of compromise form represented by ideas of drinking blood, thus regressing to the mouth level while still retaining the idea of blood. Sometimes regression went further, and the idea of blood was replaced by other foods and she would then dream of snatching drinks from married women, greedily stealing cakes and eating them in secret, stealing or being robbed of chocolates and sweets. But along with these fantasies of the fulfilment of hostile wishes there went cruel self-punishment and a sense of compulsion to give back the stolen good things, sometimes represented by vomiting or by being cut open, sometimes by the idea that others were robbing her, or by the necessity which she felt to sacrifice all her money and pleasures to her parents.

It is thus not only the neurotic's attachment to his destructive impulses because of their sexualisation but also his intense condemnation of this passionate cruelty that makes cure difficult, because he fights with the whole strength of his often very powerful character against becoming aware of what it is that he is holding down in his unconscious, and he has a very understandable horror of the process of analysis as soon as it begins to threaten the breakdown of the elaborate defensive structure against his own dreaded impulses which he has spent so much effort in building up.

Both his pleasure and his self-condemnation combine to resist the analysis. Nevertheless, it is only by taking the risk of becoming aware of the alarming impulses which he has so energetically repressed that he can gain control over them.

These impulses are often actually murderous, as appears clearly in the dreams of patients and sometimes in their waking fantasies. A patient dreamt she was cutting up her cat's dinner when suddenly she noticed that what she was cutting was the lower half of a man's body, and she was sawing it in two. Inside the penis which she was slitting was a fluid. Her mother came in and said to her: "Take care of that stuff, I want it". The dreamer thought to herself, "What a hypocrite mother is always pretending to be so unhappy, when all the time she is getting this nice stuff to eat!"

Another patient dreamt that she found in her room masses of dismembered limbs on the floor. The next day, when she was looking at her husband, she was suddenly terrified by the idea that his face had gone blank and his eyes were glazed over. This was pure fantasy, as he was, in fact, quite well, and it arose, as did her dream, from an unconscious murder impulse. On speaking of it she suddenly developed a sharp neuralgic headache, probably a form of self-punishment.

But it is not only hate that these people fear—they fear their love also, regarding it as too violent to be borne by its object. A patient who had been expressing her ill will against me, began to become aware of her loving feelings. She lit a cigarette for me and then became afraid that she would burn me. Her next idea was that she was afraid she was becoming too fond of me and I had better look out lest she did me an injury.

The fantasies which the neurotic is repressing are ferocious because of the early stage of development to which they belong. Furthermore, at that infantile stage at which the unconscious still remains, the distinction between thinking and doing is not so sharply marked as it becomes later in life. Wishing is not distinguished from acting, and this makes the patient unconsciously regard it as highly dangerous to have any feelings at all for fear of awakening the primitive love-hate, assuming, as he does, that his impulses must inevitably be carried out in action.

So far we have considered in some detail the sexual and sexualised destructive meanings of psychogenic disturbances of the bowel functions. Now, leaving the pregenital sensual pleasure and transposed genital significance of the excretory functions, I want to turn to the other reason for the great interest which attaches to these activities in childhood—one which is especially important from the point of view of character development.

Sensual pleasure is not the whole emotional significance of its excretory functions to the young child. There is also a very important psychological side consisting in pride of achievement. The child is as proud of what it has done as a hen who has laid an egg! I believe these strivings after power and self-assertion are the expression of instincts which are *not primarily sexual*, though they are originally associated with an activity which gives sensual pleasure and may also symbolise sexual potency if they become further sexualised by regression.

That excretion had all these unconscious meanings for Miss M.

is shown by the following dream. One night she dreamt she was watching another girl who danced beautifully, which she was unable to do. Dancing had for her a strong sexual significance. On account of her unconscious fears she had been forced to abandon sexual gratification, and that was why in the dream she could not dance. The girl who was dancing reminded her of various rivals whom she had envied intensely. The dream went on that she sat on a bucket and defaecated, and then fetched her headmistress and said to her with great pride, "Look what I have done!" Here there was regression from a sexual potency which she was too much afraid to enjoy, back on to what we might call a sort of infantile excretory potency.

In this dream of Miss M.'s the act of defaecation was substituted for dancing, which unconsciously signified to her more adult genital love relations. It indicated a regression from the genital level at which she felt she could not compete, to an excretory level where she could better distinguish herself. But there is also this other very important idea in her dream; for the dreamer defaecation was an achievement, a proof of her power, which must naturally redound to her credit in the headmistress's eyes.

It would seem that the child is inclined to ascribe a sort of omnipotence to its excretory powers, and that this belief often lingers on in the unconscious, especially of those who have never acquiesced in their early training in cleanliness, but have only submitted through fear. By way of illustrating this grandiose attitude Dr Karl Abraham quotes a little boy of three, who when he was at the seaside used to make water as the waves came in, enjoying himself with the pretence that he had made the whole sea. A woman patient told me that when she was a little girl she used to refer to the part of her where the water came from as the Atlantic Ocean. Traces of this attitude often persist in later life. Many adults who would pass as more or less normal are considerably preoccupied, perhaps only half-consciously, with the question whether they have succeeded in producing a sufficiently large daily motion, and when they have been particularly successful they are conscious of pleasurable sensations, and even a glow of moral satisfaction.

The child appears to over-estimate the products of the body both as regards quantity, as when a little boy persuaded himself that the wave, and perhaps the whole sea, even, was his doing, and also in the sense of supposing them to possess great and even unlimited power to create or destroy every object.

It has been suggested that this infantile megalomania is a normal stage in development which is associated closely with the period when the excretory functions are at the height of their interest. The child attributes to its excretions all sorts of wonderful powers, and imagines itself achieving all sorts of triumphs by means of them. It may be that the megalomania is itself a defence of over-compensation against the child's dawning awareness of its own powerlessness in the face of intractable and thwarting reality, and it may be stronger in those children for whom real disappointment and frustration have been especially intolerable. I believe it is this same infantile megalomania which reappears sometimes, but now in a morbid form, in insanity as delusions of grandeur In any case, whatever the origin of this grandiose phase, it seems to be a regular occurrence in the course of development, and is only to be regarded as pathological if it persists into later life.

It is suggested that a too strict and premature curbing of this necessary infantile megalomania may do serious and lasting damage to the character. In this connection Dr Abraham[1] quotes an interesting case of a woman, a patient of his, whose mother had been driven by the state of her own health and a new pregnancy to enforce very early and strictly her infantile education in cleanliness. He says, "she had earlier than usual demanded obedience regarding the carrying out of the child's needs, and had reinforced the effects of her words by smacking it. These methods had produced a very welcome result for the harassed mother. The child had become a model of cleanliness abnormally early, and showed herself surprisingly submissive. When she grew up, the patient was in a perpetual conflict between a conscious attitude of submissiveness, resignation and

[1] *Selected Papers on Psychoanalysis*, by Karl Abraham, M.D., The Hogarth Press and The Institute of Psychoanalysis.

willingness to sacrifice herself, on the one hand, and an unconscious desire for vengeance on the other".

This description might have been written on purpose to apply to my patient, Miss M. Of his own patient Dr Abraham adds, "The painful feelings of insufficiency with which she was later afflicted very probably went back in the last instance to the premature destruction of her infantile megalomania".

The psychoanalytic view, very briefly, is that at first the baby's love is directed entirely on to itself, and while this is so, it learns only by fear. By and by it transfers some of its love from itself on to other people, and then it begins to be willing to control itself "for the sake of" those it loves. At this stage, the parting with urine and faeces at the time appointed by someone else may be thought of in terms of making presents to this other person. When this person is not in favour the excretory products may be withheld as an expression of disapproval, or else are fired off as an offensive.

In the unconscious, such presents or their equivalents are believed to arouse admiration, astonishment, or terror in the recipient. Patients often equate a flow of words or a flood of tears with such excretory gifts. One patient who was unacquainted with this theoretical view suddenly decided to give me what I wanted, that is, in consciousness, to free-associate instead of preparing and choosing her words. After about half an hour she asked me if I liked it, saying that it seemed to her ridiculous, and I explained that I thought she was giving me a present of her words. She replied, "it's easy for me, I am just showering it out", and when I asked her what picture that brought to mind she reluctantly told me a joke about an aperient working so violently that a cow in the next county was hit. The ambivalence of the gift and especially the ridicule are apparent, but there was goodwill in it too, and it actually was a reconciliation token she was offering me after a prolonged period of rage and obstinacy. When I had given her my interpretation the first words that came to her mind were, "Very well then, you've asked for it now!"

Miss M. had a dream which seemed to illustrate the equation between defaecation and making presents, the attitude being ambivalent. She dreamt she had to make a present to her friend's stepmother, but when she got to the house she found to her embarrassment that she had not brought any present with her. Then, to her further embarrassment, she found that she had emptied her bowels in several places on the carpet. The friend's stepmother was a woman she did not really like, and whom she believed to be jealous of her because she was a favourite with the friend's father. This reproduced closely her early attitude to her mother, who did not get on with her father, and whom she believed to be jealous of her father's affection for herself. In the dream she forgot to bring a grown-up present and relieved herself on the carpet instead. She gave the stepmother a present, but in pregenital terms, and evidently, at least partly, with a damaging intention.

Although bowel products sometimes stand for love gifts it is striking how often they are used to express hostility. Another patient, after crying in analysis and outside for several days, upbraided me, saying, "You oughtn't to allow me to do it all over the place", the next association being "shitting", evidently in rage and with destructive intentions and then being overcome by remorse. The crying combined the hostile output and the expression of grief and remorse, and it was interesting that as soon as that explanation had been given, the patient, after laughing and obviously accepting it, ceased crying and began instead to try to win my admiration by telling me of his exploits.

This sense of power in evacuation links up unconsciously with the power of genital potency, and injury to confidence over the earlier excretory power may do serious damage later to sexual potency. The same patient unconsciously equated evacuation with intercourse, which he sometimes obviously regarded as an act not of love but of hostility and contempt. At times when he was angry, women's bodies were symbolised by lavatories, though when he was happier they would often be represented by churches.

In the free-associations of patients who are unconsciously pre-occupied with rage and revenge one gets over and over again ideas of violent explosions, dark tunnels, drownings, thunderclaps, blasts which blow everyone out of the room, and so on. These probably all refer to bowel and bladder activities, but the relation between flatus (wind) and aggressive impulses is a particularly unfamiliar notion. This may be because it is particularly primitive and very specially repressed; but the universal feeling that it is at the same time very rude and very funny suggests that we are half aware that it has some forbidden significance.

A patient, who, so far as consciousness went, was on good terms with me, came to hear me give a lecture, and was surprised to find herself attacked with such violent flatulence pains that she was hardly able to stand up. This, occurring as it did during the period when we were attempting to analyse her rivalry with and jealousy of other women, seemed to be a physical expression of her fury at my achievement.

Urination also may represent the physical expression of an emotional attitude, either destructive or passionately loving, or both these two at once.

One patient who described gunmen shooting into a crowd also had fantasies of arson—punning on the word when it occurred to him as if it were spelt "arse on". One day a friend to whom he felt some homosexual attraction offered him a cigarette. Rather to his own surprise he refused it, making the excuse that he was afraid he would set the room on fire. This fantasy of setting on fire seemed to spring not from hostility but from love, just as in the case of my patient who feared she would burn me when lighting my cigarette.

Another patient thought of rays pouring out of Paradise, and the beams of light from the cinema lamp, and then the idea came to him that cinema films often catch fire. From that he passed to death rays. His attitude here was ambivalent, but the idea of fire undoubtedly carried the symbolic significance of passionate love.

This preoccupation with setting fire to things, which is not uncommon, seems to be connected at the deepest level with bodily erotic fantasies of powerful urination. Besides the contrast fire-water, I think the burning sensation of the hot urine passing over the urethra helps to make the unconscious connection between these two ideas. At any rate there is so much evidence pointing to the reality of such a connection that its existence in the unconscious is beyond a doubt. Miss M., for example, had on one or two occasions experienced ecstasy in connection with the sight of burning, soon followed by panic.

The striking thing about the emotion, whether of love, hate, or fear, aroused in connection with the infantile excretory acts and products is their overwhelmingness and the sense of being taken up on the tide of feeling which can no longer be regulated or controlled, and indeed seems to come from outside, almost like a possession by spirits. With this comes a great sense of power when there is no need to resist, but a terrible sense of danger when attempts are made to struggle against the tide in vain.

This overwhelmingness seems to be a characteristic of involuntary muscle action, such as comes into play in peristalsis, contraction of the bladder, and orgasm, and it may be that this favours identification between them.

I have referred to the fact that patients seem sometimes to fear, above everything else, a repetition of the sheer overwhelmingness of the physical sensation which they must at some time have experienced. They seem, as it were, to dread annihilation by excess of feeling, so that they dare not let themselves go. It looks as if this overwhelming sensation which they dread (and at the same time long for, and constantly seek to reproduce) is really something like orgasm, though perhaps not the sort of orgasm which adults experience—rather something less localised and more diffuse.

Now, as I have just pointed out, one of the essential features of orgasm, over and above the erotic quality, is the way in which, once it has been started, it takes control of the organism, carrying itself through to a climax independently of volition, inevitably; and this characteristic, as well as the sense-pleasure quality, is closely paralleled, especially in childhood before sphincter control has been well established, in the physical sensations of defaecation and urination, which, once they have begun, carry themselves out in the same inevitable way, sometimes even in defiance of voluntary attempts to check them.

The neurotic's fear, which appears on deep analysis to be the fear of helplessness in the face of physical demands, may express itself alternatively either in the form of fear of loss of sphincter control or fear of sexual orgasm. The patient who has suffered humiliation and punishment or shock over learning to control his bowels or bladder may fight against loss of control when threatened with sexual orgasm; or, alternatively, one who has been overwhelmed by infantile orgasm may transpose these fears to other functions and express them regressively in the form of anxiety about defaecation or urination.

This struggle for self-control often appears to be the fundamental problem in cases of sexual impotence or frigidity. Patients of this type dread the overwhelming force of their own feelings to which they have at some time succumbed. It is no doubt true that, on account of the hostility which, for neurotics, is mixed up with all strong emotion, they fear that if they give way to their instincts they will do terrible damage, and one view is that it is this dread of doing harm and the punishment which their misdeeds will bring back on themselves which makes them afraid to let themselves go. But this does not seem to be the whole explanation.

Apart from their fear of doing damage, these patients appear to dread loss of control *in itself*, and struggle against the helplessness of being overwhelmed by loving as well as by hostile feeling. A patient who, as a result of analysis, was beginning to be threatened with a reawakening of sexual feeling which for years she had successfully repressed, had a nightmare of a runaway horse which threw a girl and killed her. She had frequent nightmares of wild animals, and the earliest childish nightmare which she could remember was of tigers chasing each other madly in circles in the garden. These wild beasts appeared to represent her own violent feelings which she had been unable to master in childhood. She had, it seems, at an early age, been exceptionally intractable. In the end she had achieved self-mastery, but only by wholesale repression, transforming herself into a sad and ineffectual adult, incapable of initiative and independence.

Another patient, in a similar situation of reawakening sexual potency, dreamt of a runaway stallion. This patient spontaneously compared her wish for self-mastery to the centaur whose human head and torso are united to the lower parts of a stallion. At other times she dreamt of being in runaway cars unable to find the brake, and once she had a very terrible nightmare of going completely mad, kicking and screaming and finally being overwhelmed by a huge wave breaking over her. In both these patients defaecation and urination were disturbed by this fundamental fear of letting go.

Mr J.'s life was dominated by fear of loss of control of his bowels. He was never easy in his mind when he was more than a few minutes away from a lavatory, the whole of London consisting for him essentially of a chain of these between which he threaded his way, hurrying anxiously across the longer intervals in great distress in case he should suddenly be overcome with the need for the next one while it was still out of reach. He had on two occasions actually soiled himself, and these were memories of the most acute humiliation.

In Mr J.'s analysis no memory was recovered to determine whether in his childhood any catastrophic events had actually occurred connected with the loss of control of his bowels, but his anxiety about this subject was at any rate enormously reinforced by anxiety over loss of sexual control expressed regressively.

I have quoted these cases to illustrate what I mean about the neurotic's dread of letting go emotionally. Whether this dread of loss of self-control, which so many patients experience, is to be ascribed to fear of their own hostility, or whether, as I am inclined to think, it has in it also the sheer terror of being run away with by their bodily functions (no matter of what kind), it is, at any rate, certain that much of the difficulty of psychogenic illness is the result of the patients' terror of losing control, and analysis shows that the instinct held in check by this terror has a sexual element, even though, owing to regression, the form which the fear takes in consciousness may be, and often is, fear of loss of control of the bowels or bladder. Sometimes the same fear is expressed as fear of running amok or having a fit.

This need at all costs to keep control, which carries with it anxiety whenever strong feelings threaten to be stirred, often goes with a history of early childish passionate outbursts, perhaps accompanied by wetting or soiling of clothes or bed, which is sometimes, especially in childhood, an involuntary physical expression of strong emotion. A patient whose whole character had been organised on stoical lines of defence against the betrayal of feeling recovered memories of intense humiliation experienced in childhood. He had suffered from bed-wetting till the age of ten, and the adults who brought him up had exposed him to public contempt, by encouraging the other children in the family to jeer at him. This patient, who on the surface was almost excessively forbearing and conciliatory, was repressing in his unconsciousness a resentment which had never been outgrown, and in the unconscious he still clung to his early pleasures. Experiences such as this child suffered may set up very powerful defence reactions, so that any threat of being run away with by emotion or by its bodily expressions is automatically checked. The patient has learnt his lesson so well that he cannot let go even though there is no reason for not doing so.

This almost reflex inhibition may produce disturbances of a variety of bodily functions: speech may be checked, producing stammer; the free evacuation of the bowels or bladder may be interfered with: sexual potency may be impaired. Along with any of these symptoms there may also go a much wider impoverishment, the loss of all the achievements into which pregenital potentialities develop. To lose this pregenital potency of the physiological functions, to exchange pleasure and acquiescence in them for dread and struggling against them, is to be in danger of a crippling of future cultural developments.

The premature imposing of self-control in the matter of cleanliness makes especially heavy demands on the child whose sensual capacity is strong. The battle which is fought out over the adult demand that, concerning this matter of passing their excretions, children should do, not as they themselves wish, but as they are told, assumes tremendous importance because these physiological acts are used to express our strongest instincts—those connected both with creative power and sex and, if disturbed, with rebellious hate and self-assertion.

In so far as they express hostile aggressive emotions, fear of consequences may lead to an excessive self-control which so effectively inhibits aggression, that, along with the disappearance of temper in ordinary life, there goes a much more far-reaching loss of all initiative and all power to stand up to opposition or to tackle external difficulties. Furthermore, to this is added a turning inward against the self of aggressive impulses which can find no other outlet. This turning of aggression inwards is the unconscious foundation of melancholia.

On the other hand, in so far as loss of control stands for a yielding to pleasure or to love, it may be resisted because of previous experiences of disappointment and frustration, the repetition of which is felt to be intolerable.

To escape either this disappointment or the repetition of remorse and punishment actually experienced in connection with yielding to sense-pleasure, the child may attempt the superhuman task of renouncing instinct satisfaction. One patient exclaimed bitterly, "I have had to be superhuman all my life". She had in fact all her life always been frustrated by her inner conflicts over achievement which, for her, unconsciously, still meant her earliest achievement of evacuation. She had also repressed sexual feeling and had never married.

I think it will be found to be a general rule that patients who are sexually cold all have an ideal of being superhuman, dating from the difficult renunciation of the early infantile sensual pleasures, the struggle often having been played out over the sacrifices demanded at a very early age by cleanliness. Sometimes this has been reinforced by punishment for early childish masturbation, thus completing the lesson, which the child may learn too well—that it must never give way to strong feeling. Loss of control is henceforth dreaded and fought against with the whole strength of the personality. Even so, however, the renunciation is usually more or less incomplete. The deep check on spontaneous sense-pleasure, which is in fact a profound deprivation, is often made as it were an excuse for superficial self-indulgence, the neurotic seeming to say, "Since I have made such a tremendous sacrifice, I must be allowed special privileges in minor matters"

In any case the renunciation is made only in respect of real life and consciousness. In the unconscious there is no renunciation, but, on the contrary, an obstinate, unmodified clinging to fantasy satisfaction of the original wishes.

This question of the ill effects which may result from making too severe demands for self-control in matters of cleanliness in early childhood is of great importance in the understanding of psychogenic illness. As the subject is unfamiliar to most people I will recapitulate what has been said. On the one hand, there is the danger of wounding the child's sense of creative power and self-esteem, so that it becomes discouraged and so ashamed of losing control that it will never again dare to let itself go. In such cases the pleasure which is normally strong in connection with evacuating in childhood and later the pleasure of genital sexuality, which follow developmentally on these and become unconsciously associated with them, are transformed into pain, pride turns to self-distrust, courage and perseverance to dread and irresolution, love to hate.

On the other hand, there is the danger that all that is achieved may be a superficially submissive attitude which masks a repressed but never overcome rebelliousness. The child has submitted to force, but has never given its consent. Indeed, though training may have been remarkably successful so far as conscious and overt behaviour goes, in the unconscious it has only resulted in fixation to the early infantile demands. And even from the point of view of overt behaviour excessive training may often defeat its own end, actually depriving the child of the power to control its sphincters, and provoking disturbances of the bowel action or of urination. "Accidents" may happen involuntarily, but these on investigation often turn out to be the work of unconscious self-will which is still determined to have its own way and to relieve itself when it chooses.

It has been explained, however, that this insistence on having its own way and defying control is usually found to refer, not simply to the pleasure of evacuation for its own sake, but to the more important instincts of creative power and sex for which these excretory acts stand symbolically, since the child sometimes feels as if, in demanding self-control of it, adults are in fact asking it to give up creative power and sexual pleasure entirely, which means asking it to commit emotional suicide Some children consent even to this, but many, while submitting on the surface, still unconsciously rebel, and this rebellion may take the form of being unable to help doing just the very thing that was forbidden and this may persist even into adult life. As usual, however, it would seem that the symptom expresses more than one impulse, and the analysis of involuntary diarrhoea or enuresis usually reveals the fact that they are also being used unconsciously as a weapon of revenge, self-assertion or self-punishment.

This problem of self-control is thus a delicate one, and obviously needs very careful handling.

I have sometimes found that people who have not a clear understanding of the psychoanalytic point of view are under the impression that what is aimed at is "to get rid of all our inhibitions", by which they mean that psychoanalysis is in favour of encouraging people always to do just whatever they feel like doing regardless of the results. They take it that the psychoanalytic ideal would be complete selfishness and disregard of everyone else, sexual promiscuity, masturbation, perversion and licence for all the behaviour which ordinary morality regards as shocking or obscene. This, of course, is a misconception.

It is true that the psychoanalyst is not concerned with making moral judgments about human impulses and does not set up before the patient any particular ethical standard. What interests him is the dynamics of the mental and emotional situation in which the patient actually finds himself—what he really wants, often unconsciously, to do, and what stops him from doing it or compels him to do it. The analyst's task is performed when all the factors of the patient's problem are brought to the light of consciousness: after that, it is the patient's affair and not the doctor's as to how he chooses to live, but he is at least now, for the first time, in a position to make a conscious personal choice instead of being driven blindly by contradictory unconscious forces over which he has no control because he has lost touch with them. What is unsatisfactory about neurotic repression and inhibition, of which people talk perhaps too glibly, is that it is so hopelessly out of touch with reality. It is a blind negative dating from the nursery, based on delusion and not on fact, arbitrarily inhibiting the patient in his activities, regardless of the real results of what his instincts urge him to do. Similarly the instincts which are his motive forces are the primitive passions of infancy which have not a chance to mature and do not properly correspond with his adult needs. The effect of raising the neurotic's problem to consciousness is that it gives him a chance to substitute for blind insistence or blind repudiation a reality attitude by means of which he may be able to adjust his demands and expectations to real possibilities and to decide how much he will try to get and how much he will postpone or renounce or accept substitutes for.

Furthermore, the lifting of repression on his hatred and resentment has the effect of liberating his capacity to love, which till then was so much entangled in conflict that it could not function. While all emotional outgoing is checked by the accompanying hostility and the fear of consequences, the patient can do nothing with his capacity for love but expend it on himself. All neurotics are more or less "narcissistic", that is self-lovers, and many are auto-erotic. But when the fear of emotion, both loving and hostile, and of its imagined consequences is reduced, patients spontaneously begin to experience love and goodwill, sometimes for the first time in their memory, and then a certain amount of altruism comes naturally.

This, it will be seen, is very different from the attitude of unbridled grasping at any and every immediate satisfaction which psychoanalysis is supposed to foster, but neither is it self-control in the neurotic sense of blind renunciation accompanied by unconscious clinging to the original demands. All these ways of dealing with disappointment are on an immature level. Adult self-control seems to consist in being able to tolerate the delay of satisfaction without falling into rage and despair, and it is noticeable that those who have failed to achieve emotional maturity have never learnt how to do this. Disappointment throws them again and again into a turmoil in which the only alternative seems to be repression, with the loss of the capacity to care, or else fury. They do not know how to wait.

No psychoanalyst, then, would dispute the importance of learning how to deal with the problem of what to do about the clash between one's own interest and pleasures and what other people expect of one, or indeed what reality has to offer. On the contrary, the successful handling of this universal problem is recognised as being perhaps the central thing in maintaining psychological health and arriving at emotional maturity. But it would seem that the attempt to force self-control on a child against its will may defeat its own ends.

Things might work out with less danger if the demands made upon children for self-control were delayed longer than is customary in our civilisation, and if these did not come up until the child was emotionally ready to co-operate over this question of cleanliness, so that making messes was not *the* thing singled out to be regarded as its first serious naughtiness. As things usually are, it is over the question of when to pass its urine and faeces and when not, that the baby extremely early in life first encounters the distinction between right and wrong, and gets its earliest experience of praise and pride or blame and guilt. Learning to be clean is the first alien standard of conduct imposed on the child in the teeth of its personal preferences.

One might even say that it is here that the child has to make its first effort to live up to an ideal, since it is here that it first takes over a standard of civilisation to act inside itself as its own conscience. Henceforth, it no longer feels easy in doing what it pleases, if this is contrary to what others demand of it. The conflict, which was originally external, now goes on within as an internal struggle of natural impulse against what may now be called conscience.

The original uneasiness may have been due either to fear of punishment or else to love and the wish for approval, and the conscience develops differently in the two cases. It is clear that for its future peace of mind it matters a great deal whether fear predominates, or love.

Renunciation may be voluntary—the child may make a

present of it out of love. In that case the standard of the loved teacher is accepted without difficulty. The child's will is in harmony with its own conscience, there is no secret defiance. But if self-control is achieved by fear and punishment, the child may submit on the surface, but underneath it may retire into covert obstinacy. It may, all the same, take over the teacher's standard into its own conscience, so that it feels guilty when it disobeys, but there will be no inner harmony, instincts and conscience will be always at war, and the child usually makes up for its defeat in reality by clinging to exaggerated fantasies of its mighty destructive powers.

This internal disharmony between superimposed conscience and instinct may give rise to such emotional conflict that the situation becomes intolerable and has to be solved, or rather side-tracked, by repression.

When such repression is resorted to, the struggle may appear, for the time being, to have subsided. Often the child may seem on the surface to have learnt self-control completely and even to be unusually docile, but if it has never really given its own secret consent and has only obeyed through fear, the difficulty of learning self-control, that is, of accepting frustration or at least of postponing pleasure, will not have been successfully dealt with, and it may merely have dissociated the forbidden wishes, while still clinging to them unconsciously. This repressed conflict then forms a dissociated nucleus to which regression may occur later on, and by and by it may reassert itself by giving rise to symptoms.

In such cases the conscience is of a peculiar kind. It is harsh and primitive, having all the marks of the violent attitude which belongs to the child itself at the early period when severe frustration over the sensual pleasures of infancy was encountered. When this type of conscience exists the resulting personality is intensely puritanical, rigid and censorious. We are apt to think of such people as being exceptionally firm and impressive and perhaps even typically adult. Nevertheless, they are in fact immature, never having developed beyond their early harsh sphincter morality.

In other cases, where the lesson is not so all too well learnt, the harsh conscience, though submitted to up to a point, through fear, always remains an alien influence, cringed to, but also evaded and defied, never adopted wholeheartedly. Alongside of this archaic superimposed conscience the infantile defiance and infantile pleasure-seeking flourishes somewhere out of sight, in an obstinate subterranean way, too much dissociated and repressed to be modified by everyday experiences.

This is the danger of repression—*there is no growing up*. People who have dealt with frustration in this way are at once too yielding or too self-sacrificing on the surface, and too obstinate and self-seeking beneath it, for satisfactory adaptation to life, and, owing to the excessive renunciations they have been struggling to make, they are profoundly destructive and revengeful, though this too may be quite out of consciousness, and they may actually appear over-sweet.

So far we have tried to explain psychogenic disturbances of the excretory functions as the result of conflict which is often started in childhood over training in cleanliness, and have shown why this conflict is so acute. Urinating and defaecating are highly valued in childhood in their own right, as manifestations of creative power and as sense-pleasures, and are also used to express childish love or hostility. Moreover, as has been explained, the impulse to evacuate the bowels or bladder is sometimes the bodily manifestation of true sexual excitement expressed in terms of its pregenital equivalents.

There is considerable evidence that young children when excited sexually, especially if the situation simultaneously provokes fear, express their excitement by a sudden incontinence which is often the occasion of deep humiliation and distress. If this has happened early, it may tend to be repeated when later sexual situations arise. I know of a case of a girl who on the occasion of her first proposal of marriage from a man to whom she was much attached experienced nothing but an overwhelming necessity to rush to the lavatory.

I should like here just to suggest a brief list of the more obvious physical symptoms not infrequently met with in medical practice concerning which it would be worth while to bear in mind that the unconscious persistence, or regressive sexualisation of infantile preoccupations, may be the whole or part cause of the illness. I have already spoken of symptoms which might have reference to mouth fantasies; in this chapter we have been concerned with the possibility of underlying excretory preoccupations.

One immediately thinks of constipation and diarrhoea; it is pretty well agreed that muco-membranous colitis has a strong psychogenic element; frequency and retention of urine may have; rectal, urethral and bladder pain, urethral spasm or involuntary enuresis or tenesmus, and perhaps even haemorrhoids may have psychogenic causes; and the same appears to be true of the irregularities of peristalsis of flatulence, colic, achlorhydria or hyperchlorhydria. In several cases I have found considerable evidence, though it has not been possible to obtain strict proof, that symptoms corresponding to the clinical picture of duodenal ulcer have been produced by anxiety expressing itself in terms of disturbance of the digestive functions. There seems no reason *a priori* why such disturbances, even when their origin is psychogenic, should not lead on to real ulceration.

The swelling of the body in attacks of flatulence has sometimes been found to be a dramatic representation of pregnancy. In such cases it would seem that interference with the physiological functions is an acting out of a fantasy, and bodily symptoms of psychogenic origin can often be explained along these lines. But I do not think this dramatisation of fantasy is the only psychogenic explanation of such physiological disturbances. Bodily malfunctioning can sometimes be explained as the direct physiological expression of some repressed emotion, and this possibility should never be overlooked in the search for more subtle symbolic explanations of psychogenic symptoms.

Vomiting, for instance, and diarrhoea, while they *may* have reference to pregenital impregnation and birth fantasies, seem also very often to be direct physiological expressions of a conflict of emotions in which fear perhaps predominates.

We are already quite familiar with the bodily manifestations of some emotions, especially the fear which we call nervousness or stage fright which attacks many people who have to face an ordeal, and which often manifests itself in the form of frequency or disturbance of peristalsis or vomiting, as many examination candidates, soldiers, actors and public speakers have reason to know. This excitement may often cause abnormal functioning not only of the alimentary system but also of other physiological systems, the vaso-motor, for instance, causing rapid pulse, sweating, flushing, pallor, hot and cold shivers; or the respiratory system, causing breathlessness.

I should think it is very likely that a great many of what pass for constitutional physiological characteristics, such as a tendency to catarrh, low or high blood pressure, vaso-motor instability, attacks of acidosis, or endocrine disturbances, especially malfunctioning of the thyroid, and probably very many more which we shall classify properly some day, are really to be explained as physiological expressions of chronic repressed emotional states of fear, rage, guilt, desire, etc. Some day the physiologists may be able to work out this side of the symptom picture. Interesting work has been done on this subject in connection with animals by Dr Cannon of Harvard[1], and more work of this same kind is being done. It should throw a great deal of light on certain classes of psychogenic illness. Until the details of the modifications of all the various physiological processes, secretory, nervous, vascular, and so on, typical of the different emotions have been worked out, we are not in a position to say definitely just what bodily disturbances go with what emotional conflicts. We can only say generally and vaguely that some correlation exists: but even this much is well worth keeping in mind and may save the doctor from a vain search for organic explanations of disturbances of bodily function for which the cause is purely emotional.

Until physiology is able to supply us with further detailed knowledge we must be satisfied with this general statement, and therefore in spite of the importance of this aspect of the subject, I have only referred to it briefly and dwelt in more detail on the other explanations of the meaning of psychogenic illness of which I have first-hand experience. The two kinds of explanation are

[1] *Bodily Changes in Pain, Hunger, Fear and Rage*, by Walter B. Cannon, M.D., S.D., LL.D., Appleton, 12*s*. 6*d*. net.

not in the least incompatible and very often I think both are true of the same set of symptoms.

Finally, I should like to point out that, over this highly significant question of evacuation, the attitude of doctors as well as patients may be influenced by their unconscious preoccupations. Medical theories which put down a large part of the ailments from which humanity suffers to intestinal stasis and toxic absorption certainly fit in wonderfully with the guilt and punishment ideas which arise out of unconscious hostile fantasies expressed in excretory terms. Fear that the contents of the body will be poisonous to the self or infectious to others is very common, especially in obsessional neurosis. In severe cases this may lead to such a fear of contamination that the greater part of the patient's life is absorbed in purifying and cleansing rituals. In insanity the delusion of inner corruption may go to all lengths. I do not wish to pretend that we are all insane, or even neurotic, nevertheless investigation of normal people reveals the fact that even those who are carrying on life quite successfully are not altogether free from unconscious preoccupations and delusions resembling those which we discover in psychogenic illness, and, this being so, perhaps the doctor should mistrust too great enthusiasm either on his own part or on that of his patients for constantly giving a "thorough clear out" with enemas and rectal douches, as possibly a rationalisation concealing unconscious fantasies which are not relevant to the medical problem in hand.

In my next chapter I shall take up the last stage of the child's emotional development, and in doing this I hope to show how it comes about that some children find development on to the adult genital level too difficult, and so are driven to fall back on regression to the pregenital preoccupations.

But I should like to put in just one word of warning. This discussion of development in stages will have been misleading if the impression has been given that these stages are distinct, or mutually exclusive. Each has special characteristics, but the child at any moment will show features of all the stages which it has reached, though probably at any given time the features of one or other stage will predominate.

SUMMARY

I have here described the second stage of childish development in which preoccupation centres round the excretory functions, and I have said that these have a primary sensual pleasure value, but that they also become further sexualised in a more adult sense by regression.

Besides this sensual value, they also have importance because they normally represent creative power and achievement in early childhood. The young child appears to pass through a megalomaniac phase in which it ascribes great power to its excretory activities and products, probably because of the powerfulness of the sensation which accompanies those functions, but probably also as an over-compensation against its own real weakness.

I explained that the early experiences of discipline, the learning of self-control, which most often centres round the teaching of cleanliness, is a critical period for the small child. If the training relies too much on fear, and too little on voluntary co-operation on the child's part, various evils may result. If the child attempts to make superhuman efforts at control, it may either fail, and lose even ordinary control, or it may control too well and ever after fear to let itself go. This loss of courage may later on inhibit not only the adult sexuality which normally develops out of earlier sense-pleasure seeking, but also all the displacements and substitutions of object through which pregenital pleasure-seeking becomes transformed into the cultural achievements of human beings.

CHAPTER VI

IN the preceding two chapters I traced the development of the baby's capacity for sensual pleasure and emotional relations, first through the suckling stage of nutrition and mouth activities and next through the excretory stage of anal and urethral activities.

I want now to complete our survey of the child's emotional development by discussing the final stage which immediately precedes full capacity for adult sexuality.

Freud has called this the "phallic" stage because it is at this point in emotional development that interest in the genitals awakens. Analysis of his patients showed him that, whatever the conscious attitude might be, unconsciously they were intensely preoccupied with the genitals, but that it was the sexual organs themselves, rather than the whole person, on which their attention seemed to be concentrated, and that the sort of emotions which these bodily parts aroused appeared to be, not adult love, but a very ambivalent attitude in which curiosity, awe, and the desire to grasp and possess conflicted with dread and aversion amounting at times to horror.

This isolation of the sexual organs appears to be a stage of development which, if it is not strictly normal, is at least of very common occurrence. It would seem to be the result of shock and consequent fixation in connection with the awakening of genital sensations and early discoveries about the genitals of adults and about sexual activities. If these discoveries are made at a time when the child is in a state of love and satisfaction, they arouse pleasure: there is no shock and fixation does not result.

Two little girls who had the opportunity of seeing their father's body about the age of two both showed pleasure in the penis, exclaiming, "Pretty". Another, a year or two older, used to admire her mother's pubic hair, calling it affectionately "your mouse".

Affection and admiration seem to be the spontaneous reaction so long as the child's attitude is loving. But if the discovery of the adult genitals and sexual activities come at a time when the child is angry, disappointed and jealous, it may arouse feelings of intense hostility and alarm, riveting the attention upon them with a sort of horrified fascination. The emotional shock may be traumatic, that is, it may be dealt with by dissociation, by which the experience is repressed, but at the cost of fixation and arrest of sexual development.

That such fixation upon the isolated genital organs themselves may persist in the unconscious is sometimes clearly shown in dreams. Miss M. dreamt that she was in her cot and her mother and sister were in the big bed. A curious little man, resembling an elf, who was hideous, with a long nose and a nightcap like her grandfather's, was jumping about the floor and leering at her. She thought he wanted to get into bed and do something to her, and she wanted to dash across to her mother's bed for safety, but she was afraid he would catch her if she moved. This dream reminded her of many night terrors, when she used to get into bed with her sister or mother for reassurance. The ugly little elf reminded her of her father's penis, which she had sometimes seen when he was sleeping and exposed himself. It also reminded her of the baby who died. She said, "I was afraid he would do *that thing* to me", meaning, in a sense, the sexual act, though not as it really is but rather as it appeared in the terrible fantasies in which it was represented in her unconscious by being soiled with excrement or urine, by bleeding to death, by infection, by being impregnated with something which would grow like a cancer and drain her life.

Mr J. had a dream very similar to Miss M.'s, but in which contempt took the place of fear. He dreamt of a ridiculous little man who leapt about and did antics. In telling me about this man the patient burst into bitter laughter.

I think both these patients were concerned rather with the penis itself than with the whole man, in both cases their father. Their attitude to this penis was fascination and dread rather than love.

Once again it is disappointment and the resulting aggressive impulses that bring such dissociation and fixation about. Just as at the suckling stage of development the attack was directed against the mother's breast, so at this early "phallic" stage it is directed against the genitals of the parents or other important figures in the child's life.

At one very modern school where the children were allowed to say anything they liked, a little girl of four, who had been prevented by her teacher from doing something, turned upon him in a rage, saying: "Very well then, I will cut off your seed pods".

The idea that the genitals are going to be, or have been, injured arises out of such hostile impulses. These supposedly injured genitals are now regarded with so strong a mixture of desire, horror, dread and compassion that the very thought of them may have to be repressed. Their image nevertheless persists in the unconscious, and any real or imaginary discoveries which lend colour to this idea of injury will now be taken as confirmation of its truth. It is out of this state of mind that the idea comes of the vulva as a castration wound and the terror of menstrual blood. All kinds of other experiences, if these, unconsciously, are taken as proving the truth of this fantasy of genital injury, may also arouse the same painful emotions. One patient could not bear the sight of blood (which was connected unconsciously with menstruation), another fainted at being told of a dark sore (which unconsciously represented the vulva) and again when a war mutilation was described to him (standing for castration): another was so filled with horror at the sight of insects, especially Daddy-long-legs, which had injured themselves by flying against the lamp, that he could never stay in the room (their quivering unconsciously stimulated ideas of sexual torture).

The injured genitals are thought of as dangerous weapons, thus giving rise to a fear of sexual contact.

The story of a giant gun which came away from its fastening on board a battleship and another of a huge fish thrashing about the deck killing the fishermen aroused in one patient fantasies of the injured penis, enraged by pain and running amok. To this patient the idea of sexual relations was so terrifying that he became impotent.

In the unconscious the dangerous genitals often appear to be represented in the symbolic form of wild beasts, hairy monsters, spiders, snakes and the like, which borrow a sense of terrific power from the strong emotions which they arouse in the child itself. When fear is great, the child's relation to them may be one of self-preservation from attack, perhaps by biting, and then, projecting its own impulses, it thinks of them as devouring monsters. Nevertheless these, even in early childhood, are the desirable parts of the body. These, therefore, are the parts of the parents' bodies which exert sexual attraction, and if the idea of them is so charged with danger as to become unbearable, this aspect of its parents may become dissociated in the child's mind, and repressed. The idea of the parents thus becomes split into two; on the one hand, the familiar everyday person with whom it is possible to enter into human relations, on the other, the unconscious picture of the huge terrifying inhuman but still exciting genitals on which sexual curiosity, desire and fear are concentrated.

When a person carries about this picture of physical sexuality repressed in his unconscious, relations with people are of a special kind. Friendly human relations may be possible so long as they remain asexual and so "pure", but when sexual feeling threatens to be aroused the object of it is at once transformed into an enemy and human feeling disappears.

The experience or sight of erection seems sometimes to be a determining factor in the great importance which appears to be attached by both sexes to the penis. As a small child Miss M. had seen her father's penis move when he was lying on his bed half-undressed. Her preoccupation with what she had seen interfered with her school work; she became dreamy and "careless". One day when she was in the infants' school she was kept in for an hour looking for the thimble she had lost, in floods of tears, quite incapable of finding it. Her next remark after telling me this was that the teacher sang such a stupid song in the sewing class, it went "thimble, stand up straight". The two associations came one after the other without her being aware of any connection between them, but an analyst would regard the juxtaposition of the two in free-association as evidence that her childish muddle over the thimble was connected somehow, perhaps even then unconsciously, with her preoccupation with erection.

This evidence of apparently spontaneous life which is in fact beyond voluntary control, together with the strong emotion which accompanies it, is felt as almost magical, strange, uncanny and tremendous. Sometimes patients describe experiences of an almost mystical nature which seem to have reference to this same theme of erection, or its pregenital urethral equivalents such as fire and water. Miss M. had moments of rapturous exaltation referring to the transfiguration of Christ, the Burning Bush and a flaming sunset, which could be traced to a phallic source. As regards the sunset in particular, she showed both sides of her ambivalence, once going into a condition of rapture, and once into a panic in which she thought, exactly as in the case of the little man in her dreams, "I must not look or it will *get* me". She had also many dreams of burning fires and red-hot smoking objects. Once it was a burning house she dreamt of and she was holding a baby in her arms which seemed to be her own childish self. She thought, "Baby must *not* see this, he must not know what 'extraordinary' means". Then her father came up as a fireman in a cart which reminded her of the tumbrils which took aristocrats to the guillotine. The representation of the genital organ in terms of burning suggested that this patient thought of it as an organ of urination, and that for her the sexual act was confused with excretion. But also this burning referred to the redness of blood and the heat of passion. It would seem that fire, the urethral equivalent of passion, can be used alternatively to symbolise the genitals of either sex, and in this dream the burning house represented not only the genital organ she had seen but also her own bodily state which the fireman was to assuage with water from his hose. She thought "only *he* can put this fire out".

Her attitude to the penis was very ambivalent. She dreamt of a smoking hot tennis racquet belonging to a man, which she took and then broke. She frequently dreamt of using and then breaking things she had taken from men, and of male symbols such as long pokers, guns, bayonets.

The female genitals also focus the same kind of preoccupations as the male organs and often appear in dreams and fantasies with the same ambivalent awe and dread. But here, as we have seen, the appearance of the vulva may be taken as evidence that it is a wound, which is thought of as having been produced by the loss of the penis. This adds a terror to the female genitals, which is absent in the case of the male organs, in that the appearance of the vulva, especially in adult women who may have suffered laceration in childbirth, is taken as a proof that the woman has actually suffered castration, thus appearing really to confirm the fantasy of genital injury of which we have been speaking.

The child is already familiar with the pain of having to part from precious things—first the nipple must be relinquished, later the faeces, to suit other people. Precious toys are continually being lost or appropriated by others. The logical inference, if you can call it so, at this stage, seems to be that perhaps the penis also may have to be relinquished.

This motif, dread of the loss of something essential to happiness, almost, as it must seem, to life itself, runs right through psychogenic illness. Freud originally named it the "Castration Complex", but actually, fear of loss of what is most cherished at each of the levels of development, mouth, excretory, and phallic, adds its contribution to the symptoms and to the fantasy picture. Threats, fairy tales and real events may each play their part in confirming these fears. The open threat of cutting the penis off as a punishment is much more common than most people suppose. Nurses will sometimes use this threat to little boys if they catch them playing with themselves. A friend who has an estate in Italy and has a good deal to do with the *contadini* children told me that she heard a man using the same threat as a joke to a little boy who was obviously terrified. She protested, but the man only laughed and said it was always done and he saw no reason against doing it. This sort of joking with little boys appears to be quite common in every country. The joke or threat of the adult is the result of what was probably once a very real fear, and to the child it is no joke at all, but a frightfully real possibility. Stories again repeat this alarming threat. It is surprising how insistently the books written for children harp upon this theme. Think of the story of Naughty Little Suck-a-Thumb, and the Great Big Scissor Man. Conrad is punished by loss of his precious sense-pleasure object because he enjoyed it when his mother had forbidden him to. The Three Blind Mice have their tails cut off simply for running after the farmer's wife. The mermaid princess had to have her tongue cut out in order to live with the prince. All these stories are about the theme of castration.

Until he actually discovers what the female body looks like the boy has no clear realisation that the genitals of girls and women differ from his own, though there seems to be evidence that, even at a very early age, children of both sexes have a vague instinctive impulse towards some still unknown bodily part which shall be complementary to their own sexual organs. The mouth sucks without being taught: and it would seem that the genitals also have instinctive knowledge of what is needed for their satisfaction. (I do not, of course, mean conscious knowledge of propositions about the subject.) Dr Zuckerman[1], who has studied the sexual life of baboons, writes that young baboons which have been reared apart from adults nevertheless display in their games with each other, long before puberty, a knowledge of the movements of coitus which they certainly have had no opportunity of learning, and when puberty comes they know without any teaching how to perform the act. It seems probable that the innate instinctive knowledge of young human beings in these matters is not inferior to that of the young baboons. Normally, then, the discovery of the real female genitals would simply reveal what was already, unconsciously, being sought, but we have seen how, to a boy who is already haunted by castration fears, the actual discovery that in women the penis is missing may be a severe shock, because he may take it as proof that the penis has been lost.

From the evidence of Mr J.'s symptoms and of his dreams, fantasies and associations, it appeared that one very important reason for this patient's illness *was* the unconscious fear of castration, thought of in terms of loss of or injury to his penis.

[1] *The Social Life of Monkeys and Apes*, by Dr Zuckerman. Kegan Paul, 1932.

He was tremendously disturbed, as a very small child, over the first sight of a girl in her bath. What disturbed him was that she had no penis. He satisfied himself that she must have hidden a penis between her legs. He often did this himself, for protection partly. He was sleeping in bed with this girl, and his anxiety was so great that he managed to lift the covers and look again, and actually seems to have hallucinated a large penis which comforted him for the time being. He also had a curious fantasy when he was little about a boy with a very long penis which he showed off, and about a woman who had a penis, and was as strong as a man.

At one point in his treatment he became extremely anxious and felt that analysis was taking away from him everything that was worth while. He suddenly broke off the treatment with the idea that if only he got away from that he would find he was well. He did not find this, and after some months he resumed treatment. He told me that at the time he broke off he was haunted by the most horrible faces, the dreadful thing being that they had no noses. He thought the faces had to do with me. He thought of leprosy as a disease in which the extremities dropped off, and of diseased people who infect others with their own complaint. He thought how awful it would be to see his own face in the glass without a nose. Then he thought of his whole body in the glass and the extent to which the penis might or might not be visible. There was a good deal more evidence all pointing in the direction of castration fear, but this is a sample. I told him I thought he might be talking about the discovery that there are human beings who have not got penises; that the frightful faces without noses were nightmare presentations of this, to him, supremely alarming fact, and the hasty breaking off of treatment was from the fear that I should want to rob him or infect him with my complaint (i.e. being without a penis). He had had the fear that some day there was to be some frightful revelation in analysis, and also that he might be going to ask the analyst some terrible question such as "What is it like to be a woman?" I suggested that perhaps really the terrible question might be, "What is it like not to have a penis?" and that the frightful revelation might also have to do with this.

Although I had told him, on earlier evidence, that I thought his anxiety might be concerned with some sort of castration fear, he had not at all connected this new set of associations with that idea. Now he laughed and said he had been thinking it would be wonderful to walk down Piccadilly with his coat unbuttoned and his hands in his pockets, and it struck him that he was meaning walking freely without the least fear that anyone would rob him of his penis, for since boyhood he had always felt it necessary to keep his coat buttoned as a protection.

All this emphasis on the presence of the penis and the urgent need to deny its absence in females seems to point to unwillingness to believe that some people have not got penises. This arises partly, no doubt, from the boy's anxiety lest he, too, might in that case lose his, as they had presumably lost theirs.

But there is a still deeper meaning in this insistent denial by the boy of the genital difference of the sexes, and that is the fear of the female genitals arising out of the belief, already referred to, that intercourse is a hostile act and that the genitals injure each other. The existence of the vagina must be denied because it is regarded as at once too vulnerable and also too dangerous to contemplate: it *must* not exist.

The root of the fear seems to be the boy's own fantasy of sexual cruelty, according to which his penis is felt to be a murderous weapon and the vagina a wound.

One patient spoke of fantasies of firing a pistol into the woman's body, another of penetration with hot needles. The sadistic perversions are the acting out of these sexual fantasies of cruelty. Fear of the vagina as a dangerous castrating organ is the reverse of this picture in which the woman is thought of as retaliating on the penis and revenging herself by destroying it.

But there is yet another side to this preoccupation about people not having penises which comes up so often in the analysis of male patients. Besides the fear, there is also something very like a *wish* to lose the penis. When Mr J. hid his between his legs, it was partly for protection, but also, I believe, partly to pretend he had not got one. He remembered trying to imagine that he was developing breasts like a woman, and when he came for treatment, already grown up and married, he still believed that it was only women who could be sexual without having to be ashamed of it, and all his exciting daydreams were about being a confident, successful girl, who led a loose sexual life. When he first came to consult me I asked him what he thought psychoanalysis would do for him, and the first reply that came into his head was, "It will turn me into a self-confident girl".

I think this idea of becoming a girl really brings us back again to his original fear. It seemed to be the penis which made sexuality forbidden. That was why it was better to be a woman, because sexuality was safe for her, but dangerous for a man since it meant castration. I have direct evidence of this because he told me that he used to think perhaps the penis had to be left inside the woman in order that it might grow into a baby. His actual words were, "Every baby meant the sacrifice of a penis". After intercourse his anxiety about whether his penis had been injured was quite conscious.

Another adult male patient, who must in childhood have been horrified at the discovery of the female genitals, was much preoccupied with women's clothes and the wish to see women undress. He also had the impulse to show women his own penis. When his castration anxiety had been lessened by analysis, he asked about the female genitals, remarking that he had never felt interested in them but only in the breasts. When I said I believed this was on account of the likeness between breasts and penises and the absence of any real penis from the woman's genitals, he exclaimed, "Don't tell me they haven't any! Surely they have a penis hidden inside".

The deeper analysis of the patient's need to believe this revealed the same dread, as appeared also with Mr J., that if women had not got penises of their own, they would want to steal them from men. This made the idea of intercourse so alarming that he could not bring himself to risk penetration for fear that the woman would never let his penis go again. He described a bad dream in which he was stuck in a muddy hole: frequently he expressed fear of being trapped and shut in. Along with this fear of suffering genital injury himself, there went also the corresponding fear of the injury which he would have to inflict, since, almost consciously, he regarded the vagina as a wound too painful to be touched. Thus self-preservation and compassion for the woman he loved played into each other's hands to forbid potency.

Soon after he had begun to grasp this interpretation he came saying he had made an important discovery, namely, that women really have genitals of their own and not simply a lack of male genitals. He felt it would now be more possible to be fond of them. This "discovery" had been made possible by some lessening of the patient's own sadistic attitude which thus reduced his fear of the female genitals so that he was able to recognise their existence.

Identifying the penis with sexual potency, male patients have expressed their pity for women on account of their lack of this organ, imagining that they must feel as if without it they had no personality at all. This pity, like the idea of the castration wound, was really a mask for fear. Potency and genitals were denied to women because they were felt to be too dangerous for their existence to be admitted. In these examples what I have tried to bring out is this *intense preoccupation*, characteristic of the phallic stage of development, with this one bodily organ, the penis, leading to over-valuation of it, and an attempt to deny the existence of the female genitals.

It was taken for granted by Freud and the earlier psychoanalytic investigators that this extreme valuation of the male genitals, with the accompanying denial of all sexual importance to those of the female, was a perfectly natural manifestation which needed no explanation[1]. Further study, however, began to throw doubt on this assumption, and many psychoanalytic investigators now follow Dr Karen Horney[2] in the view that, while the boy's pride in his own sexual organs is natural and normal, the denial of value to the sexual organs of the other sex is not natural and calls for explanation. This attitude, though no doubt it is often met with in the phallic phase of the boy's development, is held to be, not a normal phase of development,

[1] Freud himself is still inclined to maintain his original views on this question.

[2] "The Dread of Women", *International Journal of Psychoanalysis*, vol. XIII, part 3.

but essentially pathological, being the result of castration fear and directed towards the woman's genitals regarded both as a wound, the proof of castration, and also as itself an instrument of castration. The denial of value to the vagina, which may be carried to the point of a denial of its very existence, is regarded as an attempt to overcome the intense fear which this organ inspires in the boy who, as a result of his own destructive sexual wishes, believes that the woman will revenge herself by using it to castrate him.

The girl, at the phallic stage, often displays this same attitude of denial of femininity and over-estimation of masculine attributes. It was originally held that, just as it was natural for the boy to over-estimate his genital organs at the expense of those of the female, so also it was natural that the girl should share in this phallic cult and should regard her own different genital structure as a proof of her castration. This was Freud's view, and considerable evidence presented itself in apparent support of it. There can be no doubt whatever that dislike of feminine sexuality and penis-envy play a very important part in the neuroses of women. Analysis of women patients nearly always reveals a greater or less degree of resentment at the possession of the female genitals and a wish to possess the penis instead, or even quite frequently a fantasy of really possessing a penis. These ideas, which are for the most part repressed in later life, are often conscious in childhood. A friend was told by a little girl of five or six that she was expecting one to "creep out of" her. Women patients quite often dream of having penises. A friend's patient dreamt of looking at herself naked in the glass and seeing that she had one. Miss M. dreamt of a little girl whose father gave her a present of a huge thing shaped like a Zeppelin to wear in front of her, because he was so fond of her. Later she dreamt that she cut off a penis from her own body and threw it on the rubbish heap. Another patient dreamt that she had cut out a large model of the male genitals and was tying it round the waist of some unknown person.

All this points to a demand on the part of the girl for a penis of her own, and it is often accompanied by a vigorous repudiation of the vagina, menstruation and childbirth.

Boys and girls at the phallic stage thus seem to agree in emphasising the importance of the penis and attempting to deny the female genitals. The question arises as to whether this attitude is natural or pathological. In discussing the boy's phallic attitude I have suggested that it is to be regarded as pathological, and have traced it back to fear of the supposedly dangerous female genitals, a fear which is based ultimately on the boy's own impulses of genital attack.

If, in considering the girl's penis-envy and repudiation of her femininity, we are to regard these as pathological also, we may look for the explanation along similar lines.

The problem of adaptation to sex seems to be complicated in the case of girls, and this wish to possess a penis is undoubtedly complex in its origins.

One reason for it is that women do really possess in the clitoris a small homologue of the penis. Before puberty this quasi-male organ focuses a considerable amount of erotic sense-pleasure, and to this extent the girl's sexuality is at this stage partly masculine. Girls often discover the clitoris and use it in masturbation much as boys do the penis.

But the girl seems commonly to feel that the penis has definite advantages over the clitoris: the boy's genital is larger: he can direct the stream of urine with it and is permitted, while urinating, to show and handle it. For both sexes in childhood urination seems to be used both as an expression of passion and as a weapon of attack, and the girl feels that without a penis she is at a disadvantage from both these points of view: she can neither love, attack nor revenge herself in urinary terms as boys can. This early urinary rivalry is often an important factor in the penis-envy displayed by girls and women which causes them to wish to have penises of their own, but it does not explain the repudiation of the female genitals which is the other side of this "castration complex" in women.

This repudiation appears to be based on the girl's feelings of danger in connection with her femininity in so far as sexuality is fantasied in terms of soiling and mutilation. When these fantasies are strongly masochistic, the admission of the reality of the female organs is felt to lay her open to humiliation and danger. The admission of the vagina is here felt as an admission of vulnerability, or as a proof of having already been injured: the penis is needed as a *weapon of defence*. But this sense of danger and need for defence are, as we have seen, a consequence of the disappointment of very early *feminine vaginal* desires, which, by arousing hostility, transforms into something dangerous and guilty what was to begin with an infantile daydream of pleasure in the vaginal possession of the father's penis, the expression of that early impulse towards the still unknown organ of the opposite sex which would fulfil the needs of her own body. It would thus not be primary, but rather a reaction formation.

If this account is correct, then, it follows that the repudiation of the female sexual organs is pathological in both sexes. In the boy we have attributed it to castration fears of injuring and being injured by the vagina, these fears being themselves a consequence of the boy's own aggressive destructive fantasies; in the girl it would seem to be the result of mutilation fear connected with her own feminine impulses when these are masochistic, so that yielding to them is regarded as involving her genital destruction, this fear, in its turn, being the result of her own impulse to injure the penis, out of revenge for the disappointment of her early feminine genital desires, which transformed the idea of sexual contact into a fantasy of mutual cruelty. This fantasy of the injured genitals would thus explain this occurrence of a pathological "phallic" stage in both sexes. But, whereas the typical male reaction appears to be the over-valuation of the penis and the denial of the vagina, the typical female reaction seems to be repudiation of the vagina and demand for a penis of her own.

I have called these the typical male and female reactions, but actually they only reveal a part of the truth. The analysis of male patients constantly reveals, coexisting with denial of the vagina, a seeking for it also, together with a repressed tendency to wish to *be* instead of to possess the female parallel to the female wish to *be* instead of to possess the male.

And in the female, conversely, though the demand to reverse the sex is usually more outspoken, there seems always also to be repressed over-valuation of the female functions, corresponding to the male phallic attitude, with an attempt to deny the penis, accompanied nevertheless also by a seeking for it.

In considering the feminine fantasy of possessing a penis it is thus important to distinguish two quite distinct meanings: primarily there is the original normal feminine vaginal wish to possess the penis of the loved male, but this may be heavily repressed: secondarily, when, owing to disappointment, this feminine wish has become cruel and therefore guilty, humiliating and dangerous, there is the pathological repudiation of femininity and the demand, not to possess the male or his penis, in love, but either to use sexual acts to castrate him, or else, abandoning the vagina altogether as too dangerous, to *be* him, and to have a penis of her own instead.

Some of the Freudian terminology is by now fairly widely known, and those who are familiar with the idea of the famous "Oedipus Complex" have perhaps been waiting for me to discuss it. Actually we have already for some time been considering the extreme manifestation of this "incest" conflict, in the cases where the boy's sense of guilt about sexual ideas caused him to fear that sexuality would lead to the loss of his penis, and the girl, to compensate for the disappointment of her infantile hopes, unconsciously believed that she had stolen her father's penis, or her mother's baby, and had it inside herself as a secret treasure, and at the same time as a terrible and guilty burden. These are usually described as "incest" fantasies, but I do not think that it is actually the fact of incest that makes children's early sexual ideas alarming.

This so-called "Oedipus" situation, which concerns the conflicts over the early sexual love and hate for the parents, appears to matter so much for later life, not because the emotions happen to be directed to the parents, but because this is the period of first love and, as such, *sets the pattern for all later love experiences.*

In cases where it happens that the child's first love is directed to people other than the real parents the same struggle over love, hate, fear, jealousy and revenge occurs equally. No matter who may be the object of the first love, the problem of disappointment remains, and here at this phallic stage of childish love, just as we saw earlier in the case of the pregenital frustrations, what causes all the trouble is the anxiety aroused by the intolerable tension. This is reacted to by fear and the aggressive impulse to master the denied object, and these two reactions give rise to the hostile emotions of revenge, and destructive rage, setting up a passionate cruelty in place of the original condition of pure desire. From this there follows fear of the genitals of the other sex towards which this attack is directed and fear of the castrating or mutilating effects of sexuality on the child's own sexual organs which may cause it either to over-value them and despise the dreaded genitals of the opposite sex, as seems to occur very often in the case of the neurotic boy, or to repudiate and deny them and wish to possess the organs of the other sex instead, as happens most typically in the case of the neurotic girl.

This transformation of the idea of the genitals from something desirable into something bad and dangerous may make the idea of sexual contact abhorrent: the boy dares not risk his penis into the dangerous trap and dreads the pain and damage which it will inflict if it is put there: the girl dares not allow her body to be rent or burst by admitting the penis and dreads the castration she will inflict on it if she lets it enter her. That is one of the two great fears behind the flight from sexuality which characterises psychogenic illness.

The other fear has to do, not with the supposed dangers of sexual contact itself, but with the revenge from rivals which the child anticipates if it should succeed in supplanting them. The child's love attitude is possessive and does not tolerate the idea of sharing. It wants to get rid of everyone who gets in its way and it expects the same attitude from others. The principal obstacles which stand in the way of the child who wants exclusive possession of its mother are the father and the other children.

At the phallic level these both seem often to be represented by the penis or some pregenital equivalent symbols of them, and it seems that there may persist in the unconscious a fantasy that some such thing as this has to be met and overcome before any woman who is unconsciously identified as the mother can be attained. This may be the unconscious basis of the knight and dragon myths. The unconscious fear seems to be that the rival, the dragon, will bite, cut, tear the penis off, in terms similar to the revenge fantasies which the boy has himself entertained.

Sometimes the dangerous rival appears less fantastically as a huge man. Mr J., at a period of intense discouragement in his analysis, dreamt that someone was insulting his wife, and that he challenged him to fight. The man rose up, getting larger and larger till he was perfectly enormous, and it was obvious that the challenge to fight was a sheer absurdity.

At this point in his treatment, Mr J. said he wanted nothing but to be left alone. He sacrificed all desire because the conflict appeared too hopelessly unequal. He also decided at this time to give up sexuality, to "cut it all out", as he expressed it. That is to say, he wanted in a sense to sacrifice his penis (castrate himself)—and I think this was due to incest anxiety, the early, but now hidden and unconscious dread of his too powerful father, which came out so clearly in his dream.

Fear of this terrible rival may drive the boy to abandon his male sexuality, becoming impotent or changing his sex and adopting towards the rival a submissive homosexual instead of an aggressive male attitude.

In the case of the girl dread of the rival mother may produce similar disturbance of her sexual life. The little girl's struggle with her rival mother is over the desire to take from her the father's penis or the baby, and so it happens that a neurotic breakdown is often precipitated either by marriage or by pregnancy.

In the course of treatment of women patients the analyst often comes upon unmistakeable evidence of this repressed fear of the mother which may manifest itself in consciousness under various disguises. Sometimes it appears in the form of fear of sterility, or, alternatively, of having maimed, diseased idiotic or monstrous children, or again of the child dying in the womb. The analysis of such fears reveals the underlying fantasy of retribution for the early wish to prevent the mother from having other children, the patient unconsciously fearing that this hostile wish will now be turned against herself or her children.

Sometimes this unconscious fear of retribution takes the form of panic on becoming pregnant. In some cases patients may be driven to almost any lengths to get rid of the child though fear of what will happen if the pregnancy is not stopped. Those fears appear on analysis to be directed both towards the rival mother whose children the patient once wanted to destroy and also towards the baby lest it also should now retaliate by destroying the patient herself.

There seems no doubt that quite early in their lives children really *do* feel this rivalry with the parents of the same sex. They often express openly the hope that one parent may die so that they may be able to keep the other to themselves, and very many adults still remember such feelings.

Miss M. clearly remembered one occasion when she pressed herself to her father with mixed feelings of hope and dread that he would do to her what he wanted to do to her mother. When nothing happened she turned her back on him, half relieved, half furious. She was at that time conscious of a guilty feeling that she was driving her mother out into the cold, and she seems to have compensated for her disappointment by the fantasy of success and out of this arose the belief that it was she who was responsible for the estrangement between her parents, just as she felt her death wishes had killed her baby sister.

As a result of her guilt over the supposed success of this early wish to supplant her mother she feared her intensely, fantasying her revenge in terms of her own primitive childish hostile wishes, and this fear was one of the two roots of her illness, stronger, perhaps, even than her fear of the sexual act itself.

From all that we have been saying about the phallic stage of development the striking thing which emerges is, on the one hand, the extent to which children, even at a very early age, would seem to be preoccupied with genital interests and fantasies of genital contacts, and, on the other, the primitive and fantastic nature of their impulses and beliefs in connection with these. It may be wondered how they come by so much information, both true and false, on this subject, particularly as regards the sexual act itself. Children seem to get their ideas of sexuality in various ways, from watching animals, from things overheard or purposely told them, from their own fertile imaginations and from immature instinctive impulses, but it is surprising how many seem to get them directly from watching the parents themselves.

In quite a number of patients one comes upon memories or easily interpreted references to the early witnessing of parental intercourse, with strong emotional reactions. One patient spoke of it as the "night battle"; another had an alarming vision of limbs writhing under a blanket. In the cases when it is possible to find out the child's reaction, this usually seems to have been one of intense curiosity and excitement, but often also of anger and fear, the father's behaviour being interpreted as a dangerous assault, generally regarded as anal, an idea which may be strengthened by the behaviour of animals, and by the child's lively interest in that part of its own body. Miss M., when she slept in a cot in her parents' room, remembered trying to keep awake to see what they did at night. She was not able to remember exactly what she *did* see, but she had a dream about going at night to see what the fairies did (this was associated with the coming of babies), and then they were in a rage and would not let her see, and all turned into wild animals (a constant symbol for her father when sexually excited, and also for her own passionate feelings in so far as she identified herself with him). The dream ended with her pretending nothing had happened, and asking some girls for something to eat—that is, I think, regressing back to the mouth.

In all cases in which the dreams or fantasies of patients point to some early witnessing of parental intercourse, what was seen seems to have been misunderstood and thought of as a dangerous struggle. The child no doubt interprets what it sees in terms of its own preoccupations, but in so far as these are pleasurable this would not cause any revulsion. It is possible that the child's horror at what it sees may have some real foundation in cases where the relations of the parents themselves are cruel or unhappy. But I believe that the deepest reason for the surprising misconstruction which it puts on sexuality is jealousy and despair. The child who wants to take part can only look on.

A patient who was a painter spoke of two very interesting compositions which she felt impelled to paint, of whose significance she was quite unaware until they were interpreted to her. One was of Christ nailed to the Cross with two people sitting at the foot on a sofa committing adultery. In speaking of this composition she remarked, "I *hate* to see people lose control—it's their eyes", and was then reminded of her lifelong fear of her father's eyes. When she was trying to work out her other composition she said she could not think of anything except the "Temptation" in which Adam and Eve and the serpent were to be painted as seen through a network of branches and leaves. In the distance was the angel with the flaming sword and in the foreground a pool at which a hind that had just been drinking was looking up, watching through the branches the scene beyond.

There was considerable evidence that this patient had as a child witnessed intercourse between her parents, perhaps, as in Miss M.'s case, actually through the bars of a cot. In some cases, at any rate, the witnessing of such scenes appears to arouse fear and jealousy in the child, and it then turns with fury and contempt on what it sees. The logic of disappointment and revenge seems to go, "Since I am shut out, then it is not something nice at all, it is something filthy and dangerous, and I hope they will soil and injure each other". At the same time what is happening arouses curiosity and a sort of instinctive sympathetic excitement which sexualises these other emotions, producing the impulses of passionate cruelty of which I have already spoken. Sexual relations are then pictured unconsciously as consisting in acts of sexualised cruelty or degradation, and this is a very important motive for rejecting sexuality with disgust, rage or ridicule and even trying to give it up altogether.

Now and then the unconscious produces biting satires upon this subject of parental intercourse. One patient dreamt of a long scene between a man in theatrical plush kingly robes with a gold crown on curling locks but hideous thick lips, who attempted to make love in bed to a stout woman rather resembling a caricature of an opera singer, while my patient watched, tolerated, but utterly disregarded. She said, "I do not think I now know *how* humiliated I felt". She said she had some faint sympathy with the man though she couldn't blame the woman who spoilt it all by complaining that she had lost something, perhaps a bracelet, and started waddling about the room to look for it, showing pink and fat through a cotton nightgown. "She was so silly", my patient said with scorn, and then, "but she was so utterly feminine—I envy those women". On another occasion she dreamt of a huge man riding on an absurd and pathetic little donkey. This dream also was a cartoon of her parents' sexual relations.

Another patient, more bitter, and regressing to anal terms, spent a whole hour laughing over schemes for soiling a church and converting it into a lavatory, getting some such relief by joking as my woman patient found in parody. In both these patients scorn was a cover for jealousy.

Jealousy and fear between them appear always to underlie the neurotic repudiation of sexuality. From them arise the two great fantasy dangers which have to be faced before the adult genital attitude can be reached, fears concerning contact between the genitals in so far as these are regarded as instruments of castration and mutilation, and fears of genital attack from the parent of the same sex in so far as he or she is regarded as the avenging rival. These fears are what constitute the so-called "incest barrier". They are formidable enough, and if it were not for the fact that they rest on fantasy and not on reality, the neurotic's terror of sexuality would be amply justified.

One may say ultimately that analysis consists in bringing into or near consciousness these amazing unconscious beliefs, so that the deductions which have been unconsciously resting upon them may be recognised to be invalid. The neurotic is as logical as a madman, but his premises, luckily, are equally false. In fact, there is a remarkable similarity between the underlying assumptions of both.

There has been a good deal of misunderstanding about what psychoanalysts mean by these notorious "incest wishes" and the famous "Oedipus Complex". From what has been said it will be seen that what they mean is something quite different from the popular view that, according to Freud, the boy falls in love with his mother, or the girl with her father and, owing to some innate horror of incest, detest themselves for this crime. Love, it is suggested, does not do the child any harm, and it is not because the first attempts at love are usually "incestuous" that they sometimes result in the neurotic repudiation of sexuality. The reason why this first "incestuous" love is a critical time in the child's emotional development is because, in so far as it seeks satisfaction in a physical sexual sense, it is doomed to disappointment, and this mixes rage with the original love, giving rise to conflict and tension which may lead to repression, with the result that emotional development becomes arrested.

This early "incestuous" love, though it has something in common with the love of normal adult life, differs from it, as we have seen, in its forms of expression according to the level of development at which the repression occurred. But there is also an essential difference between the two in the kind of love offered and demanded. Immature love is insatiable and ambivalent. It cannot bear any delay or sharing, but demands absolute possession and mastery over the love-object. And it makes this demand because it cannot tolerate the tension to which lack of satisfaction gives rise and which threatens to transform love into hate and aggression. It is only when some measure of tolerance of the tension produced by failure to obtain immediate satisfaction has been acquired that the constancy of an adult love relation can be achieved. Those who are psychogenically ill have never acquired this tolerance, and the ambivalence into which frustration throws them is their great difficulty. At the earlier immature stages of emotional development love is not a true object-relation to the other person, which leaves that person free, but rather an attempt to deny him any separate existence. At a deep level this attempt seems actually to be fantasied in terms of devouring or incorporating the loved object, thus keeping control of the person or part of the person needed for satisfaction, and escaping the pain of separation.

In psychoanalytic terminology the child, in so doing, is described as having "introjected" its parents. Henceforth it regards itself as it regards them. So long as these introjected parents are loved this is satisfactory. But when the child's own attitude is very full of hate, identification with either parent, whether of the same or the opposite sex, at once becomes fraught with dangers and difficulties. Just as the ideal way to begin life would be for the child to identify with a parent who is loved and accepted, so the dangerous way is to take inside itself a parent who is more hated than loved and who is defied.

This means perpetual internal conflict, hating itself in so far as it has identified with the hated introjected parent, and defying and fearing itself—or, if you like, the introjected parent in itself: and again retaliating on itself. This situation is made still worse when the introjected parent hates and is hated by the other parent.

This introjection of the hated parents appears to explain some kinds of madness—I am thinking of melancholia, in which the unhappy patient hates himself and pursues himself with the most relentless enmity and continually inflicts upon himself humiliations and punishments: it is often the deep motive of suicide. This introjection of the parent lays the foundation of the child's conscience or moral standards or ideals, which I shall discuss more fully later, and the attitude to the introjected parent-figures is of the greatest importance in all subsequent emotional character development.

For the present it is enough to lay it down broadly, that *in so far as the parent is loved, identification as a step in the process of growing up will tend towards health*, and *in so far as the parent is hated, it will tend towards psychogenic illness.*

For simplicity and clarity, these early identifications of childhood are sometimes spoken of as if the boy identified with his father and the girl with her mother, and speaking generally this is true. But actually there often appears to be a tendency to identify with both parents. When its early sexual impulses towards the parent of the opposite sex meet with their inevitable disappointment, the child, in trying to make up to itself for this external failure, goes through a period in which it lives out in fantasy the supposed relation between the parents. In this it plays both parts, and if the fantasy is one of mutilation and danger it blames itself for the harm inflicted and at the same time regards itself as having suffered this harm. One might say that being the parents in fantasy constitutes the child's early sexual life, on the imaginative side, while physically its pleasures are obtained from the various bodily parts which are appropriate to its stage of development. Thus at different times the parents' sexuality will be fantasied in different ways, either as sucking, licking, biting, eating, drinking, urinating, defaecating and so on, and in *being* the parents in fantasy the child feels as if it had done these sexual things itself and had them done to it. These activities are fantasied as good or bad, life-giving or destructive, lovely or filthy, according to the state of the child's own feelings towards the parents. When the parents are "good", what they are thought of as doing is good. When they are "bad", then it also is bad.

The neurotic's repudiation of sexuality is based ultimately on identification of sexual pleasure with "bad", that is, hated parents. The parents' sexuality becomes "bad" when the child is disappointed and jealous. The child represses this idea of the "bad" parents and this makes a split in its picture of them; in consciousness the "good" parent is retained as an object of asexual affection and the sexual hated "bad" parent is banished into the unconscious. When the parents' sexuality is "bad" the child's own sense-pleasures become "bad": it repudiates them and this makes a split in its own sexual life. Being identified with its parents it condemns its own sexuality in condemning theirs.

Identification seems to be the usual mechanism for getting over the emotional crisis which the child has to face in connection with the disappointment of its first "incestuous" love, and the identifications it makes at this time leave their mark on it for life and colour all its later love relations.

If the child succeeds in identifying mainly with the parent of the same sex and loves the parent of the opposite sex, it grows up into a normal heterosexual adult. If it identifies mainly with the parent of the opposite sex and loves the parent of its own sex, it grows up homosexual. But, as we have seen, the entanglement of love and hate which transforms love acts into acts of sexualised cruelty may prevent the child from reaching any sort of sexual maturity, arresting it at earlier levels, and causing it to regress back to them. The situation may be described by saying that in such cases the child has introjected parents whom it fantasies as cruel, dangerous or contemptible and in so doing has come to hate its own sexuality.

It is this attitude of hostility to sexuality, either conscious or unconscious, and the attempt to give it up which distinguish the neurotic from the normal person.

It is a strange thing that human beings have this terrific power of denial which they can direct even against the source of all their pleasure in living. It seems almost a contradiction in terms to be capable of doing this. Where can the child find the driving force to turn against his own pleasure instinct, if it be true, as I believe it is, that we do nothing, and can do nothing, unless in so doing we somehow gratify the pleasure instinct? How then does the neurotic manage to give up sexuality and potency by saying, "I am one for whom there is no sensual feeling", "I am without genitals".

It would seem as if this was the most utter renunciation, abandoning the pleasure instinct itself; and yet, even in this final renunciation of sexuality, sexual pleasure finds its part. No doubt fear and anger are powerful checks, but in the last resort the only force which is strong enough to overcome sexuality is sexuality itself. The renunciation of sex becomes tolerable and possible only in so far as it can draw strength from sexuality itself. The neurotic who is impotent or frigid, though consciously he may hate his emotional paralysis and long to come back to life, nevertheless draws comfort at a deep unconscious level from the fantasy of a sexual experience so mighty and awful that the body has died under it. At this deep level castration of pleasure and potency represents for the neurotic the most utter abandonment to passive love. This is the same passionate attitude which, undistorted by guilt, is expressed in the words, "Father, into Thy hands I commend my spirit", or "Not my will, but Thine, be done", and "Behold, the handmaid of the Lord; be it unto me according to Thy Word".

This same capacity, which is displayed in extreme love, for

the complete surrender of the barriers of self-protection is enlisted by the neurotic in his struggle to master his own sexuality which fear and disgust prevent him from enjoying. It is only with the help of this powerful sexual force that he achieves the miracle of self-destruction whereby he succeeds in turning his back on the pleasure instinct. The power to renounce is borrowed from the very thing which is to be renounced, so that sacrifice of pleasure itself becomes the goal of the pleasure-seeking impulse. A neurosis is, indeed, a very remarkable human achievement which proves the extraordinary capacity for renunciation possessed by mankind, but it is an unnecessary heroism and is based ultimately on groundless fear. Also the renunciation is never complete; the banished impulses persist in the unconscious always pressing for satisfaction and seeking for some breach in the defence through which they may force their way back to consciousness. This pressure from their own banished impulses is a continual source of the anxiety and guilt from which neurotics so often suffer.

In my next chapter I shall discuss further this characteristic neurotic anxiety and guilt.

SUMMARY

In this chapter I have discussed the last stage of sexual development which precedes the full capacity for adult love—the "phallic stage" in which sexual preoccupation and the desire for sense-pleasure have passed on from the pregenital erotogenic zones to the genitals themselves. This phallic stage differs from the adult attitude in that sexual interest seems still to fall short of complete love of the whole person, being focused rather on the genital organs and sexual activities. Shock at the sight of the adult genitals, or the witnessing of sexual intercourse, or the discovery of the pains of childbirth, or the appearance of menstrual blood, seem to favour fixation at this level of partial love.

At this stage the child's strong sexual interest in the parents lays it open to bitter disappointment and tormenting jealousy: because of the pain it suffers it may now wish to separate them and to rob them of what they give each other. With this fantasy of robbing and separating there goes the dread of being robbed and abandoned. The child who wishes to take the penis or babies away from its father or mother will begin to fear for its own penis or for its fantasy babies, and it is here that the so-called "Castration Complex" arises. Jealousy also causes the child to wish that the parents' sexual activities should injure them, and to believe that they have in fact done so.

This makes the child's sexual fantasies terrifying and this terror may be intensified and, as it were, confirmed by real experiences, or stories, or vivid dreams, or actual catastrophes such as accidents or deaths which are taken symbolically as proving the reality of what has already been imagined.

The name "Oedipus situation" has been given to this early sexual interest which the child feels in its parents, and psychogenic illness is sometimes said to be the result of this Oedipus situation. This is misleading.

The Oedipus situation is important because it is the child's first experience of love and sets the pattern for the loves of later life. According to the way in which the child succeeds in dealing with the difficulties inherent in this first love situation it learns how to love and is able to go on to healthy sexual maturity, or else its power of loving becomes impaired by entanglement with hostility, and it attempts to give up sexuality, fails to mature, and remains emotionally crippled and fixated to its early love disaster.

The state of psychogenic illness, when it occurs, is not the result of early sexual love itself but of the various difficulties with which that love inevitably has to contend. These are:

(i) The tension set up by disappointment, rejection, and the need to wait and postpone satisfaction, leading to fear of strong feeling and to an entanglement between sexual love and hostility and fear.

(ii) Jealousy, leading to hostile fantasies against rivals, together with fear of the rivals' revenge which is pictured in the same omnipotent and destructive terms as the child's own vindictive wishes.

(iii) Cruel or degrading ideas of what sexuality means, springing from this disappointment and jealousy which lead the child unconsciously to prefer to believe that the pleasures from which it is shut out are dangerous and filthy.

The difficulty and danger of the early love situation is proportional to the intensity of the child's own disappointment, jealousy, rage and fear.

The dangers inherent in the Oedipus situation are most successfully avoided where the child really loves the parent of the opposite sex and is able to identify itself with (or "introject") a loved parent of its own sex who really loves the other parent. In this way the child learns how to love, by sharing in fantasy the parent towards whom its early sexual wishes are directed, while it can still also love the parent whom it has introjected and escape the pains and hostility which come from rivalry and jealousy. The boy can now *be* father and love mother, the girl can *be* mother and love father, thus enjoying the sense of personal value and security which is needed as a starting-point from which a wider love of other things and people can develop.

When the parents who are introjected are hated and despised, the patient attempts to renounce sexuality altogether and develops a psychogenic illness.

CHAPTER VII

OUR brief outline of the stages through which the pleasure-seeking instinct passes on the way to full adult genital love has now been completed, and an attempt has been made to show how it sometimes happens that people fail to reach full maturity. Throughout all that has been said we have returned again and again to our central theme, that emotional growth is arrested as a result of the entanglement of sexuality with the originally non-sexual instincts of fear and hostility which disappointment arouses. The conflict between the original primitive desires which, though disappointed, have not been relinquished, and the hostile impulses with which they have become entangled, produces an inner frustration which perpetuates disappointment and hostility. This internal deadlock creates a state of tension which may be dealt with by repression, but which then forms the unconscious foundation for the development of neurotic symptoms. These begin to appear when repression threatens to break down. There is now a danger that the repressed conflicting impulses will force their way back into consciousness and demand satisfaction, and this danger, unconsciously recognised, gives rise in consciousness to the feelings of anxiety and guilt which are so characteristic of neurotics.

We may think of neurotic anxiety as being of three different kinds. The first, *primary anxiety*, arises simply from the state of psychic helplessness into which the child is thrown by failure to obtain satisfaction for urgent instincts. This failure produces a heaping up of psychophysical tension which mounts and threatens to become unendurable. Anxiety might arise from the damming up of any instinct—food-hunger, for instance, or pleasure-hunger, aggression or fear. Such a situation of tension seems to be the ultimate danger which must, at all costs, be avoided.

The second kind of anxiety is one stage removed from this primary anxiety and is a danger signal set up to protect the organism from falling into primary anxiety. This kind of anxiety tends to develop in any situation which, if not somehow modified, would be liable to lead on to the original condition of psychic helplessness in the face of undischarged instinct tension. If primary anxiety has led to repression of the instincts which failed to find satisfaction, there is always the danger, whenever new situations occur which resemble the earlier ones, that the old intolerable instinct tension will reappear. Any *weakening of repression* or, what is equivalent, *strengthening of the repressed* is therefore the signal for an outbreak of this second kind of anxiety.

The third kind of anxiety is "*castration*" or better "*mutilation*" *anxiety*. Unlike primary anxiety which results simply from the damming up of undischarged instinct tensions, this "mutilation" anxiety results from repressed sexualised cruelty. It is an expression of the patient's dread that the repressed mutilation fantasies, which arose as a sort of compromise out of the conflict between love and hostility, are now about to break through the barriers of repression and carry themselves out in action. Since from the primitive point of view, at which the unconscious has remained, being aware of any impulse means carrying it into effect, and since the external world is expected to behave as the child itself feels and wishes to behave, two things are dreaded: the danger from within of the threatened outburst of uncontrolled primitive impulses of love-hate which have become entangled and now appear together, and the retaliation from without which is expected to follow. The anxiety is an expression of the terror of losing control of the repressed instincts lest these fantasies of injuring and being injured should actually come true.

Anxiety about the return of the repressed finds expression in a sort of parable in a variety of fairly typical dreams and fantasies. One patient dreamt of being in a car: the brakes would not work and it was backing downhill out of control; another dreamt of rushing downhill in a car beside a mad driver; another of a speed boat; another of a terrible explosion; another had a waking fantasy of logs being whirled down a rushing torrent; another dreamt that someone was screaming in terror; another that she was riding a horse which went mad with fear.

Sometimes conscious fear is experienced of committing acts of violence, going mad or running amok, assaulting or being assaulted. More commonly the fantasies are not so near consciousness and then the anxiety may attach itself to real events or possible dangers which may seem more or less to justify it. In such cases the patient is usually very unwilling to admit the possibility of unconscious reasons underlying his distress, and insists that reality accounts for it all. Sometimes, however, it is more like the nameless horror of a nightmare. It takes the form either of painful apprehension and restlessness and uneasiness, consciously experienced, or else of the circulatory manifestations of strong excitement such as palpitation, rapid pulse, chilliness, sweating, flushing and giddiness, divorced from conscious emotion.

The unconscious source of neurotic anxiety, whatever form it may take, is the dread of the failure of repression resulting in helplessness in the face of the demands of primitive instincts.

Although it is often not difficult to recognise in general outline from a patient's symptoms, dreams and free-associations, what his repressed impulses are, in what fantasies he is seeking to gratify them, what sort of retributions he fears and how he is attempting to defend himself, the actual concrete details of the repressed fantasies which make up the unconscious delusional system on which his illness rests become clearer if one can understand what he must have believed himself to be doing in childhood by early masturbation activities which combined love, revenge and punishment so inextricably. It is here that emotion most often entrenches itself, and this is the most carefully guarded of all the child's secrets.

When a child discovers that exciting sensations can be produced by stimulating particular parts of the body, those which we have called the erotogenic zones, it may provoke these sensations in itself simply for pleasure. Such masturbation activities would not arouse conflict. But observation and analysis show that masturbation is often used in childhood, and may again be used later, as a refuge from disappointment and to let off the tension, and when it is used in this way it is inspired by anger and revenge as well as by the original pleasure-seeking or love, and is accompanied by fantasies of cruelty.

One of my patients experiences a compulsion to masturbate when she was in danger of receiving rebuffs. At such times she suffered a disturbance of appetite, either complete lack of any wish for food, the parallel of the surface repudiation of her violence, which made her gentle and retiring; or else ravenous hunger, the parallel of her secret sense of devouring strength. When she was thwarted she would bite her fingers, and when she masturbated she thought of herself as a ravening wolf, dark-skinned, hairy, dirty, and having a strong smell which the other women of her family had not. She was really of medium colour, her hair was not particularly thick, she had no marked smell, and she was clean and elegant. This sinister picture of herself, as became clear after some months of free-association, was the male side of her masturbation fantasies, and stood for an extremely primitive picture of her father's sexuality.

She had abandoned her femininity very young, fearing the rivalry with her mother which lay along that path. She was embarrassed and wretched in the pretty clothes in which her mother dressed her, and hated her mother to look at her body, unconsciously dreading retaliation for the envious hostility which her mother's body had once aroused in her, and which was the theme of her sadistic masturbation attacks upon her own body.

Tormented by guilt and anxiety about the sexualised hostility provoked by her early disappointments, first with her mother over the birth of a younger child, and then with her father over the rejection and failure of her childish love, she had been driven first to abandon her own sexuality as a girl, taking refuge in a ferocious travesty of male sexuality directed towards her mother, and then, when this proved too dangerous, she was forced to give up her aggression also, and remain a limp but rebellious burden on her parents' hands.

Of all these primitive fantasies nothing appeared on the surface. The patient on ordinary acquaintance made a charming impression as a reserved, modest, appealing young girl. At home, it is true, she was difficult, rather untidy, lazy and un-co-operative. She seemed to have little interest or ambition, but the only striking abnormalities she displayed were, on the physical side, mild chronic digestive trouble, constipation and disturbances of appetite, and on the mental side unreasonable shyness with occasional outbursts of temper if she was thwarted, in which she would fling herself down and scream with rage.

Since she had never reconciled herself to her original disappointments and held her early violent reactions to these in a state of precarious repression, any new rejection was liable to touch off an uncontrollable explosion of primitive fury, which, to her shame and horror, was sometimes discharged by masturbation accompanied by fantasies of sexualised cruelty. These mutilation fantasies were the unconscious delusions which were distorting her outlook and spoiling her human relations.

The characteristic thing about these masturbation activities is that even when they begin with excitement and pleasurable physical stimulation, when they are of this compulsion type they usually end in great distress and disillusion, often with an unbearable sense of waste and wanton destruction. A patient, whose case is fairly typical, said, "When I have done it, I feel I have killed something". What she had killed symbolically was her parents' bodies and her own which was closely identified with both of theirs—indeed, in the deep primitive unconscious her parents' bodies and her own were not distinguished from each other, nor was there a reality limit to her destructive powers. Her masturbation *meant* to her unconscious the literal mutilation and death of the three all-important bodies—mother, father and self. When she began to love anyone, she felt that they feared her and that she would be compelled to destroy them, and their destruction was also equivalent to her own. She had a permanent conviction that her own body was irreparably damaged, and that it was an object of distaste to others, in spite of the reality, which was, as it happened, in flat contradiction to this, since she was unusually prepossessing.

It was her repressed unconscious belief that she really had the power to carry out these fantasies and that in the masturbation acts which symbolised them she had really done so. Her guilt over this was responsible for her illness.

Neurotic guilt, a painful emotion which in some form is always present in psychogenic illness, thus results from the presence in the unconscious of repressed sexualised hostility.

The neurotic behaves as if he had a bad conscience. He suffers either from feelings of insufficiency, for which he blames himself, or else from a heavy sense of responsibility which forces him continually to justify his existence. His activity may be paralysed by his own inner self-contradiction, or he may be driven on continually to undertake fresh tasks; but these are carried out with effort and friction and he knows no peace or satisfaction. This is because he is divided against himself and because all satisfaction is unconsciously repudiated as wicked and dangerous.

Very often the patient is conscious of these feelings of guilt and worthlessness, and such feelings may weigh crushingly even on people whose lives are apparently blameless or even estimable. Sometimes they are dealt with by over-compensation, so that in consciousness there is an appearance of exaggerated self-satisfaction and even callousness in circumstances which normally might be expected to arouse shame: but this superficial lack of conscience is found to be a bluff, assumed, often quite unconsciously, because the sense of guilt is so intolerable that it has to be ignored.

Psychoanalytic theory as to the orgins of this neurotic guilt has undergone considerable modifications recently, largely as a result of the further light thrown by child analysis, in which Melanie Klein[1] has been a leading pioneer. Her play technique, which makes it possible to study directly the conscious and unconscious reactions of young children, has added a fresh field to psychoanalytic research which formerly had to base its ideas about the early stages of human development upon inferences drawn almost entirely from the study of adults[2].

The older psychoanalytic view on the subject of guilt and conscience was that they were derived from the punishments inflicted by parents and nurses for "naughty" behaviour. It was held that we acquire our consciences by introjecting these early commands, taking them inside ourselves, so that what was formerly an external prohibition now becomes an internal one,

[1] *The Psychoanalysis of Children,* by Melanie Klein, Hogarth Press and Institute of Psychoanalysis, 1932.

[2] The views put forward by Mrs Klein are still under discussion in the psychoanalytic world, but by many psychoanalysts they are regarded as the most important contribution since Freud.

the sanction being either fear of punishment or the desire to please the grown-ups by obeying them. The neurotic, it was held, does not outgrow this early nursery morality and still unconsciously fears punishment and tries to "be good" at this nursery level of values. Thus the neurotic adult who, as a child, was severely taught not to let itself go, physically or emotionally, ever after unconsciously regards letting itself go as wicked, and fights against doing so at a deep involuntary level which acts automatically without reference to the entirely different later situations. At this level the old nursery standards still rule, and the impulse to let go arouses the very same old shame and guilt which were originally experienced over such "naughtinesses" as, for instance, soiling and bed-wetting.

There seems still to be much truth in this earlier psycho-analytic explanation. The conscience of the neurotic does seem to be infantile and to reproduce the severity of early training, as if it really was the harsh parent or nurse taken inside the patient and still scolding or terrorising him. His attitude towards this conscience is also in keeping with this explanation: he resents it, defies and evades it, but all the time fears it and does not doubt its authority. For the most part his submission to it is only a compromise: he placates it with lip-service and self-punishment, but in the disguised form of the symptoms he still gets his own way.

This old theory of guilt, however, is not adequate to explain all the facts; guilt cannot all be due to harsh training, since it appears as strongly, or even more strongly, in children who have been brought up with great lenience. The view now being taken is much more that the root of the trouble is the child's own destructive impulses, with which it reacts to frustration.

If to the hostile child the whole world seems to have become hostile and punitive, its guilty fears will depend rather on its own attitude than on what other people do to it. Children would thus seem to have, in their own capacity for resentment at interference with pleasure, an inner tendency to develop guilt spontaneously, apart from outside teaching or the experience of deliberate punishments. And it does not even seem necessary that their temper should have actually done serious damage: it is enough that they *intended* to do it, and in their omnipotent fantasy they will seize upon outside events for which they were not really responsible and claim the guilt for these. The death of parents or brothers and sisters is taken by young children in this way as a proof of the efficacy of their own death wishes, and may set up lasting guilt, remorse and fear.

This happened, as we have seen, in Miss M.'s case when her baby sister died. Even though no one knew of her hatred of this child, and no punishments had been threatened, she felt herself responsible for the catastrophe and for her mother's illness which followed it. Henceforth she went in dread of her mother, fearing she would thrash her to death. Actually her mother had never beaten her: it was she herself who, at the time of the baby's birth, had wished to attack it and her mother, out of jealousy and revenge, and now she expected punishments corresponding to her own hostile impulses. She was so much afraid of her own power to do harm, which the baby's death seemed to her to prove, that she made a vow never to allow herself to be jealous again, and in fact her guilty terror did give her the strength to banish the greater part of her hostile feelings from consciousness, though only at the expense of turning them against herself, causing her to hate and despise herself and unconsciously to punish herself by developing her painful and disabling symptoms. In later life, when the repression gave way, her repressed feelings broke out again in their old form of murderous hate.

Here guilt, leading to a repression which laid the foundations of psychogenic illness, was brought about by a distortion of real events in the light of the child's own death wishes, unaided by outside blame.

It would, of course, be folly to deny the importance of real experiences of threats and punishments, but these do not in themselves seem enough to explain neurotic guilt; even the most real experiences appear to depend for their effect, in a large measure, on the person's own attitude at the time, so that one who was already "guilty" on account of his own hostility would be much more impressed by them than one who had a clear conscience. It would seem, then, that neurotic guilt usually arises from a combination of fact and fantasy, early experience being interpreted in the light of the projection into the outside world of the child's own impulses. If these are very hostile they may act more powerfully in producing a sense of guilt than any punishments that may really be inflicted. Indeed real punishments seem sometimes to relieve the burden of guilt, and children who do not get them may seek them of their own accord.

Very soon after the baby's death Miss M. changed from a good child who did well at school into one who was always in disgrace. She felt she *must* talk on purpose to lose an order mark though she had nothing she wanted to say. She lost it and went home crying, to forestall her mother's anger, but I think unconsciously she wanted to give her mother something to punish her for. This seemed to be because a real punishment which turned out to be tolerable would act, unconsciously, as a reassurance against the fantasies of punishments, too frightful to contemplate, which she felt might overtake her on account of the baby's death. I think her guilt had been too great to be borne without some overt retribution, and when she really got herself punished she felt better. This talking in school was only one of a number of similar "naughtinesses" which she developed at this time in order to incur punishment.

Another of my patients, whose hostility in childhood was strong, but heavily repressed, used to delight in getting himself wrongfully punished because this eased him of his own secret self-reproach. Grown up people, too, who are depressed or anxious, sometimes seem to feel better when they have a real disaster to worry about. An asylum patient of mine, who was full of repressed hatred, when he was thwarted would sometimes say recklessly, "I think I had better just go and commit a murder so as to have something real to be punished for". I had never suggested this theory to him and he knew nothing of it.

This need for allaying an existing dread of retribution by *real* punishment should not be forgotten in considering the problem of apparently unmotivated and unprofitable crime. The crime in such cases may be, not the *cause* of any sense of guilt the criminal may suffer from, but its *effect*, an unconscious attempt to get real punishment, and get it over, rather than remain in perpetual dread of the retribution pictured by his own lurid fantasy. If nothing happens, in order to forestall this retribution, which is felt to be inevitable and even justified, the child, and later the neurotic, may be driven to almost any lengths in the way of self-punishment. When people keep perpetually falling, cutting, bruising and hurting themselves, apparently by accident, it is possible that these "accidents" have an unconscious purpose behind them, the need to find an outside punishment to satisfy the inner feeling of guilt. Even serious accidents leading to permanent injury or death may come about in this way.

The greater the child's repressed hostility, the greater will be his unconscious fantasies at the phallic level of some sort of mutilation, and the self-punishment inflicted sometimes even symbolises the forestalling of this by self-mutilation. In insanity this is sometimes literally carried out by the patient in the form of actual self-castration; I think this was very possibly the meaning of the compulsive idea "Cut it off" which, it will be remembered, so much alarmed the patient that he had to change it to "Sussex Gorse".

The impulse towards self-castration in the literal physical sense seems not infrequently to exist in the unconscious even in people who are not in the least insane, and occasionally it comes to consciousness. More than one patient has expressed the conscious wish to rid himself of his penis as being the source of all his self-reproaches.

This impulse sprang from mixed motives of hate, protection, guilt and sexual pleasure-seeking. Being castrated unconsciously meant to them, on the hate side, castrating the father, with whom they were identified; on the preventive side, it meant making it impossible for themselves to carry out their sadistic sexual wishes, and also protecting them from the counter-attack which they fantasied as coming from the woman: on the guilt side it meant punishing themselves and forestalling punishment.

The same impulse towards self-punishment, expressed in less concrete bodily terms, appears in an enormous variety of forms, and sometimes neurotic guilt weighs so heavily that patients allow themselves no pleasure at all but spend their lives looking for suffering in order to make their burden lighter. Usually they fail completely to recognise what they are doing and believe themselves to be the victims of circumstances beyond their own control, though in fact they are bringing upon themselves the disasters that befall them.

It is not easy to realise how important self-punishment can be as a motive for human conduct. The nineteenth century idea, which many people have not even yet outgrown, was rather that we all act from motives of enlightened self-interest. To believe any such thing would be very misleading, at least until it had been so restated as to be unrecognisable as the same idea.

Nevertheless, it is actually true that we will not act at all unless we get some pleasure from what we do, only we have to reckon with *the pleasure that can be got from pain.* Even in self-punishment, though guilt is a terrific driving force, the motives appear always to be over-determined, and somewhere, though perhaps only in a very distorted and disguised form, pleasure is always present too. It was present even in the case of the patients who experienced the impulse towards self-castration: even this had in it sexual pleasure, since unconsciously it meant becoming women and so enjoying their masochistic sexual fantasy.

The pains which Miss M. endured for years were unconsciously self-inflicted. The motives included guilt, but there was also strong, though disguised, erotic pleasure. Without the erotic pleasure, distorted though it was, I do not think she could have developed the symptom. At times she would feel an irresistible desire to flog herself, but even this punishment became sexualised, for in flogging herself she experienced an erotic thrill from the fantasy of sexual maltreatment at the hands of some man who represented her stern father. The same mixture of passionate self-chastisement and sexual ecstasy is to be found in perverts, and also in some of the lives of the Saints, and a rather similar attitude is expressed now and then in hymns. There is one that runs:

Oh to be nothing,
Only to lie at His feet,
A broken and empty vessel,
For the Master's use made meet.

Of course this passionate abasement and welcoming of pain and annihilation is not true adult feminine sexuality, any more than passionate cruelty and murder are true adult masculine sexuality. Both these impulses are on the ambivalent pregenital level at which love is entangled with hostility, but, by regression, they may become charged with the whole erotic feeling of which a person is capable, absorbing all the sexual energy which, in happier circumstances, might have gone into adult love or sublimations. The whole of Miss M.'s sexual capacity seemed to have been perverted in this way so that she could only obtain gratification unconsciously, under the disguise of pain. Disappointment had given this cruel form to her unconscious sexual wishes.

Again we come back to our main thesis, that those who develop psychogenic illness are those who could not stand disappointment. They could not accept this piece of reality, and much of their subsequent illness can be understood if we interpret it as their defence against this admission.

Like the fox in the fable, the neurotic may defend himself from the pain of disappointment by asserting that the inaccessible grapes are sour. This is the source of his degradation, hatred, fear and contempt for sex. "I cannot get it so I hate it, and think it dangerous and filthy", is one way in which he comforts himself for the denial of his early love wishes.

The picture of the parents as dirty, coarse and dangerous can at least partly be explained in this way. The disappointed, jealous child thinks of its parents: "They have this thing I want and won't let me have it: let them keep it: people who enjoy that sort of thing are not nice, they are filthy and ridiculous and will suffer for it".

Such fantasies have a double use, in that they satisfy the child's revenge impulses and at the same time spare it the admission of its own failure. If the parents are degraded and injured they are punished, and if the pleasures they keep for themselves and deny the child are not pleasures at all, then the child has not missed anything.

Much of the neurotic's distortion of reality is directed unconsciously towards these two aims: the satisfaction of hostile impulses against those who inflicted disappointment, or against rivals, and at the same time the denial of the disappointment. But sometimes he achieves these aims only at a heavy price, since he deprives himself of the pleasure of love and, moreover, finds himself dogged ever after by a feeling of guilt. If this in its turn becomes intolerable he may succeed in repressing it, but he does not thereby rid himself of it, and whether it is conscious or not it may destroy his happiness and force him to waste his life in pain and self-punishment.

The intensity of the guilt is in proportion to the omnipotence of the hostile fantasies by means of which the child originally attempted to over-compensate against its real helplessness to satisfy the urgency of its early desires and pleasure-cravings.

The denial of disappointment, usually also accompanied by the satisfaction of the impulse of revenge, may be achieved by a reversal of the original situation. The disappointed child wishes to take by force from the loved person or the rival the things for which it has asked in vain. In order to deny its own powerlessness and failure, the original situation, "I wanted to injure and rob them but I had not the power", becomes turned round into "I *did* injure and rob them". But this brings with it fear of retribution, and so the triumphant affirmation of success becomes changed into guilty self-accusation and may be formulated as "I *did* injure and rob them and I can never do enough to atone for it". This was Miss M.'s case. Her belief that she had killed her rival and hurt her mother sprang, ultimately, from her strong wish that this should in fact be true. Throughout her childhood she was burdened by the need to atone for this guilty success. To recognise that she was *not* to blame meant giving up her secret triumph, and she was unwilling to do this. Similarly with the fear that she was pregnant, which haunted her whole life and appeared in a disguised form in her symptoms. To relinquish this belief and the symptoms meant giving up the secret with which she had comforted herself in her childhood for her real failure to have a baby of her own and, unconsciously, she preferred to keep her illness.

The reversal which denies the disappointment may take a

slightly different form. Instead of a denial of the failure to get what was wanted, by an assertion of success, the disappointment itself may be reversed. The reversal runs: "It is not you who make me suffer, it is *I* who make *you* suffer". This again achieves both the neurotic's unconscious aims, wiping out the pain of failure and at the same time satisfying revenge by turning the tables. Miss M.'s self-reproaches for having been unwilling to give her father what he wanted were really in order to deny the truth, which was the other way round, that *he* had refused her what *she* wanted.

Both these ways of escaping the pain of admitting failure thus involve those who make use of them in guilty self-accusations, and these are strengthened by the revenge satisfaction which the reversal of the original situation usually achieves. Although they appear as guilt, such self-accusations are really the expression of reproaches originally provoked by outside disappointment. The guilt here is about cruelty, but there is a confusion as to *whose* cruelty. One might say that really it was the father's and mother's cruelty in disappointing, but these reproaches have been directed back on to the self which, being identified with the child's picture of the cruel parents, has itself become cruel. Such people go through life re-enacting their original disappointment the other way round, now playing the part of the cruel and heartless love-object and inflicting, instead of suffering, disappointment.

To this type belong the seducers and coquettes who win love only to throw it away. The deep revenge motive is sometimes masked in consciousness by compassion. Such lovers, weeping over the hearts they have been obliged to break, remind one of the Walrus and the Oysters:

> With sobs and tears he sorted out
> Those of the largest size,
> Holding his pocket handkerchief
> Before his streaming eyes.

In a sense, of course, this compassion is as real as the revenge itself, but it is made hypocritical by the task of over-compensation which it has to perform.

Such reversals from disappointed to disappointer, that is from child to parent, are made possible by the fact that to begin with the child seems actually not to distinguish clearly between itself and them. Identification with the parents seems normally to precede the development of a separate consciousness of self, and later, as we have seen, there appears to come a stage at which the child again reverts to this attitude by pretending in fantasy to be them. In so far as the parents are loving and loved, such introjection of them helps to establish the child's inner security. It is harmful in proportion to the child's fear and hostility towards them.

Unfortunately it seems that it is just when the parents are arousing the child's fear and hostility that the need to introject them is greatest. The child suffers from constantly being at the mercy of other people, and it may react against the danger to which this lays it open by focusing its energies and its fantasies on the aim of keeping its environment under its own control. The motive may be either love or fear. To introject loved or needed parents is to keep them safe inside and not to lose them. Such introjections are often made when a parent has really been lost either by death or absence. Again, in so far as the parents are feared, the purpose in introjecting them seems to be to obtain a sort of magical control and mastery over them. But here again, as in the attempt to escape the pain of disappointment, the mark is overshot, producing lasting internal maladjustment, since the fear and hostility are now taken inside along with the introjected parent, and henceforth there can be no escape. The child now feels towards itself what it felt towards its parents or rivals and believes about itself what it believed about them.

The reversal by way of identification runs, "It was not your fault it was mine, since I am you, but since you are wicked so am I". We have seen that the need to make such reversals of blame springs from a mixture of love and fear. To blame the parents is to attack them, and this, from the point of view of omnipotent fantasy, is to destroy them. To substitute the self and attack that means protecting the parents as well as escaping and forestalling their retaliation. The child who needs and loves its parents wishes to preserve them even in the midst of its hostility to them. If it takes the blame on itself, it can still love and be loved by its parents. If it blames the parents instead of loving them, it feels that it will suffer the loss of their love and be abandoned by them as a punishment.

One of my patients had seen another patient of whom she was jealous leaving my house. She began her hour with me by saying she was too angry to scold me; she dug her nails into my cushion and said she wanted to strangle me. Then she asked me if I was still there. I said I thought she wanted to destroy me and was afraid of having done so and thus being left alone. She said she thought I had stopped loving her, and immediately began accusing herself of being contemptible and worthless. This was an attempt to protect me, the faithless love-object, as well as to forestall my revenge (which was anticipated in the form of the withdrawal of my love) by diverting her attacks on to herself. Really it was *I* whom she felt to be contemptible, or rather, originally, her mother for whom I stood. She went on to say that the other patient she had just seen was coarse and ugly, and then she said it was she herself who was ugly and that she loved this other patient. Here she was protecting her rival, the other patient, and over-compensating against her hostility by exaggerated love. This repeated her attitude to her younger brother, the original rival.

This patient seemed to have made an identification with her mother, in which she took upon herself the heartlessness of which she had originally felt her mother was guilty. She had deeply resented the birth of her younger brother, regarding this as a withdrawal of her mother's love from herself. Her identification with her mother caused her to feel that she herself was cold and heartless. She was ashamed of this and tried to conceal it under a great display of kindness. She sometimes spoke of a mental picture of a vast frozen sea over which shone a grey cold light. It was beautiful, but terrible and pitiless. She was bi-lingual and when I asked what that sea was she replied, "c'est la mer de glace", and then added with strong emotion, "Oh, I see now, c'est la *mère* de glace". One of her most terrible memories was of her mother's face looking at her accusingly and unrelentingly.

Her own emotional life was frozen by the introjection of this ice-cold mother.

This feeling seems to be widespread in patients. They often accuse themselves of an emptiness in their emotional life which may actually amount to a sort of depersonalisation. I think what has happened is that in the early phase of identification the loved person appeared so cruelly heartless that the child, in taking this parent figure inside itself, deprived itself of the power to feel, and then directed against itself the blame which it was struggling not to feel against the original love-object.

Miss M. believed herself an outcast, soiled, infected, ulcerated. This picture of degradation was the product of her jealousy and really represented her attitude to her mother in so far as she was her successful sexual rival. She took this upon herself, partly to protect her other loving picture of her mother, and partly in order to deny that she had not got the thing for which she envied her mother. She and not her mother was the filthy and degraded one, meaning *she* and not her mother enjoyed sexuality as represented in the pregenital form to which her anger had degraded it.

In these strange twistings back on the self of what appears to be suffering we must not forget the concealed element of gratification and the ultimate advantage secured by denying the original disappointment, whatever the cost.

"Mother or Father is hateful and filthy", which is the child's expression of its jealousy, becomes, by identification, "I am hateful and filthy", and under this lies the love gratification denied by reality—"my rival's success is mine"—together with the hate gratification—"in my destruction my rival is destroyed".

In consciousness the hate has reversed pleasure to pain, so that the shame and agony endured no longer appear openly as wish-fulfilments; nevertheless patients cling to their sufferings very tenaciously because by these they are still asserting the fulfilment of their disappointed childish wishes that something should have been done to them, and denying the truth that nothing really *was* done, which is more intolerable than the pains they endure.

Many of the mechanisms which underlie psychogenic illness, and the deep needs which they satisfy, are now clear.

These needs are:

Pride: the necessity to deny the pain and humiliation of the early love disappointment.

Revenge against the disappointing love-objects and against successful rivals.

The need to protect the love-object and to go on loving and being loved.

The need to escape retribution and to forestall it.

The need, in spite of everything, to go on enjoying sexual pleasure.

The neurotic attains these aims in the following ways:

By reversal of the disappointment situation.

By the sexualisation of cruelty, humiliation and pain.

By degradation of sexuality and of the sexual parents.

By identification with the degraded parents.

In attaining his aims by these methods, the neurotic, though he evades some suffering, involves himself in heavy losses, since he condemns himself to a life of guilt and pain and sacrifices his chance of happiness. In the attempt to evade one pain he only substitutes a greater and more lasting one.

Reversal of the original disappointment situation enables him to imagine that he has succeeded in robbing the parents, but it also arouses guilt, and while he clings to his fantasy of success this feeling of guilt may force him to sacrifice all later real satisfactions.

Sexualisation of cruelty, humiliation and pain transform sexual desire, so that real conscious satisfaction becomes impossible.

Degradation of sexuality forces him to repudiate love and happiness and degradation of the original sexual love-objects causes him henceforth to despise and fear those who arouse his love.

Identification with his degraded love-objects leads to self-contempt and more guilt. From these spring self-punishment by means of which he carries out a vicarious revenge, while at the same time atoning for his guilt and forestalling retaliation.

The attempt to avoid accepting the reality of disappointment thus involves the child in a distortion of reality which may ever after stand in the way of any real appreciation of itself or of other people as they actually are.

At the height of its hostility aroused by its early disappointment, the child seems regularly to replace the figures of its own real parents by fantastic creations, called, in psychoanalytic terminology, "Parent Imagos", which are really modelled on its own hostile fantasies projected outwards. The supposed intentions of these Imagos reflect the child's own, and that is why the violent destructive child falls a prey to guilty terrors, no matter how mild the real parents have actually been.

Unless one is familiar with the delusions of insanity, has actually listened to a number of analyses, and come to realise what neurotics' unconscious fantasies are, it is almost impossible to believe how strange and monstrous these Parent Imagos can be. Even the sex is obscure: often the Imagos seem to combine characteristics from both sexes. Thus one may find fantasies, usually unconscious but sometimes conscious (as in the case of Mr J.), of a woman with a penis, or more often with many penises, and sometimes like a Medusa with the many snakes (penises) displaced to her head. In this connection comparison with the older gods of India is illuminating.

Miss M. had a nightmare on this theme in which she came up to a platform banked in flowers, on which sat a woman (representing the Mother Imago) with snakes for hair, holding a jewelled sword (all these representing penises). The dreamer dared not look, and tore her own teeth from her mouth. This was a reaction to her own overwhelming biting fantasies.

The fantasied male Imago may have female attributes. One patient dreamt of a small boy (standing for herself) paralysed with terror at being threatened by a huge man with a vast open mouth full of dangerous fangs, representing the female genital displaced upwards.

Since patients identify with their Parent Imagos in their sexual fantasies, it is not surprising that unconsciously they loathe sexuality. But the unkindness of the Imago which is the source of neurotic guilt is not all fantasy. Children are certainly not altogether blind to some of the real truth about their elders. What the child seems intuitively to react to is, not so much the parents' conscious intention towards it, as their unconscious attitude, so that it may suffer from the repressed hatred or jealousy of its parents even though they may have over-compensated this attitude in consciousness by demonstrations of love and solicitude. Perhaps the so-called "spoilt" child is often suffering in this way, being the object not so much of love as of remorseful atonement. Children are also quick to react emotionally to the deep relation between the parents, and often suffer acutely when the marriage is loveless. In such circumstances the difficulties of healthy emotional development are increased, since, if the parents do not in fact love each other, identification with them means the prohibition of love itself.

But it still remains true that even in cases where the hostility or actual cruelty of the parents is fact and not all fantasy, the forms in which the child imagines this will be expressed are quite unlike anything that ever could really happen. The existence of hostility, then, may not be a delusion, but the form in which the child expects it to be expressed *is*. It is true that hatred exists as well as love, but it is not true that this hatred will in reality be expressed by mutual devouring, castrating, disembowelling and the other still wilder assaults which the child's imagination creates on the model of its own infantile fantasies. It is fear, not simply of the element of hostility which exists in the real world, but of its expression in these frightful, dangerous, fantastic forms, that underlies neurotic anxiety and guilt.

This neurotic sense of guilt differs from the conscience of everyday life. The self-punishments it may demand are primitive and savage because it is itself primitive and savage; it enforces prohibitions which the normal adult has long ago discarded; it does not distinguish real from fantasy dangers; it is rigid, acting automatically rather than in the light of reason; it rules like an external force without conscious consent, and, in the case of hysterics, it even controls the physiological processes so that if they attempt to do what it does not permit they may be driven by their terror to strike themselves dumb, blind or paralysed, or lose the power of feeling.

The severity of this archaic conscience paralyses the neurotic's life, and prevents him growing up. His submission to it depends on his belief in the omnipotent destructive powers of the Parent Imagos, and this belief in its turn follows from his unconscious claim to being himself omnipotent and able to satisfy all his demands.

Real emotional growing up begins only when the unconscious attempt to deny the early disappointment is given up. The insistence upon its own omnipotence was the child's reaction to its own real powerlessness to achieve either satisfaction or revenge, and when some limitation of power is accepted this need to claim omnipotence diminishes. But the dangerousness of the Parent Imagos, together with the archaic conscience which is derived from them, were both modelled on the child's own omnipotent destructive fantasies, and so, when once the renunciation of omnipotence has been accepted, the terror of the Parent Imagos and the severity of the conscience diminish correspondingly. They become humanised. But it was to a large extent the dangerousness of these Parent Imagos which made it necessary for the child to hate them and also to punish itself for this. The unconscious sexual fantasies of the neurotic still reproduce this childish attitude to the Parent Imagos, and so, as these become more human, the fantasies become less dangerous and aggressive and the neurotic's need to repudiate sexuality diminishes, thus making satisfaction possible and so lessening the tension and further diminishing the aggression. So a benign circle begins to replace the old vicious circle of deprivation, fear, hostility, more fear and still more deprivation and fear. With the disappearance of the need to be so afraid, the guilt and anxiety which sprang from the hostility diminish. Thus the situation seems to turn on the acceptance of the reality of disappointment. While this cannot be admitted, every fresn suggestion of the failure to achieve satisfaction is reacted to by denial and omnipotent hostile fantasy, thus simply repeating over and over again the child's attempt to escape the pain of realising its limitations, which the neurotic has never outgrown.

He is cured when he is able to discard this attempt at flight from reality, to risk failure and accept what he can get. The difficulty of cure lies in the neurotic's intolerance of frustration. His early helplessness in the face of urgent instinct demands, which he had no power to satisfy, drove him to fall back on the fantasy of his own omnipotence, and he is loath to relinquish this fantasy, even though in clinging to it he saddles himself for life with the shame and guilt of his supposed success and with the fear of fantastic omnipotent penalties.

One might say that he has to learn to be disappointed in order that he may not need to continue to be so, for he seems to have such an exaggerated dread of finding himself powerless to get what he wants that he dares not risk real wanting. Fearing disappointment excessively, he reacts with excessive violence to any hint that his desires may not be granted, and then, fearing his own violent reaction, he represses both the desires and the fury. So of necessity he goes unsatisfied, and desires and fury mount up instead of being assuaged by satisfaction, thus creating the vicious circle which underlies neurosis.

The problem of real emotional growing up, then, is to be able to tolerate frustration well enough to endure desire without immediately reacting with a mixture of fury, despair and omnipotent fantasy and terror which in its turn leads on only to more frustration and still more fury, despair, omnipotence and terror.

In this fundamental sense, the neurotic, dissociated by early disappointment and panic, has never grown up.

SUMMARY

In this chapter I began by discussing the nature of neurotic anxiety, explaining that there were three kinds of such anxiety: primary anxiety, resulting directly from the damming up of undischarged instinct tension; secondary anxiety, which is a danger signal giving warning that such a situation of undischarged tension is threatening; and finally castration or mutilation anxiety, in which what is feared is that the barrier of repression may fail and the repressed fantasies of sexualised cruelty may be carried out in actual fact.

I went on to discuss neurotic guilt, which I explained as the result of the need to deny childish disappointment and powerlessness, and the desire to be revenged. However much suffering it may cause in consciousness, the neurotic clings to it unconsciously rather than admit his failure. From this neurotic guilt arises the need for sacrifice and punishment which play such an important part in human life.

I explained that the strength to inflict pain on the self is derived from the sexualisation of suffering. In the case of some neurotics the whole force of their sexual capacity has been enlisted in the service of self-punishment, so that this affords them their sole gratification in life. It is not easy to restore such people to health.

To be really healthy I said that it would be necessary to give up denying the early disappointment of the Oedipus situation, since, if this were admitted, omnipotence would become unnecessary and so the neurotic anxiety and guilt inspired by the omnipotent delusions of destruction and retaliation would disappear.

What stops the neurotic from getting over the early disaster is his excessive fear of disappointment and of his own reactions to this. He grows up when he has acquired the power to tolerate delay without reacting immediately so violently that he has to give up or repress his desires, for until he can tolerate some delay he can never achieve the real satisfactions which would relieve him of the tension and frustration that stand perpetually in the way of his recovery. With the acquiring of this power, satisfaction becomes possible, and this begins to break the vicious circle of disappointment of desire leading straight to aggression which arouses fear and turns what is wanted into something terrifying which must be rejected, this leading inevitably to more disappointment, more aggression and more fear—the vicious circle of psychogenic illness.

CHAPTER VIII

ACCORDING to psychoanalysis, the people who develop psychogenic illness are those who, in the face of the emotional conflicts produced in childhood by disappointment, have reacted to their real helplessness by a denial of the disappointment and the assertion of their omnipotent power to satisfy their pleasure-seeking and destructive instincts. This flight from reality takes the form of fantasies of terrific mutilations (the so-called castration complex) which arouse in them a mixture of triumph, terror, rage, remorse and sexual feeling, bringing with them the fear of monstrous retributions which may be too terrifying to be faced and so are repressed. In extreme cases *no* outlet for the pleasure-seeking instinct escapes this taint of sexualised cruelty so that none can be indulged with an easy mind. *Any* satisfaction of theirs now unconsciously appears to them to mean the destruction and ruin of all concerned, their own aggression destroying that which they desire and involving themselves in the disaster as a just retribution. When Oscar Wilde wrote "For each man kills the thing he loves", I suppose he was talking about his own ambivalence. A patient burst into tears and said, "Whenever I touch anything beautiful, I have to spoil it".

Because of this entanglement with destructive impulses, pleasure-seeking has to be repressed, and so sexual development is arrested at an immature and primitive level. Anxiety tends to appear whenever the barrier of repression weakens or when pressure from the repressed impulses is increased. It is a question of the equilibrium between two opposing forces. If the pressure from the unconscious threatens to outweigh the repressing forces, the only alternatives are either to give up the claim to omnipotence, which means admitting the reality of the early failure, but at the same time being released from the anxiety and guilt which this claim to omnipotence brings with it, or else to keep the omnipotent guilty fantasies, by means of which the failure was denied, and find some *modus vivendi* with them which shall allow them to disturb consciousness as little as possible. The first of these ways of dealing with the problem is the only one which can rightly be regarded as completely healthy. No one can be considered in perfect mental health while he cherishes repressed delusions and needs to defend himself against fantasies of omnipotence which threaten to erupt, and so constitute a potential source of anxiety and guilt having no foundation in external reality.

Complete contact with reality, however, is a counsel of perfection which mankind has certainly not yet attained: everyone does cherish unconscious delusions and is therefore not ideally sane. The degree of mental health depends on the proportion of the total energy which is being used up in repressed fantasy, and in the effort needed to keep it out of consciousness. It might even perhaps be measurable, at least theoretically, in terms of the amount of anxiety and guilt, conscious or unconscious, against which defence is needed. Even when a great deal of energy is being wasted in the repression of omnipotent delusions, it does not follow that the person will be obviously neurotic. Granted that the presence of repressed sexualised hostility is causing considerable unconscious anxiety and guilt, this only means that there is a need to find ways of preventing what has been repressed from upsetting the rest of the personality which has maintained contact and adapted itself to reality.

One way of meeting the difficulty is by the creation of *psychogenic symptoms*. This defence has already been discussed. The alternative defences against interference from what has been repressed are *more repression*, further reinforced perhaps by a protective scheme of life, or else the easing of tension by *sublimation*.

Among all those people who would ordinarily be counted as normal, or even as remarkably well balanced, I believe a surprisingly large number are making use of the whole scheme of their existence as an unremitting defence against unconscious anxiety and guilt. This defence is often so successful that no suspicion of uneasiness reaches clear consciousness, and yet their whole career may really have been unconsciously inspired, and still be dominated, by the need to neutralise anxiety. These lives differ from real normality and health in the restless drive which seems to force them on. Such people cannot enjoy relaxation. Here it is not a matter of giving an outlet to repressed fantasies by any particular substituted activity, as occurs in symptoms or sublimations: the whole of their lives seems to be a grand organised phobia, designed to avoid finding themselves in some type of situation which to them is intolerable. For some, the intolerable situation might be helplessness, and it might thus be necessary for them at all costs to avoid being in any situation which they could not control. For others, the danger situation might be envy or jealousy, and life has to be arranged to avoid the possibility of ever coming into conflict with a successful rival. For others, what cannot be tolerated is disappointment; they must not ask and fail to receive. Others must never meet with contradiction and risk having their temper roused. Others, on account of their unconscious guilt, must spend their lives making restitution.

All these anxiety situations have much in common and could be related back to the emotional conflict provoked by the original disappointment of early pleasure-seeking, that is, either to dread of being left in a state of unsatisfied desire, or else to castration or mutilation anxiety.

They may be avoided in two opposite ways. Failure may be ensured against, either by limiting the demands made on life, withdrawing from the struggle and avoiding competition, taking no risks; or else by making demands, but seeing to it that they are always satisfied. In the case of those who take no risks, the limitation of their ambitions may perhaps suggest something amiss, though for the most part they pass as ordinary inconspicuous people; but those whose lives are pathologically organised round success are usually regarded as patterns of health. They may make use of all the normal outlets and appear to lead full and satisfying lives.

An analyst reported a case[1] of this sort who would be held up as a pattern of normal womanhood. She devoted her life to home pursuits, childbirth, and the education of her children, and

[1] Case of Miss Ella F. Sharpe reported in *The International Journal of Psycho-analysis*, vol. XII, "The Technique of Psychoanalysis".

seemed a conspicuously well-adapted wife and mother. Nevertheless, her feminine activities were all compulsive. They were not followed simply for their own sake, but were as necessary to her in defending herself against the anxiety connected with her deep rivalry with other women as a phobia is to a frank neurotic. If she could not produce babies, she fell into anxiety as severe as the anxiety of a claustrophobic patient who is forced to go into the Underground, or is shut up in a cupboard.

Throughout their lives such people are dominated, just as the neurotic is, by the need for security against anxiety, but, whereas in symptom-formation the patient's energy is dissipated in symbolic performances which have little or no real use, this other type of defence is often played out in terms of real achievements. It falls short of true mental health because, however real the achievements may be, they are inspired, not so much by reality considerations, as by the delusion of dangers which do not in fact exist. The driving force is not healthy pleasure, but fear.

I feel sure that the analysis of a great many personalities who have achieved the most brilliant successes would bring to light some such state of affairs. Their achievements would be found to rest, not so much on the happy realisation of their instincts, as on inner compulsion; they do not merely enjoy what they do and so do it well, they *must* succeed on penalty of falling into acute morbid anxiety, and any check which threatens their defensive scheme of life throws them into a fury or panic. Many brilliant students and prominent men of affairs belong to this class. Some of them carry on successfully right through life—every now and then one breaks down from what is called "over-work", and then the inner strain of their terrific achievement becomes apparent. Such people cannot really be regarded as in perfect mental health, even if no breakdown ever comes to betray them, but they belong, obviously, to a different class from the neurotics or the insane. Indeed they constitute an important section of the population which, in our civilisation, is regarded as entirely, and even typically, normal.

The other "normal" way of dealing with unconscious anxiety and guilt is by *sublimation*. Sublimation consists in the transferring of the value with which the pleasure-seeking instinct normally endows the objects of its desire on to other objects not in themselves sexual. Simple sublimation would result if the instinct transferred was nothing but pleasure-seeking or love, and such sublimation would no doubt play an important part in complete mental health. But while unconscious anxiety and guilt persist sublimation is necessarily more complicated, since, besides being carried on for its own sake, it has also to be used defensively. Used in this way, however, it is far more practically successful than the other alternatives of symptom-formation and repression. Both allow a partial outlet for repressed impulses, but whereas the symptom, though it may compensate by denial and punishment for the forbidden gratification, yet always manages somehow to include an element of destruction and revenge which perpetuates the guilt and demands always more and more repression, sublimation, while it also gives expression to repressed ambivalent impulses, yet neutralises the guilt which gratification arouses by perpetually making restitution in symbolic form for the destructive wishes. Surgery may be an obvious example of such sublimation, in which cutting up the body combines injury and cure, and the giving of anaesthetics is another illustration, since here the patient is overpowered and reduced to a condition resembling death itself, but yet this is done to spare him and is indeed an act of mercy.

The lives of many people are, I think, built up on this plan. From their dreams and all their creative work it is clear that they must still have in them somewhere the same sort of unconscious preoccupations as also find expression in neurotic symptoms and insanity.

The analysis of all those socially permitted activities, such as art, literature, philanthropy, music, cooking, cleaning, typewriting, agriculture, learning, science, research, teaching, singing, business, finance, and so on (that is, any of the vocations that a healthy person may take up), strongly suggests that they are often transformations of our early primitive preoccupations no less than symptoms are. Furthermore, they would often appear to be used as acts of restitution designed continually to allay the guilt which torments those who unconsciously cherish great hostility, and unconsciously believe that their destructive fantasies have succeeded[1].

One case in point was a woman of thirty, who had been determined from childhood to become a painter and had succeeded, against a good deal of opposition, in getting her parents to allow her to give up her other education and go to an art school when she was fifteen. She seems to have shown considerable talent, but she became discouraged after a year and spent the next fifteen years of her life taking up one thing after another and then dropping it.

After a few months' analysis, she came to the decision, which she had always been secretly hoping to make, but had always put off, to return to her painting. She liked especially to draw women, but complained of the *flatness* of her work. She could not get the contours *rounded*. She was evidently ambivalent about women's bodies, and in her drawing alternated between bad days when the figures seemed to be squashed out flat, and good days when they were full. At a later period she was worried for a time by an exaggeration of roundness in which she complained that her paintings looked as if they were "blown out and too full".

In this outlet of art she seemed to be working out a mixture of impulses, some destroying, some restoring and recreating the bodies which she drew. The unconscious struggle between flatness and roundness turned on the subject of pregnancy.

I made some interpretations to this effect, which roused feelings of guilt and alarmed her. She found it difficult to follow what I said, appearing not to have understood, and she told me plainly, in her next association, though without realising consciously that she was doing it, to leave her alone and not to make her aware of what she meant unconsciously by her painting, and then she said, defensively, and with embarrassment, "Do you know what I really want to paint is a picture of Mother Earth, which shall represent her as quite perfect".

During a period of less repressed hostility to women's bodies she took to chopping pieces of wood and felt that she would like

[1] See also an article in the *International Journal of Psychoanalysis*, by Ella F. Sharpe, vol. XI, part 1, Jan. 1930, "Certain Aspects of Sublimation and Delusion".

to change over to carving or stone-cutting, thus unconsciously attempting to utilise her aggressive impulses in the interests of creation.

Prior to her return to painting she had been turning her hostility back on herself, sometimes in the form of masturbation with fantasies of torture, sometimes in the form of acute self-depreciation which even led her to threaten suicide.

As she gained further insight into the ambivalent conflict which disturbed her painting, and which had formerly driven her to abandon it, an improvement appeared in her work, the incentive to paint shifting over, from the need to make restitution, towards creation, inspired by more unmixed love and pleasure. This is only a single case and comparatively simple. I agree that we have no right to generalise from it to theories about the unconscious meaning of art, or still less of sublimations in general. But analysts are all the time collecting material about this subject, and it appears to point in the direction which I have indicated, namely, that both psychogenic symptoms and sublimations give indirect expression to the pleasure-seeking instinct which has become repressed because of its entanglement with destructive impulses: but that, whereas in symptoms the destructive impulses appear, deflected but essentially unchanged, in the useless form of self-inflicted pain, in sublimation of this defensive kind the destructive impulses are turned to advantage, in that the very activities whereby the destruction is symbolically achieved—as for instance, the cutting or soiling of the material in sculpture or painting—are used to make symbolic restitution—as in creating a statue or picture—thus making the sublimated activity acceptable in a way that the mere symptom could never be. Even the destructive component is now made use of, whereas with symptoms it is destructive only, and so has to be atoned for by pain.

Symptoms thus fail to meet the problem of anxiety and guilt, while sublimation solves it. It remains true, however, that so long as the delusion persists of the magical power of destructive fantasy and the supposed retribution which it will bring, such repressed fantasies remain as a constant menace which must always be met by some measure of defence.

The ideal solution would be to get rid of the delusions and gain contact with reality.

Even in perfect mental health the hostile and destructive impulses which disappointment and jealousy arouse would still, to some extent, remain, but instead of being endowed with all sorts of monstrous omnipotent destructive powers and expected to provoke murderous retributions, the everyday acts in which they find daily expression with all of us would be recognised as the attenuated and comparatively harmless pieces of cruelty or spite which in fact they are, and so would no longer give rise to morbid anxiety and guilt. And, indeed, when the unconscious reasons for the delusional fears from which so much of our hostility actually springs became conscious and were seen to be unfounded, much of the cruelty and spite would disappear automatically.

The absence of these delusions and of the morbid anxiety and guilt which follows in their train might be taken as the criterion of perfect normality. Such a normal person, having really outgrown the delusions produced at the time of his early struggles, would be able to see situations as they are and react to them in a way that was really appropriate. Real dangers would, I suppose, arouse fear and efforts to protect himself, even in the ideally normal person, but he would not be constantly imagining danger when it was not there, nor seeking self-destruction. He would not be afraid to experience living, and he would escape the neurotic guilt which comes from the persisting unconscious infantile belief in the omnipotence of his own hostile impulses, and the chastisement which the archaic conscience inflicts upon most of us on this account.

Possibly it may be felt that such a person would be inhuman. I have heard people express alarm that analysis might too successfully relieve people of their endearing weaknesses. But fantastic anxiety and guilt are not endearing weaknesses! There would be no danger of dullness or tediousness resulting from being relieved of such a bugbear, and I wish it might be possible to be entirely rid of it. Actually, however, analysis can hardly hope to do more than relieve the patient of the excessive burden which he carries over from the past as compared with that of the average man, so that he need not check himself at every turn, but can at least dare to permit himself a glimpse of things as they really are, divested of fantastic terrors.

For, as it is, the neurotic hardly comes in contact with reality at all. Because of his excessive unconscious dread of renewed disappointment and the conflicting passions into which he fears this would again plunge him, he has never given himself the opportunity to grow beyond the primitive outlook of his unconscious, which still dominates his adult relations with the outside world, as it did in infancy with all of us. The fundamental thing about the neurotic outlook is that essentially it has remained primitive. It is still profoundly ambivalent, still believes in its own omnipotence, still projects its own impulses and its own omnipotence on the outside world.

Thus, it is clear that there is a great deal in the neurotic's deepest attitude towards life which has simply never grown up at all, however adult and intellectual and cultivated he may seem in ordinary social encounters. We all, it is true, in our customary relations with people tend to put up some amount of bluff, though perhaps our bluff succeeds better in disguising us from ourselves than from them. This is much truer of the neurotic, and the more severe his illness the more true it becomes. The neurotic's conscious social personality is necessarily always a kind of bluff: what really governs his life is something quite different, something quite unconscious, because deeply repressed; and, however civilised and philosophic and tolerant the surface personality may be, this repressed unconscious is invariably primitive.

It is this repressed primitive part which is responsible for psychogenic illness and speaks through the symptoms, dreams, fantasies and free-associations of patients, and obviously these expressions of the unconscious will not be properly intelligible until we have some idea of how unconscious mental processes work and how they differ from the normal adult thinking with which we are familiar. I believe it is possible to formulate a few essential characteristics which distinguish primitive mental processes from the thinking of more adult type. They depend on the relation to reality.

The first and perhaps the most striking characteristic of primitive thinking is that it is *not hampered by any need for consistency*. While disbelieving and denying, it can also, in the same breath, believe, or it can believe contradictory things simultaneously. Logicians of the unconscious might call this the first law of unconscious thought, but it is the exact opposite of the first law of thought in conscious logical mental operations.

The second distinguishing characteristic of primitive thinking is the belief in the *omnipotence of thoughts and wishes*.

The third is the *confusion of fact with fantasy, thinking with doing*.

The fourth is the *small importance attached to knowing and the all-importance of wishing*.

The fifth is the *complete failure to distinguish from one another things which are somehow emotionally identified*.

The mental operations of the unconscious seem to be primitive in all these senses. With regard to the first point—its disregard of consistency—the neurotic's ambivalent attitude is a striking example of this type of self-contradiction, and again and again in dreams, symptoms and fantasies we find that contradictory wishes and contradictory attitudes and beliefs are being expressed simultaneously by the same symbol or action without the contradiction being felt as any difficulty.

As regards the second point—the feeling of omnipotence—the unconscious fails to recognise the limitations of its own powers. This primitive belief in the omnipotence of thought is what makes the child's megalomania, his belief in magic, his fantastic image of the parents which, failing to distinguish between the self and the outside world, he constructs on the pattern of what he believes himself to be. This omnipotent attitude characterises the savage, the madman and the dreamer, and it persists unconsciously in the neurotic too. The advantages from the point of view of pride and the denial of disappointment and helplessness are obvious, and on account of these advantages the belief in omnipotence is hard to give up. To give it up is to admit the danger and humiliation of powerlessness and is felt as reopening the door to all the intolerable pain and anxiety which once belonged to the psychophysical helplessness of unsatisfied infantile needs.

On the other hand, the belief in omnipotence brings with it its own terrors and anxieties. For the primitive mind believes in the omnipotence of *all* its wishes, including the revengeful, destructive ones. The savage works magic to make rain, to make the crops grow, to bring success; but also he works magic to destroy, and he believes in this black magic quite as much as, or more than, the other, and so lives always in dread of black magic turning back against himself. In the neurotic this sense of his omnipotence leads to feelings of guilt and terror, as well as to excessive self-glorification, both inflated in proportion to the persisting strength of the delusion of omnipotence.

The third characteristic of primitive thinking is the failure to distinguish fact from fantasy, thinking from doing. It, too, brings with it its own special advantages and dangers. At the most primitive level of all, this failure is complete when fancy reaches the vividness of actual hallucination. The madman, reverting to his early attitude, withdraws his interest from reality and substitutes his own delusions. In doing so he escapes the disappointments of real life. But, since the wish is not distinguished from the deed, mere fantasies of destruction are enough to arouse all the guilt and terror, which, at the adult level, could only be justified by the doing of real damage.

In dreams, delirium or fantasy reality is similarly forgotten and we are taken up with the productions of our own unconscious. Sometimes these are pleasant compensations for reality disappointment, but here, once again, panic may come out in nightmares. This withdrawing from contact with reality marks a regression to an earlier kind of mental process which is preoccupied exclusively with wishing and has no interest in true perception.

The most primitive level of the mind would seem to be entirely taken up with pleasure-seeking, and if what it seeks is not forthcoming in reality, it supplies the deficiency by imagination or even hallucination. The repressed unconscious of the neurotic appears to function at this level and we can never understand its creations, such as dreams, fantasies, hallucinations, delusions, psychogenic symptoms and sublimations unless we remember that the driving forces behind them, no matter how self-contradictory or painful or senseless they may appear to be, *are always ultimately wishes*. Usually what is wanted is so unfamiliar or actually unwelcome to adult thinking, and so disguised and over-determined and condensed, and often contains such a large element of pain and punishment, that the wish-fulfilment is by no means obvious. But occasionally in dreams the simple wish-fulfilment is clear and no conflict disturbs the satisfaction.

Otto Nodenskjold in his book *Antarctic* (1904) tells of the experiences of the crew who passed the winter with him. He says they all dreamed vividly. "Eating and drinking formed the central point around which most of our dreams were grouped. One reported in the morning that he had had a dinner consisting of three courses. Another dreamt of tobacco, whole mountains of tobacco."

Freud quotes the dream of a friend while he was a medical student. This young man had been vigorously called by his landlady but was most unwilling to get up. Instead of waking and going to hospital he dreamt of a room in a hospital with a bed in which he was lying. A chart with his name and age was pinned over his head. Reassuring himself with the thought, "Since I am already in hospital, I need not go", he turned over and slept on.

The superficial wish-fulfilment in these dreams is obvious. To interpret them fully no doubt one would need to go deeper and look for wishes more important and more repressed, whose fulfilment in the dream is correspondingly disguised. But the point I am concerned with in these illustrations is to remark that the dream fulfilment of such innocent wishes as here appear can be represented quite openly just because there is no harm in them. It is when pleasure-seeking and destructive impulses are aroused simultaneously that there comes in conflict, and with it the need for greater distortion.

The final essential characteristic of primitive thinking is the *failure to distinguish things which are emotionally similar*. The meaning of reality is all in terms of instinct satisfaction. Whatever arouses the same instincts *is* the same. To the baby all men are, to begin with, "Daddy", all furry things "pussy". If one original pussy frightened the baby, all the other pussy things frighten it and it does not attend to the difference between them.

Analysis and discrimination seem to be later achievements at a more adult level which the unconscious has never reached. Situations which have little unconscious significance may be nicely discriminated; but when anything really stirs a repressed emotion, the reaction to it is primitive—it is not distinguished from the earlier situations to which that emotion remains attached.

The emotions which the neurotic has repressed being essentially his love and his hate (or, more accurately, his sexualised hostility), anyone who later stirs this emotion is at once unconsciously assimilated to the earlier love-hate objects.

All men and women who become important to him, in his unconscious fantasy are simply father and mother over again. All aggression tends to have the unconscious significance of murder of rivals or of frustrating love-objects, all disappointment the significance of weaning, early discipline, or the first frustration of love. The Oedipus situation, which has been described in the preceding two chapters, is confused with all later important relationships so that these are reacted to, not on their own merits, but as if they still were this first one, thus unconsciously re-animating the old omnipotent fantasies and the old mutilation terrors.

It follows that he will repeat the same failures over and over again, because, in his unconscious, which governs his life, he fails to recognise that there is any alteration. The unconscious is still in the nursery; it is fixated there.

But there is an important reason for this fixation and the repetition which it brings about, and this is that with all their pains and frustrations and disappointments, these early nursery emotional experiences remain for these people the type of sexual satisfaction, and they fly towards them again and again, inevitably, like a moth to a candle, always getting stunned and scorched, but perpetually returning to renew the attempt. Such perseverance of instinct striving which still goes on and on inevitably seeking its object, learning nothing by its failures and never daunted, is more like the blind persistence of insects than the intelligent adaptations which characterise human beings;

and indeed in this matter the neurotic, as long as his repression holds absolute, is reduced to the inevitable and hopeless instinctiveness of creatures much lower than himself in the evolutionary scale. No matter what the cost, he seeks the old Oedipus situation of frustration, which for him means sexuality, seeing nothing in any new situation of life, but still always the same old figures of father, mother, brothers and sisters, or rather, not even these, but only their Imagos, wildly distorted by the projections of childish fantasy.

Thus to the extent that anyone is actuated by repressed unconscious drives he behaves like a mechanism rather than like a living creature. He is utterly determined and can do nothing but fatally repeat one reaction. It is only in so far as he escapes repression, or is later able to lift it, that he chooses freely in the only sense in which freedom seems to have any meaning, that is, he makes his choice with his whole self, recognising his present situation and using his past experience to secure the most complete satisfaction of which reality admits.

Having now completed my statement of the psychoanalytic theory concerning the origin and meaning of psychogenic illness, I cannot end without saying something more about its treatment, though what I say on this subject must be brief.

I have explained that the neurotic, dominated by his earlier emotional attitudes, which were repressed during his "Oedipus" struggles, will endow everybody with whom he comes in contact with the attributes of the Parent Imagos either consciously or unconsciously. Schoolmasters, employers, officials, will all be reacted to as if they were the original parental figures as they then appeared to the small child. A 'bus driver who will not stop when he is hailed may call up a passion of fury: a policeman may evoke terrible feelings of guilty dread.

It is an essential characteristic of neurosis to make such emotional confusions or, as they are technically called, "transferences", all the time, on to everyone, and it is to be expected that this will still happen when treatment is attempted. The patient who has already made transferences to the policeman and the 'bus driver will now make one to his doctor. If he has defied or cringed before his father and later before schoolmasters or employers, he may do the same before his analyst.

It would be foolish, of course, to say that the neurotic is incapable of any appreciation of reality: this may be true in extreme cases of insanity, but the neurotic is only partly deluded, and is mainly in contact with the outside world. Nevertheless, it is true that the neurotic patient shows considerable lack of reality sense in human relations when his fantasies are allowed to develop unchecked, as happens in the analytic situation. The analyst is loved, feared or hated for quite other than reality reasons.

What made the patient ill originally was not his love but his hostile emotions, and it is these which still stand in the way of cure. Because of them he mistrusts himself and everyone with whom he comes in contact. This mistrust, which runs through his whole life, naturally appears also in the analytical situation. Here too, as elsewhere, the patient will manifest his terror of human contact which springs from his repressed mutilation fantasies. When the delusions on which this terror rests are understood and seen through as they reappear in relation to the analyst, the barriers between the patient and the rest of the world are also removed and he can make what contacts he pleases. The neurotic mistrust of human contacts rests on the repressed mutilation fantasies of mutual injury by devouring, strangling, burning, cutting or whatever it may be. It is these which interfere with reality contact and cause the patient to make stereotyped transference reactions of aggression or fear.

The successful outcome of a Freudian psychoanalysis consists in the patient being released from the need to make transference reactions and enabled instead to react to present-day reality.

It might be supposed that a patient would welcome the attempt to discover these fantasies in order to dispel them and that he would relinquish them gladly, but this is by no means the case. On the contrary, he clings to them because, unconsciously, they still represent the fulfilment of his sexual and hostile impulses, and he *wants* them to be true. At the same time, he is terrified of them, and puts up every conceivable defence against becoming aware of them, and this, for the same reason as he originally fell ill and still remains so, namely that the repression of these fantasies appears to him to be the only possible way of escaping mortal danger and intolerable pain. His life has been spent in fighting the danger of becoming aware of them, and the fight continues throughout the analysis. At every turn he holds himself in check lest, in becoming aware of what he unconsciously dreams of doing, he should be impelled to carry it out in actual fact.

The analysis progresses to the extent to which the patient gains insight into these repressed fantasies. But encouraging him to dare to relax his repression and risk becoming aware of what, unconsciously, he still wants, is, of course, not the same thing as inviting him to *carry out* the primitive urges against which he has all his life been struggling. He advances in his cure essentially by knowing what he wants to do, whether he does it or not. Mere acting out of his wishes blindly would not be of the slightest use. But in so far as his unconscious cannot distinguish between thinking a thing and doing it, he is bound to fight against the analysis, regarding it as a direct incentive to the actions he most abhors, because they are actually his strongest temptations. There are certainly times when the analyst, around whom his unconscious fantasies have entwined themselves, must appear in the disguise of the Arch Tempter.

Transference is not a new phenomenon created by analysis: and it did not occur for the first time in this relationship; it intrudes continually into the patient's daily life also and colours his relations with everyone. He has his own ways, in ordinary relationships of dealing with the situations which these fantasies produce, and he will use them again in analysis. If he fears disappointment and the fury which this rouses in himself so that he dare not enter into any close contacts, he will mistrust the analytic relationship also, hold his body stiffly, speak softly, and keep the doctor at arm's length. If he is dominated by unconscious starvation so that he needs in all relationships to get as much as possible, he will try to *get* things once more in this new situation, demanding explanations perhaps or being hungrily determined to get his utmost out of every hour. If he resented being made to part with his faeces he may refuse to give his free-associations and upbraid the doctor for charging any fees.

All these characteristic ways of behaving to present situations under the influence of past conflicts or repressed fantasies are instances of transference.

In ordinary life he may manage to get a fair semblance of outside justification for the fears, resentments, remorses, suspicions, contempts or passionate devotions which he experiences, and there may of course be considerable reality grounds for all or at least for some of them. But in the analysis, reality contact is reduced to a minimum, and so here the part played by fantasy in what he feels and thinks stands out with especial clearness.

Under the influence of the fantasies which begin to emerge consciously in the analytic situation, the patient's idea of the analyst's character and probable reactions and even of his appearance will at times turn out to be surprisingly wide of the mark. A friend, who is exceptionally thin and fair, tells me that one of his patients, who had actually seen him daily for many months, believed him to be portentously fat and so dark that she thought he had negro blood. The patient's idea of the analyst's character is also continually altering in accordance with the fantasies which are uppermost. He may, for instance, transfer on to the analyst the same horror and condemnation which he really feels towards his own repressed sexual fantasies, or towards the monstrous Parent Imagos on whom those fantasies were modelled. Mr J., it will be remembered, thought of me as some sort of a vampire who was trying to drain his vitality and who might rob him of his penis. To him, at that time, I appeared depraved and dangerous. At other times the analyst, who is identified either with the patient's idea of his parents or of his own self, may appear ridiculous or contemptible, or, on the other hand, when love is transferred, he may appear angelic.

The patient's impulses towards the analyst also vary similarly in accordance with fantasy, and sometimes the pregenital nature of what is wanted is quite clear. One patient, warning me not to encourage her to express her real feelings, told me she would be too much for me if she let herself go, and would separate me from everyone else, feeling as if she would actually devour me. That night she had a nightmare in which she found herself in my house uninvited eating something she was not entitled to. At another time she felt as if she might strangle me.

The analyst's room becomes involved in the aggression which must originally have been directed towards the bodies of the people who figured in the early situations. Patients have had the impulse to burn up all my books or smash my furniture. The patient of whom I have just spoken expressed her jealousy of another whom she saw leaving my room by slapping the cushion on which the other's head had been lying. Another patient mentioned at the end of the hour that she had had a parallel train of thought going on all the time she was talking, which consisted in imaginarily chiselling off ornamental excrescences which decorated my mantelpiece. Her intentions towards me must have been hostile, for just before mentioning this she had remarked, "I can see that it is only because I am holding myself back that I haven't been downright abusive". I think the bits which were to be chiselled off my mantelpiece represented deeper fantasies of chiselling bits off me.

In the course of this acting-out of earlier repressed situations, the transference is continually shifting so that the analyst stands now for one of the original figures, now for another, and for these figures in different aspects, sometimes loved, sometimes hated, or again he may stand for different aspects of the patient's own self.

The close identification of the patient himself with the other figures, love- or hate-objects or rivals, who were involved in the early emotional conflicts, is very striking. His love, hate and blame are continually being shifted, now inwards, now outwards, and in all the various parts played out the analyst has his share. It is just this re-enacting of the old drama that gives the opportunity for new and valuable insight, and it can thus be seen how very important it is that the analyst should be detached enough to recognise the repetition meaning of all the various attitudes that are from time to time attributed to him or felt about him.

I am not denying of course that the patient and analyst have some real relation to each other also, but it is essential for the progress of the treatment to distinguish what is real from what is transferred and based actually, not on present reality, but on the confusion of this with repressed fantasies carried over from the past.

To the unconscious of the patient the new situations appear naturally as opportunities for gratification, in so far as the old impulses which are now re-animated seem to hold out a promise of pleasure. On the other hand, in so far as the new situations revive old mutilation fantasies, bringing with these old terrors, there may be from time to time accesses of panic. The analysis now appears to the patient's unconscious not as an opportunity for gratification but as a danger terrifying in proportion to the terrors of the fantasies which are being re-lived again in connection with the figure of the analyst. At such times fear of the treatment may severely tax the patient's determination to persevere with the cure. At one time Mr J. did in fact break off treatment for three months in an access of castration terror. Another patient, whose castration fear was also very severe, jumped up and left the room twice in a sudden outburst of rage which masked his terror, but, summoning up his courage and dimly recognising the fantasy nature of his fears, came back within a few minutes and resumed his analysis.

It is the analyst's business to keep firm hold of the transferred significances of the patient's various attitudes towards the treatment, and, in spite of appeals, threats, or panics, to keep steadily to the single object of using this transference situation to bring to light the unconscious fantasies upon which all the patient's transference reactions rest, that is, the unconscious sources of his illness, so that he may at last be convinced that the need to react in this way has no objective justification, but springs from an internal compulsion, based ultimately on the delusion of his own omnipotent dangerousness and the corresponding dangerousness of other people.

Progressively with the renunciation of this delusional belief anxiety and guilt subside, and he becomes able to tolerate erotic and hostile impulses in himself, as these occur, without immediately dissociating them in a panic, as he has been accustomed to do all his life. Gradually, as he tests reality, as he finds it in the analytical situation, it begins to dawn upon him that his fantastic terrors are groundless. He hates the analyst, and nothing happens, the analyst neither dies nor turns upon him and destroys him. He loves the analyst, and again nothing happens—no avenging rival appears, neither does love burn him up. Slowly he begins to be able to allow his attention to rest upon his own real situation, and so at last he gives himself a chance to know it.

It is this change in the lifelong panic reaction to reality which is aimed at. When that is accomplished, real satisfaction and pure sublimation become possible, and the symptoms cease to be necessary.

Thus in Freudian analysis the transference of the repressed infantile beliefs, wishes and terrors, which the patient has in fact always been making throughout life, and which constitute his illness, is recognised and accepted by the doctor as it occurs once again in relation to the analysis, and is used to cure the patient by enabling him, in the midst of re-living it once more in the consulting room, at last to see through it and finally free himself from it.

Before Freud, the whole question of transference in neurosis had never been given due weight: it was Freud who first recognised transference, not as a mere symptom occasionally occurring perhaps in certain types of hysteria, but as universal and inevitable in all neurosis. And it was Freud who devised the method of analysis by which the transference can be used to get rid of itself.

Unfortunately, there are still many psychotherapists who fail to recognise how inevitable transference is in neurotic patients, and how great a part it plays in all their relationships with the outside world, and, in failing to see this they necessarily also fail to realise the valuable use to which transference may be put in the treatment of psychogenic illness. Some doctors, while they admit reluctantly that transference does occur in some cases, regard it as regrettable, and pride themselves that with their *own* patients at any rate they do not let it arise.

On the Freudian hypothesis concerning the neurotic's unconscious distortion of all his later relations in the light of his unconscious preoccupations, this can only mean that, failing to recognise it, they do not allow the open development of the transference to take place, which can only mean that it remains unexpressed; it cannot help being there, since, so long as the neurotic clings to the unconscious delusions which underlie his repressed mutilation fantasies, he is bound to misinterpret reality, and this misrepresentation *is* transference.

The fantastic fears which, according to our hypothesis, underlie transference form the basis on which much of what passes for normal life really rests. We have seen that they may be the driving force in primitive conscience. These fears may give rise to a submissiveness which can be, and often is, utilised to enforce obedience and conformity. This same submissiveness and infantile docility to authority has long been used consciously and unconsciously in medicine. Many forms of therapy depend on it and by means of it it is sometimes possible to induce patients to give up their symptoms. Hypnotism and suggestion probably work, in so far as they do work, by taking advantage of this transference attitude. But while the cure depends upon this infantile docility, based ultimately upon fear and delusion, it cannot dispel these and thus cannot free the patient of his neurosis: it may modify symptoms, but it leaves the underlying cause untouched. It may alleviate the patient's condition in some respects, but there is a danger, as I have pointed out, that, in losing the symptom outlet, by the help of which anxiety and guilt were kept at bay, the patient may only suffer more severely. The mere removal of symptoms, while the underlying mutilation fantasies remain, will do nothing to alleviate the anxiety and guilt, and hence it happens that patients who have been cured in this way may later develop anxiety attacks or else protect themselves from these by a fresh outbreak of symptoms. Sometimes the result may be both anxiety and new symptom-formation, leaving the patient considerably worse off than before.

An interesting example of this occurred in the case of a woman who had suffered from heart attacks ever since her father's death from heart disease. Although she was to some extent invalided, she had led a fairly normal life until she was induced to see a specialist about her heart. After a thorough examination he decided that the disturbance of the heart's function was psychogenic, that organically the heart was healthy, and he succeeded in persuading the patient that this was the case. The heart attacks disappeared, but in place of them the patient developed severe anxiety, while a tendency to agoraphobia, which had occasionally worried her, now became so much increased that she was absolutely incapable of leaving her house and remained shut up in it for years without once venturing out.

It is the possibility of such unwelcome results as this that make one cautious about using transference merely to deprive the patient of his symptoms, without doing anything to dispel the mutilation fantasies out of which the symptoms arise.

The way in which the transference is used in psychoanalysis is not open to these objections. The cure of symptoms is here not the primary consideration, but rather the cure of the condition which makes symptoms necessary, the removal of the anxiety and guilt and the mutilation fantasies which caused them and against which the symptoms have been erected as defences, since it is these which are making the patient ill.

In all circumstances transference consists in reacting to present situations and people as if these repressed fantasies applied to them, as if the attacks and revenges with which these fantasies deal were really about to occur in connection with them. Transference to the analyst is used in psychoanalytic treatment to bring these repressed fantasies to light in the actual situation of the treatment on which they now become focused, so that, by simultaneously experiencing what all the anxiety and guilt were about, and at the same time recognising how little they now apply, the patient may rid himself of them.

It is thus clear what an ambitious attempt psychoanalysis is—the attempt to undo the unconscious delusions and unnecessary safeguards of a lifetime, the attempt to set the patient free to grow up. When people are apt to blame it for taking so long, and for its failures, perhaps they do not understand how colossal is the task it attempts.

Certainly, it is a serious undertaking which should not be entered upon by anyone not qualified to handle it, since it involves dealing with highly explosive material. It is not possible to avoid arousing anxiety at times during the bringing to light of alarming fantasies before the relief afforded by recognising their delusional nature has been obtained. From time to time the patient, in the throes of his struggle with the anxiety which may have been thus aroused, will produce temporary exacerbations of old symptoms or a variety of new ones, which would alarm a doctor who did not fully understand what he was attempting to do for the patient and which he might not know how to interpret.

When, for instance, unconscious mouth fantasies are stirring, the patient may become ravenous, or defend himself by refusing all food, or vomiting. When the fantasy is connected with the stolen faeces-penis-baby inside the body, accompanied by the fear of being robbed of this, there may be complete constipation: rage may be expressed in terms of flatulence giving severe abdominal pain. At times the patient may experience open anxiety, but sometimes he has no conscious awareness of the emotion, producing instead some of its psychological bodily expressions such as palpitation, cold sweats, giddiness, nausea, diarrhoea, trembling. The correct handling of all these transitory symptoms depends upon an ability to recognise the underlying unconscious fantasies in each case, so that by bringing these to consciousness the need for defence by symptoms may be removed and the anxiety concerning them dispelled by recognition of their unreality.

Merely to stir up such fantasies without helping the patient to see through them is to inflict useless suffering and may even be dangerous. Finally, the correct handling of the transference, which is so fundamental in psychoanalytic treatment, can only be done by one who understands thoroughly all the ways in which it manifests itself and is himself sufficiently free from guilt and anxiety to accept calmly whatever extremes of primitive hate, fear, aggression or love the patient may direct upon him. While admitting the emotional reality of these attitudes for the patient, he must be able always to recognise clearly the elements of transference and fantasy in the analytical relationship, since it is one of his main tasks to enable the patient to discriminate between what is transference and fantasy and what is real, and thereby to free himself from the delusions which are the source of his illness.

Only one who has himself been thoroughly analysed is properly equipped to undertake such a task.

Psychoanalysis is a serious undertaking for patient and doctor alike, and should not be begun lightly but only when there is need, and a determination, once having begun, to carry it through to the end.

Nevertheless, there is no doubt that, when at last the repressed unconscious delusions of neurosis are seen through and discarded in favour of reality, the need for symptoms is gone, and the patient is healthy in a sense in which only very few are healthy even among those who have never thought of themselves as ill.

SUMMARY

In order to prevent anxiety and the feeling of guilt from developing, those who suffer from repressed omnipotent destructive fantasies need to make use of defences. In earlier chapters we considered the recognisably abnormal way of defence by symptom-formation and the more common defence by repression, and in this chapter I have spoken of what might by contrast be called the "normal" defence mechanisms *by character reaction and by sublimations*.

I have pointed out the advantages which these defences have over symptom-formation, but have added that the ideal solution would be to outgrow the repressed infantile fantasies and not to be in need of defences at all.

I went on to enumerate the essential characteristics which distinguish the primitive infantile outlook of the unconscious from adult thinking. I explained that the unconscious has a complete disregard for consistency, believes in the magical power of thoughts and wishes, is taken up entirely with wishing and not concerned about knowing, confuses fantasy with fact, thinking with doing, and makes the same reaction to all situations which resemble one another, emotionally failing to discriminate one from the other.

I have concluded with a short description of the way in which psychoanalysis uses the transference of the patient's unconscious fantasies on to the analytical relationship to enable him to free himself from his unconscious delusions and gain contact with the real world.

For EU product safety concerns, contact us at Calle de José Abascal, 56–1°, 28003 Madrid, Spain or eugpsr@cambridge.org.

www.ingramcontent.com/pod-product-compliance
Ingram Content Group UK Ltd.
Pitfield, Milton Keynes, MK11 3LW, UK
UKHW010339140625
459647UK00010B/702

* 9 7 8 1 1 0 7 4 7 5 3 9 7 *